To Anna

TWENTY-FIVE THOUSAND SUNSETS

The Autobiography of

HERBERT WILCOX

South Brunswick
New York: A. S. Barnes and Company

TWENTY-FIVE THOUSAND SUNSETS.
© Wardville Productions Ltd 1967.
First American edition published 1969
by A. S. Barnes and Company, Inc.,
Cranbury, New Jersey 08512

Library of Congress
Catalogue Card Number: 69-14890

SBN 498 06985 0
Printed in the United States of America

TWENTY-FIVE THOUSAND SUNSETS

CONTENTS

Prelude   xiii

1   *Christmas 1965 – the early years – my religion – my mother*   1

2   *Brighton and hunger, 1901 – sausage, potatoes and onions at Harris's – J. B. Joel – the Prince of Wales – Queen Victoria – billiards – 'Boys of the Chelsea School' – memories – death of my mother – running away – cricket and soccer – my father dies*   5

3   *Camberwell and the gangsters, 1907 – Charlie Chaplin – I learn the facts of life – the 'Casanova' of Camberwell – my health collapses – Gibraltar – outbreak of the Great War, 1914 – I enlist*   17

4   *The Great War – my younger brother – I learn to read – J. A. Spender and Rupert Brooke – commissioned – romance – the Irish Easter rebellion, 1916 – my 'dance' with the Queen*   24

5   *My marriage, 1916 – pilot in the Royal Flying Corps – my divorce – Stamford airbase – Rhys-Davis – Air Marshal Billy Bishop – my second marriage, 1918 – von Richthofen – a Christian war – Rosa Lewis – Armistice Day – the first Hendon air pageant*   33

6   *Demobilised – I enter the film industry, 1918 – from 'bottle' cinemas to Wardour Street – the little old lady of Stamford Hill – Wonderful Story and Flames of Passion – Chu Chin Chow and Southern Love – The Only Way and Martin Harvey – Rex Harrison*   46

7   *Nell Gwyn and Dorothy Gish, 1928 – J. D. Williams and 'Hopie' – Elstree studios built – British and Dominions founded – Dawn and Sybil Thorndike – Lord Northcliffe and the press chiefs – George Bernard Shaw – arrival of 'talkies'*   65

CONTENTS

8   *Charles Laughton – Chaplin – Tom Walls, Ralph Lynn and the Aldwych farces – Anna Neagle and* Good Night Vienna, *1932 – Jack Buchanan –* Escape Me Never, *Elisabeth Bergner and J. M. Barrie – Galsworthy, Monckton Hoffe and Gene Fowler – Noel Coward –* The Little Damozel, *1932 – I fall in love with Anna*   84

9   Nell Gwyn *with Anna, 1934 – banned in America – D. W. Griffith –* Peg of Old Drury, *1935 – Lord Portal – I negotiate purchase of Universal Pictures – Montagu Norman – I open Pinewood – Mr Boot of Nottingham – the Hon. Richard Norton*   100

10   Victoria the Great, *my greatest gamble, 1937; would it be completed? –* Sixty Glorious Years, *1938 – Sir Robert Vansittart – H. G. Wells – Marie Lloyd and Cary Grant*   111

11   *The Second World War –* Nurse Cavell *with Anna Neagle, 1939 –* Irene *– Lord Lothian and* Forever and a Day *– President Roosevelt – lemons, eggs and bacon – Louie and Maudie –* They Flew Alone *and Robert Newton, 1941 – Geniuses: Yehudi Menuhin, D. W. Griffith, Orson Welles, John Logie Baird, Peter Ustinov, Ralph Richardson, Alec Guinness, Noel Coward, Laurence Olivier, Charlie Chaplin – Brigitte Helm*   124

12   *My plans for my children – Emerson – A. P. Herbert – my wedding to Anna – 'Auntie'*   140

13   *The 'London Series' –* I Live in Grosvenor Square, *1944 –* Piccadilly Incident, *1946 – Michael Wilding and* Spring in Park Lane, *1948 – my C.B.E. and our voyage on the* Queen Elizabeth *– Michael Wilding in America – Marlene Dietrich – Elizabeth Taylor – a breathless wedding*   144

14   *Claridges – honeymoon hotel – V-bombs and David Sarnoff – Luigi – Alex Korda – royal showing of* Spring in Park Lane *– Mary Poppins – my children today*   152

CONTENTS

15   The Beggar's Opera, 1952 – *Sir Laurence Olivier and Peter Brook* – pre-*première for the royal Coronation guests* – *Jack Warner pays* 700,000 *dollars* – *what the Governor of the Bank of England said* – *Audrey Hepburn, and actresses I missed* – *Elinor Glyn*   163

16   '*Worth-whiles*' – *Air Marshal Billy Bishop, V.C. and the Canadian tour* – *Group Captain 'Poppie' Pope* – *Lord Beaverbrook*   172

17   Odette, 1950 – *Anna's greatest dramatic performance* – *with Odette, Anna and Peter Churchill in France* – *the royal* première – *the royal garden party* – *unusual* premières: Victoria the Great *in Venice and Hollywood; the London* première *of* The Lady with a Lamp, *Princess Elizabeth and the Mountbattens*, 1951 – *Isaac Wolfson and commercial television* – *Roy Thomson* – *end of spring and the years of plenty*   183

18   *Autumn and the lean years* – *the reasons why* – *British Lion* – Yangtse Incident *and* Earl Mountbatten – *Sir Arthur Jarratt* – *Sir John Reith* – *Harley Drayton* – Ross, *Terence Rattigan and my £100,000 cheque*, 1960 – *bankruptcy* – *Vivien Leigh* – *the taxi-driver and the 'Oscars'* – *end of the famine period* – *Anna on tour*   196

19   *Full cycle* – *husband and wife C.B.E.* – *thirteen awards* – *the need for a musical* – The Glorious Days, 1952 – *near to death* – *recovery and Anna's triumph in* Charlie Girl   209

Postlude   221

Index   223

ILLUSTRATIONS

Frontispiece   The author

Between pages 30 and 31

1. Anna Neagle.
2. The statue of Queen Victoria at Hove.
3. King Edward VII walking on Hove front.
4. Harris's 'Sausage, Potatoes and Onions' shop in West Street, Brighton.
5. A. G. Vanderbilt's London-Brighton coach outside the Metropole.
6. The author aged twelve, winning a five-mile walking match.
7. As goalkeeper of a cup-winning school team.
8. Aged thirteen, as a page-boy in a Brighton hotel.
9. As a junior billiards champion.
10. K. S. Ranjitsinhji demonstrating his 'leg glance'.
11. Private Wilcox H.S., Royal Fusiliers, August 1914.
12. As a pilot officer, Royal Flying Corps, France, 1916.

Between pages 62 and 63

13. The German First World War ace, Baron von Richthofen.
14. The end of Richthofen's 'Red Devil'.
15. Air Marshal W. A. Bishop, V.C., D.S.O., M.C. with Winston Churchill.
16. Mae Marsh with C. Aubrey Smith in *Flames of Passion*, 1921.
17. The author with Werner Kraus, Lionel Barrymore and Emil Jannings.
18. With Betty Blythe in Berlin for *Chu Chin Chow*, 1923.
19. Sir John Martin Harvey in the final scene of *The Only Way*, 1925.
20. One of the bills for *The Only Way*.
21. An extract from the *Sphere*, 3rd October 1925.
22. The author with J. D. Williams, founder of Elstree studios.
23. Nelson Keys, Dorothy Gish and Will Rogers in Gershwin's *Tip-Toes*, 1928.

ILLUSTRATIONS

Between pages 94 and 95

24 The author with Dorothy Gish, star of the 'silent' *Nell Gwyn*.
25 With Tom Walls in 1930.
26 Anna Neagle with Jack Buchanan in *Good Night, Vienna*, 1931.
27 The author directing Brigitte Helm in *The Blue Danube*.
28 Anna Neagle in *The Little Damozel*, in the dress which shocked the critics.
29 The famous 'cleavage' picture of Anna Neagle as Nell Gwyn, 1934.
30 Two cartoons by Low depicting the U.S. ban on *Nell Gwyn*.

Between pages 126 and 127

31 Anna Neagle with Cedric Hardwicke and Jack Hawkins in *Peg of Old Drury*, 1935.
32 The author with Anna Neagle and Anton Walbrook during the production of *Sixty Glorious Years*, 1938.
33 At Balmoral, rehearsing a scene from *Sixty Glorious Years*.
34 Anna Neagle as the old Queen Victoria.
35 At the Ottawa *première* of *Victoria the Great*.
36 The critics' reaction to *Victoria the Great*.
37 The *Daily Express* leader on *Victoria the Great*.
38 The American Institute of Cinematography's award.
39 The author rehearsing Anna Neagle in the first scene of *Nurse Edith Cavell*, 1939.
40 Directing a scene from *Nurse Edith Cavell*.

Between pages 158 and 159

41 The author and Anna Neagle on their wedding day.
42 Anna Neagle with 'Auntie'.
43 The author and Anna Neagle with their thirteen awards.
44 With Anna Neagle and Michael Wilding at the Dorchester, receiving triple awards for *Spring in Park Lane*.
45 A memorable voyage in the *Queen Elizabeth*.

ILLUSTRATIONS

46 The author, Peter Ustinov, Anna Neagle, Odette Churchill and Trevor Howard during the production of *Odette*.
47 Anna Neagle in the title role of *Odette*, 1950.
48 The author and Anna Neagle congratulated by King George VI at the *première* of *Odette*.
49 Alexander Korda.
50 Korda's extraordinary letter about *Odette*.
51 The author with Laurence Olivier during *The Beggar's Opera*.

Between pages 190 *and* 191

52 A good friend and wise counsellor: Lord Beaverbrook, by Walter Sickert, R.A.
53 The royal *première* of *The Lady with a Lamp*, 1951.
54 Anna Neagle and Michael Wilding talking to Princess Elizabeth.
55 Elizabeth Taylor and Michael Wilding.
56 A presentation cigarette-box, marking the raising of £50,000 for nursing.
57 Anna Neagle presenting the crest of H.M.S. *Amethyst* to Commander Kerens, D.S.O. after *Yangtse Incident*.
58 T. E. Lawrence with Captain Liddell Hart, military adviser on *Ross*.
59 The £100,000 cheque to Terence Rattigan for the film rights of *Ross*.
60 The letter enclosing £5 which the author received following the news of his bankruptcy.
61 The first day out of bankruptcy.
62 Anna Neagle in the living-room in Park Lane.

PRELUDE

I was born starry-eyed on 19 April, with Aries at its zenith, and I've lived with stars in my eyes ever since. The influence of Aries has on occasion reduced unscalable mountains to molehills, transformed some of my geese into graceful elegant swans, and often prompted me to attempt the seemingly impossible—sometimes with success.

I star-gazed my way through adolescence to the Great War, when on sentry-go as a private infantry soldier I established personal contact with the all-important North Star, the Great Bear, Orion complete with Sam Browne belt, Jupiter and Venus. Venus took aggressive possession of me during those momentous war years, particularly when I was commissioned as a pilot in the Royal Flying Corps and learnt at first hand the meaning of 'Per Ardua Ad Astra'.

The Great War behind me, I found myself in a strange new world, surrounded by stars of every description: would-be stars; temperamental stars; great stars; rising stars and fallen stars.

Dorothy Parker, the American writer and wit, is reputed to have instructed her butler to bid certain dinner-guests 'God speed' as they took their departure, and to hand him or her a little note.

'Miss Parker,' the butler would say, 'has asked me to tell you how much she has appreciated your charming company and has requested me to hand you this list of the names you have "dropped" during the evening.'

I must here and now crave your indulgence for the number of names I must 'drop'. But in recalling, over a period of sixty-six years, my thoughts, aspirations, achievements and failures, these names and people are integral pieces in the mosaic of my story.

I

Christmas Day, 1965.

The dawn is just breaking over the dome of the chapel of the Hospital of St John and St Elizabeth in St John's Wood, London.

A toneless church bell tolls three times, proclaiming that the good sisters and the nurses are receiving their customary daily Holy Communion.

I have been a hospital patient here since 4 December. Less than a mile away, in a little mews cottage, my wife Anna Neagle is, I trust, sleeping the sleep she so desperately needs. For the first time in twenty-five years we shall not be having our Christmas dinner together. Anna and I have shared Christmas dinner in Hollywood, Paris, Scotland, Brighton, New York, London, Elstree and many other places, right back to 1941.

That year is memorable; that dinner unforgettable. In those days, when rationing was down to one egg a month, there was little chance of something special—even for Christmas Day. But on my way to Gerrards Cross, where I was spending Christmas with Anna and her aunt, a man got into my carriage just as the train started to move. After a few minutes he asked:

'Could you do with a tender young goose for Christmas, gov'nor?'

'And a turkey?' I queried.

A quick glance down the corridor he gave, then from the luggage rack he took down a brown paper parcel.

'I'm not kidding—here it is! Killed this morning, weighs six pounds. Dressed and ready for the oven.'

'How much?' I asked.

'A pound a pound—dead cheap.'

Anna's aunt was an extremely good cook and I am an extremely good carver. But Auntie's cooking and my carving were no match for that goose. I couldn't even penetrate the breast with a razor-sharp knife. Not a morsel of that tough old bird did we eat.

Today, twenty-five years later, I shall be offered tender breast of turkey with stuffing, vegetables, Christmas pudding and a mince pie. But I shall not be eating a morsel. I can't eat: haven't eaten for nearly three weeks; haven't read—not even a newspaper, or listened to the radio. Couldn't be bothered. Just wanted to lie still and sleep. Three weeks in the shadows. I've been as near to death as I could go—without going. Periods of delirium, during which—like the kaleidoscopic impressions of a drowning man—the important and trivial events of my life have flashed across my mind in lunatic disorder.

Whilst these impressions are still with me—some clear, some confused—I will set them down and also tell here, for the first time, the real facts of my illness which so nearly wrote 'finis' to me and to this book and robbed Anna of her greatest hour in the theatre.

Let's go back to the beginning. Twenty-five thousand sunsets ago—to 19 April, 1892.

I was born Wilcox and christened Herbert Sydney. There is some doubt about my birthplace—whether it was Cork in Ireland or London in England. My passport says London. However the accident of birthplace matters little, for I am as Irish as the Blarney Stone itself. My mother, Mary Healy, of Cork, saw to that and I'm sure that in whatever part of England our home might have been situated, it outmatched for Irish sentiment, superstition and prejudice any peat-warmed cottage in the wilds of Connemara.

I am, and always have been, religious—not aggressively so, and not bigoted. A Roman Catholic myself, I respect the point of view of all denominations since, in their various attitudes, they are all believers. I believe in God completely and utterly, and I must confess I have no time for the professed unbelievers, so waste no time in trying to convert them. If the miracle and mystery of life itself—of the seasons and the elements—has not converted them already, I am sure nothing I could say would make any impression.

I stress my personal attitude since religion has played an important part in my life, particularly during the difficult formative years.

My mother was extremely beautiful, tall and patrician, with Ireland written all over her raven hair and sky-blue eyes. Many likened her to Lily Langtry. My memory tells me there was no resemblance but, if I may endeavour to conjure up an image, if those who knew or have seen photographs of Kathleen Ferrier will add two inches in height (to make 5ft. 11in.) and those bluest of blue eyes—that was my mother.

The image in my mind is no doubt sharpened by my recollection of her at the piano, either accompanying herself or unaccompanied, extolling in a deep rich voice the beauties of the Vale of Avoca or bringing to life the frightening *Shan Van Vocht* with its warning of invasion by the French:

> *'Oh! the French are on the sea,*
> *said the Shan Van Vocht,*
> *They'll be hear without delay,*
> *said the Shan Van Vocht!'*

And, of course, sung in her beloved Gaelic. When my father suggested (which was rarely) something he would understand—in English—it would invariably be:

> *'Let Erin remember the days of old,*
> *Ere her faithless sons betray her;*
> *When Malachi wore the collar of gold,*
> *Which he won from the proud invader.'*

In truth, the invader was Danish and not English. But that was a point my mother did not emphasise!

She was related to Tim Healy—later Governor General of the Irish Free State—and was, of course, a Roman Catholic. My father, from the west country, was a Protestant. My mother was devout. My father was not. I can well imagine the scene when my father asked my mother to marry him. I am confident she said neither 'No' nor 'Yes' but:

'What's your religion, Joseph John Wilcox?'

'I'm a Protestant,' he would have replied.

'Then I can't marry you.'

'Why not?'

'I'm a Roman Catholic—and strict.'

'Does that make any difference?'

'All the difference in the world.'

'But I love you and want to marry you.'

'I love you, but I can't marry a Protestant—except on my own terms.'

'And they are?'

'We are married in a Roman Catholic church—by a priest.'

'Agreed.'

'And the children will be brought up as Roman Catholics.'

'That's agreed too.'

'All right, Joseph John Wilcox—I'll marry you! But it's a pity. A great pity!'

Well, they married and lived happily together and there were five children. But as a topic of conversation between my father and my mother, religion was taboo in the home.

My mother saw to it that my sister, my three brothers and I were brought up as Roman Catholics and as strict as she herself was. When only seven years old I would walk five miles every Sunday to serve at mass. And every night, on my knees at the bedside in company with my brothers and sister, I would say interminable prayers—in Gaelic. My mother did not like the English, but loved the Irish and particularly those of Cork. She once admonished me: 'Wherever you are, be it at the ends of the earth, you will always be able to tell a Cork man—but not much!!'

It was in County Cork, at Fermoy, during the 'Trouble' at Easter 1916 that I was shot—fighting for the British! I can imagine my mother looking down, as I feel sure she was, turning in her grave and saying: 'Herbert, it's no son of mine you are—you're a traitor, in the trappings of the enemy when you should be wearing Malachi's collar of gold!'

Rest her soul, she would not be so country-proud today if she could see Cork, or the new Dublin, in parts indistinguishable from Streatham or Brooklyn, with not a beggar in sight.

My earliest recollection of my home life in London is that there was sufficient, if not ample, money. I remember distinctly, during the coldest spell in the history of England—the late nineties, when water had to be drawn from stand pipes in the street—that I and my sister and brothers were called away daily from the convent where we were at school to rush home and serve hot soup, followed by spotted dog pudding made in the washing copper, to twenty or thirty ragged and hungry children. Ravenously hungry and cold ourselves, we were not permitted to eat until all the children had been fed and left the house.

And with empty, rumbling stomachs we would all intone our thanks to God for what we had been longing for and which was overdue. Not a very Christian attitude, but I think understandable. But the 'Good Samaritan' attitude of my mother was halted abruptly. Something had gone amiss financially in my father's activities, and whilst mysterious changes were being planned—moving to a smaller house, dispensing with all domestic help and other things that meant little or nothing to me—my mother's health broke down and T.B., in those days the dreaded killer, threatened her.

On the advice of the doctors, we moved to Brighton. It was about the turn of the century and I was eight years old.

2

Our problems now became very serious indeed, since my father had to leave his work in London, and we were a young family of five ranging from six to thirteen, with an invalid mother needing both nursing attention—in the pre-Welfare State period—and nourishing food. My father's resources soon ran out, with not a glimmer of work in sight.

But throughout this period, at a time when belief and faith were sorely tested, I recall we never missed mass on Sunday. Our church was St John the Baptist, at Kemp Town. Living as I do now within a short distance of it, I often go in for a quiet moment or two of reflection, and nothing about the church seems to have changed since 1900. Still there is the tablet of remembrance to Mrs Fitzherbert, flanked on either side by the panels of the Stations of the Cross.

When I attended mass in my youth my attention often wandered to this tablet when I should have been deeply immersed in meditation. How could a Saint be called 'Mrs', I wondered. I made inquiries and found out that Mrs Fitzherbert, despite her position among the pictures of the Saints, was herself no Saint at all!

My father's inability to find employment at that time literally meant the breadline for all of us. We all knew real hunger. As a matter of fact, my predominant recollection of Brighton in those days is of hunger.

It was in West Street that Harris's cook shop was situated. Dominating the window was a picture of Mr Harris himself in full evening dress, looking rather like King Edward VII, wearing a shiny silk top hat, with a glistening diamond in his shirt front, a scarlet silk cummerbund, and smoking a very big cigar. Underneath the picture the legend ran: 'Harris's sausages are the best.'

The only dish served at Harris's was their speciality, 'S.P.O.'—sausage, potatoes and onions. It cost fourpence. Underneath the picture of Mr Harris were three large tin dishes, all piping hot. In the first were delicious brown sausages, swimming in fat; in the second, a mound of potatoes; in the third, onions, also swimming in fat! The smell of the onions made a walk past a tantalising experience. Often I lingered and sniffed, but never did I go in. I never had fourpence.

But one day a stranger stopped me and asked the way to Brill's Baths, the famous sea-water baths in Pool Valley, now the Savoy Cinema. It was difficult to describe the way, so I offered to show him. He came from Bath, where they had other kinds of baths, I learned. For my pains, he gave me a shilling. I looked at it, and then set off—to Harris's.

I seated myself on a high chair at the counter.

'What can I do for you?' the man in a high white hat asked.

'S.P.O.' I said.

I watched him serve it and put down my shilling. I finished almost before he brought my change. Never had I tasted anything so good. I picked up my eightpence and went out and down towards the sea. But my mind was still at Harris's.

I looked at the eightpence and back I went and sat on the same seat. The man was serving so he did not notice me. But then he asked the same question, still without looking.

'S.P.O.' I told him.

He stopped—then looked at me.

'Didn't I serve you just now?' he asked.

'Yes,' I told him—'but I want some more.'

'Your name Oliver Twist?'

'No, it's Herbert Wilcox,' I answered.

He served me and looked as I dived into it at once, completely ignoring him.

'Hungry—aren't you?' he inquired.

'Yes! I am—and it's lovely.'

He went over to the pan and forked a piping hot sausage and dumped it on my plate.

'With the compliments of Mr Harris.'

My whole body glowed as I ate that second helping. On my way out I asked the kind man in the high white hat who Oliver Twist was. He told me. The next day I was back for 'more'—and Mr Harris was richer by my last fourpence.

Since those days I have eaten in the best hotels and restaurants in the world and tasted many specialities: oysters 'Rockefeller' at Antoine's in New Orleans; 'Baby Bear' cooked by the great Sovrani himself; terrapin in Baltimore; Boston clam chowder at '21', New York; and (as a guest of Zsa Zsa Gabor) jacket potatoes stuffed with caviar at Les Ambassadeurs in London. But these are faded memories beside that S.P.O. with the bonus sausage at Harris's, which I shall never forget.

But strangers dispensing shillings were not everyday miracles. At the Convent of the Sacred Heart in the Dyke Road, where I was a day scholar, I heard some of the boys talking about sandwiches being given away at Sweetings, the restaurant at the bottom of West Street, Brighton. So off I went.

A few other kids were there, and knew the ropes. I was grudgingly admitted to the gang. We waited until the restaurant closed—about 11.30 p.m.—then we were let in and given the left-over cut sandwiches. Strange tastes! *Foie gras*, smoked salmon, tongue and sardine. The *foie gras*, after one taste, was a total loss and I dodged those in future. Smoked salmon was the favourite.

One night, whilst we were waiting for the closing, a group of four came out. They had apparently had a gay time, judging from their laughter. Two hansom cabs were waiting for them. One couple was a gentleman with a shining silk hat and a most beautiful woman in white fur. 'J. B. Joel, his name is—millionaire,' one of the gang told me. 'Made a million pounds in South Africa, all out of diamonds—got racehorses, four big houses, everything.'

At that time I often saw and admired a strange conveyance (I learned later it was called a phaeton) drawn by high-stepping horses and driven along the front at Hove by a rather severe-looking gentleman. Sitting beside him with arms folded was the coachman. 'That's Walter Winans, the American millionaire,' I was told.

Another sight that fascinated me was the coach and four which plied between the Hotel Metropole, Northumberland Avenue, London and the Hotel Metropole, Brighton. On the box seat, with white pipeclayed whip, sat the handsomest man I had ever seen, in grey morning coat, grey Ascot tie, wide wing collar and grey topper, with a deep red carnation in his button-hole. He was Mr A. G. Vanderbilt, another millionaire whose hobby was to drive his coach himself in both directions. The coachman, at the rear end of the coach, sounded his post-horn to the clatter of the horses' hooves. Several halts for refreshment and changes of horses *en route* made Mr Vanderbilt's hobby a very costly one.

J. B. Joel, Walter Winans and A. G. Vanderbilt, each obviously knew how to extract the most from life; they were millionaires all.

The die was cast. I decided I too would become a millionaire.

Jumping ahead to 1921, my great friend and film partner, Nelson Keys—with whom I spent many gay nights in London—said: 'I've been invited to breakfast with someone. Come with me.'

'Will it be all right?' I asked.

'Quite all right. Nice fellow. Won the Derby yesterday and the bubbly will be flowing like water.'

'For breakfast?' I queried.

'Yes,' said 'Bunch'. 'Wonderful with eggs and bacon.'

So to 34 Grosvenor Square we went, and I met our host. J. B. Joel, known to all as Jack!

'You're Herbert Wilcox, the film producer?' he asked.

I told him I was.

'Come and have lunch with me at the Ritz tomorrow. I have a problem and I think you can help me.'

He had a problem, with his millions, the Derby winner—and I could help him! When I arrived for lunch at the Ritz, J. B. Joel was there with his problem—a young lady, obviously with film aspirations. After a champagne cocktail, he ordered lunch, starting with smoked salmon.

'Best in the world,' he told me. 'Try some.'

I said I would. My mind went back to the left-over sandwiches at Sweetings in Brighton where the first millionaire I saw turned out to be my host today. I couldn't refrain from asking him, with a smile: 'Did you ever taste smoked salmon at Sweetings?'

'At Brighton?' he asked.

'Yes.'

'In its day, very good, but I haven't been there for years. The curing has improved since those days. Now it's smoother and not so salt.'

After another cocktail, he said: 'Now Herbert—may I call you that?' I nodded. 'And I'm Jack.' I thanked him.

'My horse, Humorist, won the Derby yesterday and (putting his hand over the lady's) here's a filly who will win the Oaks for you if you give her a part in one of your films.'

'A star part,' the filly murmured sweetly. I might have known! I was seldom invited out before being asked the same question. 'I'll arrange a test,' was my stock answer.

The lunch turned out to be abortive so far as the 'filly' was concerned. But I enjoyed enormously, whilst eating the smoked salmon at the Ritz, allowing my mind to go back to Sweetings and remembering how Jack Joel had triggered off my aspirations. And here I was at the Ritz as his guest and calling him Jack . . . ! But we had better get back to Brighton in 1901.

I had an idea to make a little money, and my elder brothers also took it up. Before going to convent in the morning, and after leaving, I sold newspapers—then a ha'penny—and was often given the change from a penny. I also got commission on the sales and in this way I made as much as half a crown per week.

It was the custom for some of the children at convent to go straight to the sea-front after school. I was curious to know why.

'The Prince of Wales—he's sometimes asleep on a seat.' So one day I joined them. Sure enough, there he was. Panama hat pulled down almost on his nose, and directly behind him the statue of Queen Victoria.

One day, to my delight, he was not asleep, but walking along the Hove sea-front. No personal bodyguard, save a young, slightly interested policeman in the distance, with a dozen or so gapers looking on. As I gazed, spellbound, at the approaching figure of the Prince a man beside me took his photograph and, having done so, raised his hat in respectful thanks to His Royal Highness for having paused for a moment in his walk to assure his getting the best result.

'Do you sell those?' I asked the man with the camera. 'Half a crown each,' he replied, 'ready in two weeks,' and he gave me an address. Half a crown! I did not get one. But I remembered the incident whilst writing this book, and made inquiries through the Brighton and Hove press. The editor put me on to an insurance executive who possessed a unique collection of old Brighton photographs and, sixty-five years later, I found it! It is reproduced here.

Soon afterwards, with papers selling like hot cakes, I was calling out on my rounds: 'Argus—death of the Queen.' A costermonger stopped me and bought one. He forgot his ha'penny change as he muttered: 'Cor—won't it seem funny without the Queen.' I used these very words, spoken by Alexander Field playing a Cockney, in my film *Victoria the Great*.

I am sure the seed of interest was planted there and then which eventually emerged in the film.

And then things must have taken a turn for the better. My father was a very fine billiards player and, hearing that a saloon needed a manager, he applied and got the job. So, one way and another, we managed to keep the wolf from the door.

After school, and on Saturdays, I would help my father by marking billiards for customers and so earned another shilling or two each week. Waiting for customers, I would take out the billiard balls and on a small stool, which enabled me to look over the top of the table,

I tried to emulate the customers. I showed an aptitude for the game, which made me a freak attraction for my father's saloon.

It was at Brighton at this time that I made my stage début at the Hippodrome and added five shillings a week to the kitty. George Layton, a singer of patriotic songs, had one number which called for twenty young boys. 'Boys of the Chelsea School,' it was called, and George Layton as an old Chelsea pensioner sergeant would sing as we marched on to the stage in our Chelsea Red uniforms:

> '*Boys of the Chelsea School*
> *Are sons of the men we admire.*
> *In every heart—in every vein*
> *Runs the blood of a soldier sire.*
> *Children they are—maybe*
> *But wait till a few years fly—*
> *Heroes brave they'll show us*
> *How to behave*
> *As their fathers did in days gone by.*'

We marched and formed fours and all the time to the music and to thunderous applause.

Many, many years later I told Tom Arnold about my stage début. 'That's funny,' said Tom, 'that's how I started.' And we proceeded to sing the chorus together. Another echo during the formative years.

I wonder if that inspired the Nell Gwyn idea, involving the foundation of the Royal Chelsea Hospital, which I showed in my two films of *Nell Gwyn* and which was repeated in Tom Arnold's stage play with Anna—*The Glorious Days*.

A curious thing is the human memory. I have naturally had to draw on it extensively in the writing of this book, and I am grateful that by and large it has served me well. But, since most of the happenings make sense and must have been worth mentally recording at the time, why was I able to remember the jingle of the above song without any reference to Tin Pan Alley or the publishers?

Even more remarkable is a song that was popular in the music-halls at the turn of the century—with the Boer War still going strong and sentimentality running high. It was the custom at that time for the working classes to name their newly-born after some hero serving in South Africa—some general or V.C. If British names were not enough, then Boers. If not enough Boers, then places.

In this particular case the scene on stage was a mother with her new-born babe in her arms. Her name was Blobbs. Mrs Blobbs' neighbours arrive. What was she going to call the new Blobbs? Jack or Richard—both popular names at the time.

Mrs Blobbs shook her head as she rocked the baby in her arms and sang with loud applause greeting each name:

> '*The baby's name is . . .*
> *Kitchener, Carrington, Methuen,*
> *Kekewich,—White,*
> *Cronje, Plumer, Powell, Majuba,*
> *Gatacre, Warren, Colenso, Kruger,*
> *Cape Town, Mafeking, French,*
> *Kimberley, Ladysmith, Bobs,*
> *The Union Jack and Fighting Mac,*
> *Lyddite, Victoria—Blobbs.*'

Non sequitur gibberish, yet sixty-five years later a print emerges from the mental negative in my brain—and I assure you without any help from reference books. For something so unimportant, I doubt if they would be of assistance.

On the other hand, I cannot recall certain events of forty years later which would prove more profitable and worthwhile than the gibberish of 'The Baby's Name'.

At the ripe old age of forty-two, my mother died.

The murderous T.B., the doctors stated, had claimed another victim. But in my opinion the cause was not T.B. but a very ordinary upright piano—a status symbol of those times and the only one in our street.

My mother was not only very beautiful, she was very sensitive. And when a horse-drawn van pulled up at the door of our modest house in a modest Brighton street where all the neighbours looked upon my mother as someone much superior to them, as indeed she was—it was the shock of this which hastened her end, even if it did not actually kill her.

The van had called to take away our piano because the instalment payments had fallen behind. A small crowd of neighbours had gathered round our front door and the van. My mother tried to explain but the van driver had his orders: payment in full, or the piano.

My father was at work and we children crowded round mother, bewildered by the whole affair. When my mother lost the battle and they started to move the piano, she went to the window and saw the crowd outside. She then drew the blinds so that neither she nor her children should see the prying eyes of the neighbours as the piano was taken away.

That same night she took to her bed, and next day she talked to us and told us that whatever setback we might meet in life we must never lose our faith in God.

Perhaps she protested a little too much. I wonder.

Shortly afterwards she died, with her last conscious breath intoning the 'Hail Mary' in Gaelic. I had lost both my mother, whom I loved very dearly, and also our piano, on which I had made good progress and which had encouraged dreams that one day I might be in the Paderewski class. One of many dreams.

Within weeks the family disintegrated. My elder brother just disappeared into thin air. My father later traced him; he had apprenticed himself to a racing trainer—the Hon. Aubrey Hastings—as a jockey!

My brother Charles was taken care of by some friends in the country. My youngest brother went to live with my mother's relations, and my sister, at sixteen, took over the house and caring for my father and me. And what a problem I turned out to be! Perhaps it was because I had received too much attention and notice for my billiards—maybe, I don't know—but I must have nearly put my dear sister, who adored me, into her grave.

I would suddenly think of J. B. Joel, Walter Winans and A. G. Vanderbilt—with Aries egging me on. How and where to make that million? Certainly not in Brighton. Then London. I must get there, but how, without money?

I would walk. Had I not, on my twelfth birthday, won a walking race from the Plough Inn at Pyecombe to the Aquarium in Brighton, a distance of five miles, and collected the coveted first prize—three 'Eton' collars, made of India rubber and washable! Yes! *I would* walk to London. True it was fifty miles and not five and would, of course, take longer. Where I would sleep when I got there, or how I would exist, did not enter my head.

After tea, when my sister was in the kitchen washing up, I set out for London—and that million.

When night closed in I felt cold, ravenously hungry and quite a little frightened; but I pressed on. Hassocks and Burgess Hill were gaily passed, but after thirteen miles I could take no more. I found a soft mound of grass and, almost before I could lay my head down, fell fast asleep.

I was awakened by a bright light shining on my face. It was a 'bulls-eye' and behind it was the biggest policeman I had ever seen.

'Walking to London,' I told him in answer to his question. He picked me up like a very small child and made for the police station. There they heard my story and gave me steaming hot cocoa and thick slices of bread and butter covered with plum jam. They contacted my father and sister, who must have been frantic, and told them they would put me on the morning train and would they meet it.

It was past midnight when I settled down to sleep in the only cell—reserved for drunks or petty offenders—and early next morning the kindly policeman saw me off on the Brighton train and gave me sixpence. 'That's the start of that million pounds you're dreaming about!'

Within a week the entire operation was repeated, but this time the police were not so sympathetic. They still dished out hot cocoa and 'doorsteps' of bread and jam, but warned me and my father that the next time I would be put on the charge sheet.

My sister found the solution. When I came home from school for tea she took away my shoes! I was not as crazy as all that, so it was effective.

Then they changed my school and that really changed my life. At the new school my class master, a Mr Douglas Hawkins, was also sports master. He must have seen something worth salvaging in me.

'I hear you play billiards,' he said one day. 'How good are you?'

'I've made a hundred "break",' I proudly told him.

'King Edward once said that making a hundred break under twenty-one was the sign of a mis-spent youth,' he replied.

This was a bit of a blow.

'There are other games,' he went on.

'Snooker?' I queried.

'No! Games where you can breathe fresh air while you play.'

He doesn't approve of me; well, it's mutual, I said to myself. 'Such as?' I asked rather rudely.

'Cricket. Come to the Level with us and try your hand.'

Grudgingly I did so, and before the practice was over I was mad keen.

'I'll give you a trial in the second eleven.'

Within a month I was in the first eleven and doing well with batting and bowling. Mr Hawkins also took me to see Sussex and the

Australians at Hove and from that moment cricket ousted all other sports. I have never lost my appetite for it.

I saw all the giants of those days—C. B. Fry, Ranjitsinhji, G. L. Jessop, George Hirst, Wilfred Rhodes of Yorkshire, Victor Trumper the Australian. I devoured Wisden's book until I could reel off the names of teams and their achievements by heart.

One of my most treasured memories is of being at the Hove ground early and watching the net practice. Perhaps because of my lack of inhibition, I spoke to 'Ranji' and asked him about his famous 'leg glance'. In this the bat would almost touch the left side of his left foot to meet the ball, then invariably make a boundary all along the 'carpet'.

To my delight, he asked me to come into the net where he did a 'leg glance' for me, demonstrating the importance of the turn of the wrist. I followed what he was saying very closely, and he asked me to try it while he held my hands in position. George Cox, sen. was bowling, and to my joy I did it first time. The laugh that went up from everyone looking is something I shall not forget.

When I told Mr Hawkins about it, he said: 'That you can really boast about—being coached by "Ranji"! Never mind your hundred break at billiards!'

Then winter and soccer arrived. Once again Mr Hawkins told me to join the team at practice. It was on the Brighton Race Hill and bitterly cold with a north-east wind blowing. Nothing can equal the South Downs in a north-east wind, except Siberia. The goalkeeper passed out in the cold, and Mr Hawkins told me to take over. I was delighted. Anything to keep warm.

For some reason I found I could anticipate shots, and I saved several. As a result I found myself in the reserves. Before the season started, I was promoted to the first eleven and that year we won the Sussex Schools Cup with an extraordinary record:

Played 12; Won 12: Lost Nil: Drawn Nil; For, 89: Against, Nil.

We had gone through the entire season without dropping a single point—and as goalkeeper I had not conceded one goal.

As a reward for this record Mr Hawkins took the team to the Goldstone Ground, Hove, to see the Corinthians play Sussex, and Brighton and Hove Albion play Derby County.

This is how I came to see two of the greatest soccer centre-forwards of all time. The Corinthians were invincible with the Farmfield brothers, S. S. Harris, and their centre-forward, G. O. Smith.

As vividly as at the time, over sixty years ago, I remember the kick-off. Smith made the usual move to pass to the inside man. Three of the Sussex team rushed at the ball. But he hadn't passed. He moved forward to meet another trio of Sussex defenders. This time he kicked the ball and once again the Sussex defence pounced. But the ball had not left his foot. Smith made a bee-line for the goal, swerving and weaving with the ball 'laced to his boot' as one critic put it. Past ten men, there was only the goalkeeper who came out to the penalty limit, narrowing the goal all the time. Smith lobbed the ball over the goalie's head, swerved his way past, caught the ball with his foot as it landed, and walked it into the net. A goal with a ball untouched by any other player. No great demonstration, no kisses from his team mates; just a few polite handclaps.

By comparison with Smith, the aesthetic-looking scholar, Steve Bloomer of Derby County, with his bullet-short cropped head and massive shoulders, was like a broadsword up against a rapier. But he scored three goals and, on one occasion, he behaved in a way that would be incomprehensible these days. He knocked a Brighton player flat during a run for the goal, forgot the ball and tended the player until the trainer took over. A handshake and the incident was closed. No fuss, no ill-feeling—those were the days!

Compare this with an incident I once saw at Wembley in an international match. The visiting centre-forward made for goal with the sole of his right foot aimed at the midriff of England's goalkeeper, Frank Swift. Although Swift caught the ball and cleared, he still got the boot in his stomach. The imprint of the studs must still have been there when Swift was tragically killed flying with the Manchester United team at Munich.

Now soccer, like cricket, had become an obsession with me, and billiards receded farther than ever.

Meanwhile my sister married when she was seventeen. No doubt I contributed to her wanting to find security and stability, and to get away to a home of her own.

I was now alone with my father and our home became a lodging. At the same establishment as his billiards saloon was a very sweet woman who attended to the 'Silver Grill'. She took one look at me and decided I needed attention. She cooked for me, did my laundry and generally played the mother to me. Very soon that is what she became, for my father married her and our house was a home once more and not a lodging. I was now happy at school and comfortable at home.

But not for long. T.B. struck again, and my father had to leave his work and enter a sanatorium.

Money was now needed desperately since my stepmother had also given up her job. Permission was sought and granted for me to leave school before the official leaving age of fourteen. I got a job as a page boy at Brighton's Harley House Hotel—half a crown a week plus tips and a seven-day week of ninety hours. But fifteen shillings a week in tips was a help.

My father died at the same age as my mother—forty-two. Now I was really on my own.

My stepmother had to go back to work, of course. Then, from out of the blue, came the offer of a job at the 'Bodega' in Ship Street, in the billiards room. I thought of Mr Hawkins—but well, one had to eat, so I decided not to tell him, and took it.

In those days the 'Bodega', whether in Brighton or Glasshouse Street, was a rendezvous of the racing and theatrical worlds.

Since my interest in cricket and football had not diminished my skill on the billiards table, but rather improved my game with the health from fresh air and a fresh outlook, I was fastened on by the 'smart boys' who would challenge some loud-mouthed braggart to play me for a fiver. I was so small and the braggart usually so big that it became quite a joke—and a valuable one—to watch me 'playing ducks and drakes' with them.

My breaks went up to 200 and my fame spread to London.

Teddy Webb, owner of the Metropole, Camberwell Green, saw me play and immediately offered me the then magnificent sum of thirty shillings per week plus food and a bedroom. Fortune at last.

3

Camberwell Green! The name itself conjured up a picture of tranquillity and old-world charm. But I found it the most violent atmosphere I had ever encountered.

The race gangs would meet in the public houses, order a pint of bitter, drink it in one breath, break the rim off the top and jab the jagged weapon in the face or throat of one of the opposing gang—unless he saw it coming and made his getaway. Blood and woundings galore, but, strangely enough, seldom a fatality.

My billiards skill spread to the London racing and boxing gangs, and I was soon in their hands. My size—I was fifteen years old and about five feet—was a great gimmick on which they could win easy money with 'mugs' who fancied themselves, and also against rival gangs.

It was in Camberwell that I first met the music-hall and theatrical profession. The Camberwell empire, headed by Cissie Lawson, my boss Teddy Webb, and Vesta Victoria—a great favourite whose song 'There was I, waiting at the church' was tops in those days—was a serious challenger to the Palace, which was run by the 'Syndicate'. There, at the top of the bills, George Robey, Little Tich, Eugene Stratton, Florrie Ford and Marie Lloyd were regulars. Fred Karno's 'Mumming Birds', including the drunk in the box, Charlie Chaplin, was a highlight.

I first met Charlie Chaplin in Camberwell and was astounded that a man as funny as he was as a drunk on the stage could, in real life, be so serious and abstemious.

I did not meet Charlie Chaplin again until the 'twenties, when I was in Hollywood with Dorothy and Lillian Gish. Mary Pickford and Douglas Fairbanks, sen. gave a dinner in my honour at their home, Pickfair.

Although I was the guest of honour, Chaplin, from the moment of his arrival, like a magnet attracted the attention of all present and exuded interesting ideas on many subjects, holding the dinner guests spellbound with his witty comments. A long haul, I thought, from the 'Mumming Birds' at the Camberwell Palace to such a gathering at Pickfair, the Beverly Hills 'Holy of Holies'.

I was delighted to find that Mary had seated me next to Chaplin. Apart from the usual inaudible introduction on meeting, Chaplin seemed to know nothing of my background, and I had very little chance of bringing him into the picture.

He addressed himself entirely to me and began discoursing on various subjects, mostly serious or political, and frequently used the word 'determinism'. I had never heard it before and wondered if he had tripped up—but no—he came back to it at least twice, demonstrating with his hands the meaning of the word, which apparently was allied to a corkscrew.

I was out of my intellectual depth and, having enjoyed some of Mary Pickford's excellent wine, decided to break down the barrier.

'Do you remember playing the Camberwell Palace and Uncle Fred?' I whispered to him. He shut up like a clam!

'There are things in life worth remembering—others I prefer to forget,' he answered.

He never spoke to me again during dinner.

Since reading his superb autobiography, in which he is so frank and warmly honest about his early life, I have now come to the conclusion Chaplin did not resent my reference to 'The Mumming Birds' and Uncle Fred Karno, but resented my not being sufficiently interested in his discourse on 'determinism'. Having recently had some time on my hands, I looked up the word and found that it was 'a theory of action determined by motives themselves determined by causes irrespective of the will.' So now I know!

We've meandered from Camberwell Green to Hollywood, let's get back.

My time in Camberwell was exciting enough, perhaps too much so, and my billiards skill spread abroad. I had made a break of 315. Offers were coming in for me to compete for the Junior Championship of the World.

All over London I played exhibition games and received as much as five guineas a night. That was a lot of money in those days. One of my opponents at East Ham was Tom Newman who afterwards became Champion of the World. I narrowly missed beating him. I regret that. It would have been nice to say: 'I once beat Tom Newman at billiards.'

My fixed objective was to reach the top as a professional billiards player, and my reputation was such that many good judges predicted I would become World Champion before I was twenty-one. I knew, and was encouraged by, the top men of that time—H. W. Stevenson,

Melbourne Inman, Tom Reece and George Dawson and J. P. Mannock.

I practised for several hours every day; took long walks up Denmark Hill; never smoked or touched any drink—despite the Irish and Aries influences; and never gave girls a thought, although I realised afterwards that many had given *me* some consideration. I was oftentold I was good-looking and my photograph (reproduced here) I trust bears this out.

I noticed that on more than one occasion a very beautiful woman, aged thirty-five or more, attended several of my exhibition games. She was the first to applaud any good shot I made or a big break, and when I caught her eye she always smiled at me.

She was apparently well off because she invariably drove up in her motor car—a rarity in those days. After one match, she congratulated me on winning and told me she would like me to play an exhibition game for her guests after one of her dinner parties. I said I should be delighted. And so I was, for the fee she suggested was ten guineas! She fixed a date and told me her address in Dulwich Village.

'You have a full-sized table?' I asked. She said she had. 'I'll arrive a little early and have a short practice on my own.' I told her.

When I arrived, she opened the door to me herself and led the way up the main staircase of her beautiful house. I shed my hat and coat and she led me into the 'billiards room'. I followed her in and looked round.

There was no full-sized billiards table but a magnificent bed!

'What would you like to drink?' she asked.

I told her I did not drink.

'You will tonight—just to please me—won't you? Come and sit down.'

When I left her house it was almost daylight. I was feeling terrible and utterly bewildered. In addition, the drink she had given me had left me very giddy and ready to die. I'd never had an alcoholic drink before so she had achieved a double seduction. I was overwhelmed with remorse. Then I was sick and felt better. I vowed I would never touch gin again!

Instead of taking a tram, I decided to walk home to Camberwell. The air would do me good and I wanted time to think. The more I thought, the more I hated myself.

My first and last. Never again, I vowed. I pondered how best to wipe out the memory. After a sleepless hour or two I decided. The Oval. Surrey were playing Sussex.

The clean refreshing air, my love of cricket, and Jack Hobbs scoring a century did the trick. I arrived at my work that evening refreshed in body and soul. I decided to forget the whole sordid occasion.

But I couldn't. Before it happened I had a one-track mind: to reach the top, and make some money in getting there. Now I found my attention divided. I looked at girls—and in an entirely new light. Before long, I was responding to them as they were to me, and the Irish and Aries were having full rein.

Affair followed affair. The 'Camberwell Casanova', they dubbed me; and I'm afraid I felt flattered. But my game suffered. So did my health. What would have happened had the Metropole not been condemned as redundant and closed, I cannot imagine.

Then followed a vacuum of interest in my life until my old boss of the Metropole invited me to take charge of the billiards saloon at the Swan and Sugarloaf, in Croydon. I accepted, and tried hard to pick up the lost time. But my billiards form would not come back, and all too soon I found myself drifting back to my friends at Camberwell in an effort to forget my fading chances of real success at the game.

I indulged in a whirl which included visits to my 'tutor' at Dulwich. Wild week-ends we spent together. Plenty of drink and now fifty cigarettes a day. I seldom played a good game of billiards. I felt dejected and I guess more than a little ashamed of the hell of a life I was leading—which now took me to the fringe of West End society, and to having what is facetiously known as 'a good time'. Too good.

One day I found myself facing a doctor in his consulting room, hearing him say: 'Unless you give up *entirely* the life you are leading and get right away, I give you three months!'

'As bad as that?' I asked.

'As bad as that,' he answered.

'Couldn't I cut down?'

'No! Get right away from London; from England if you can. Find some sunshine. No smoking. No drink. No women!'

'T.B.?' I asked.

'Just round the corner,' he told me.

So, in July 1914, all hopes of making an important mark in the billiards world having evaporated, broken in health and morale, I swallowed two strong drinks and flung myself—or the bits and pieces left of me—on to an upper bunk in the *Orsova* as she pulled out of Tilbury.

I woke up at Gibraltar.

I went ashore and seeing a church door open, I looked in. Mass was taking place. After a moment's hesitation, I did what I should have done long before: I knelt and prayed for the strength to follow the abstinence decree of my doctor. Despite my depression, I did not touch a drink and I cut down my smoking to five a day, although allowed ten.

Cairo depressed me. Egypt depressed me. Everything about it was ancient—dead. And I was feeling terrible. I missed my friends—bad for me as they may have been. But at least they lived. Everything around me here was dead. Better to live three months back home, I thought, than to die here in a strange world.

I was on my way back to England on the next boat. I arrived on 1 August, 1914, and went to stay with my sister.

My chums heard I was back. They were soon on the 'phone.

'Come and join us tonight—we're going out on the town.'

'Why, what's happening?' I asked.

'Going to Buckingham Palace to hear war declared.'

After a wild evening when, for the first and only time in my life, I got really drunk, I found myself outside Buckingham Palace cheering like mad. I knew not why or wherefore but I joined in a wild serpent dance, being trodden underfoot one moment, and lifted shoulder high the next. But this was living.

I heard war declared, but not much more. When I woke up next morning I found myself in a strange room with other men like me fully dressed and lying on the floor.

'Where am I?' I asked.

'You're in the Army—that's where you are!' someone told me. And I was. I have no recollection of enlisting, but as my health was bad I knew they wouldn't accept me. Yet they did.

'When do we go?' I asked.

'You'll soon find out. Now go home and we'll let you know, and when you speak to me or ask any sergeant-major a question in future, say "Sir".'

'Yes—sir,' I replied.

How I was to know that someone in the near nude was a sergeant-major foxed me.

I knew my sister would be worried about my being out all night with my health so poorly. But how to tell her I was in the Army!

Aries and the Irish came to the rescue. I painted a picture of the deep patriotic urge which made me do it. I really went overboard. My sister was almost on the point of tears. Rudyard Kipling would have hailed me had this been the Boer War.

My call came. And such an affectionate and sentimental farewell I took of my sister, that to come back alive was unthinkable.

It was in Green Park, opposite the Ritz Hotel, that the 17th Battalion of the Royal Fusiliers fell in. I was one of them. The park was closed to the public until we marched off to Victoria; from there to an unknown destination, and perhaps glory. As we were being 'numbered' I looked ahead and—park closed or not—there was my sister, waving to me!

We marched off—down Piccadilly and Constitution Hill, and past Buckingham Palace, where we were halted for a few minutes as a battalion of the Grenadier Guards, smart in their khaki, made their way to St James's Palace. They were led by a mere stripling of a Lieutenant. It was the Prince of Wales.

At Victoria, we were marched on to the platform where our train was waiting. And there she was again—my sister! When we were stood easy, she rushed over—and again a most sentimental scene took place between us. 'Hope France won't be too cold,' she said.

No, there must be no return, I thought, after such farewells.

The train moved off. I could see her still, half waving with her handkerchief, half wiping away a tear.

Well, we were on our way to France! It was raining in torrents and the countryside looked grim. Within half an hour, the train slowed up at a little station and then stopped. The platform became alive with men jumping from the train. Probably on fire, I thought.

'All out! And fall in—at the double!' someone was shouting. I recognised the voice. It was the sergeant-major who had insisted on being called 'sir'. Yes, there was no mistake about it as our carriage door was snatched open. We got out and fell in!

'What's wrong, corporal?' asked one brave fellow. 'Engine trouble?'

The face of the sergeant-major indicated apoplexy. He turned and decided I was the culprit. Fixing his eye on me—and his look left no doubt in my mind that here was a man who without doubt and without reason hated me—he replied:

'The trouble starts tomorrow at reveille—if you know what that means! If you don't, you'll soon find out. And take a good look at that hill—it's one of the highest in Surrey. The view from the top is without parallel and you'll be seeing plenty of it for some time to come. You'll be going up and down that hill until you love it. Now, left turn! Quick march!'

Up the hill we went in the drenching rain, slipping back a pace every other step. No overcoat; wet through—I wondered what the doctor who gave me three months would say. We halted at the plateau on top of the hill where, like mushrooms, bell tents were growing out of the ground.

We were broken up into groups of thirteen and allotted a tent. Mine was number thirteen. Not too good a start, I thought.

I looked round to take in my tent mates. Good heavens! One was my young brother, whom I had not seen or heard of for many years! He'd grown taller than I and was very serious. After a few words together we wandered out of the tent, the rain having eased up. I stopped in my tracks.

'What's wrong?' asked my brother.

'That's her house,' I told him.

'Whose?'

'Lil—our sister.'

'Good! We'll get some decent grub.'

'But I can't face her again.' I explained.

My brother as a tent mate and within a stone's throw of my sister's house!

In this way the Great War began for me.

4

Weeks of foot-slogging, never-ending rain, blue serge uniforms, forage-caps that made us look like convicts and which, in the rain, oozed soap down our faces and bodies because some patriotic profiteer supplied the uniforms and caps and they were *stuck* together at the seams instead of sewn!

Beds wet through. Food uneatable. Ice-cold water for washing and shaving, and a bath for the brave ones. And it was under civilized conditions that I had been given a few short months to live!

My instinct about the sergeant-major's hatred of me proved to be only too correct. The dirtiest fatigues frequently came my way, despite the fact that alphabetical order governed the exercise; being a 'W', I should have been way down the list, and then only named once in twenty-six days. My brother, P.W., was never on the roster. In one week I was named twice. Lined up for fatigue duty, I endeavoured to stand dead still and make myself inconspicuous, but inevitably I heard his voice.

'Private Wilcox—latrines!'

He rolled and relished this word. It nauseated me—and still does. He never let up and my association with latrines became the popular ribald joke of my tent mates.

In desperation I stopped our young 2nd lieutenant, saluted smartly and asked if I could speak to him. Before he could answer, my tormentor's voice boomed in my ear.

'Private Wilcox—you know you never speak to an officer unless taken to him by an N.C.O.?'

I told him I did not.

'Well! Now you do—left turn—quick march and report to me at reveille tomorrow!'

That night I decided to desert. When all in the tent were asleep, I started to gather my things together. My brother opened his eyes and saw me. I explained.

'That's just what he wants you to do. He'll get promotion and you'll get time. Get back to bed.'

Shivering outside the sergeant-major's tent next morning for what seemed like an eternity, I was eventually dismissed by our young

2nd lieutenant. My tormentor had been caught red-handed selling some of the men's rations to the camp caterer!

From then on there was a chance that I might emerge and be a useful soldier. Strangely enough, despite everything, I felt and looked better than I had for some time.

My brother, who I found possessed a strong character, looked at our sister's home and said: '*You* may have overdone the soldier's farewell, but I didn't. I'm hungry; I need a bath; and I'd love to see Lil again.'

'But I can't,' I protested.

'Get our hair shaved off first. That will show her we're really in the Army.'

So, with convict clothes and cropped hair, we presented ourselves at her door and our welcome was as emotional as our farewells. We had hot baths and ate until we were almost bursting. It was the first of many such occasions.

Route marches with full pack, early morning P.T., night manoeuvres —in all weathers. My chest measurement had increased by inches. I slept under canvas with one blanket and ground sheet, under incessant rain and with sentry-go at all hours. I could march ten miles, and was one of the best boxers in the battalion. That's what the Army had done for me. Not only physically, but mentally and character-wise.

When exactly the moment of truth came to me, I don't quite know; possibly on sentry-go in the silence of the night, as the stars shone down. If I got through this war safely, I thought, I must do something with my life.

During the hectic years I had forgotten or neglected my religious beliefs. One Sunday morning when church parade was voluntary, I heard the call: 'All Roman Catholics fall in.' I fell in and walked five miles to mass, led by Lieut. Stanley Wootton—now one of the stewards of the Jockey Club, and respected far and wide wherever a racecourse exists.

I felt better for that mass. I didn't notice until afterwards that my young brother was with us. We fell in next to each other and marched back to camp over the lovely Surrey Hills to the singing of 'Tipperary'.

That night in our tent, whilst faro was being played by most of our tent mates to a background of ribald chatter, on subjects ranging from triumphant sexual conquests to venereal disease (the latter apparently a success symbol of virility), I suddenly heard the quiet intonation of 'Hail Mary'—in Gaelic. It took me swiftly back to the whole family, except father, on their knees led by mother.

Yes, I had lost a lot and gained nothing in my search for life and a million. I was disturbed and puzzled. Then the truth hit me hard: I was primitive, uneducated, with no standards of life or living. This must be put right; but how?

Later, on sentry-go, with the lights twinkling down in the valley, I found the answer. I would write. I confided in a tent mate who was always reading.

'How much reading have you done?' he asked.

'Practically none,' I told him.

'Try reading first—then write.'

Good sense, of course. On his advice, I started reading as greedily as I had eaten S.P.O. in Harris's S.P.O. shop. On Kipling, Chesterton, Belloc, Jack London, Spender, Conan Doyle, Oliver Lodge and finally Rupert Brooke.

It was a line out of J. A. Spender which gave my sense of values a shock and made my trudging to Bolney in search of a phantom million seem rather pointless: although then I had been only twelve years old, and J. B. Joel with his beautiful lady-friend, Walter Winans with his high-stepping horses, and A. G. Vanderbilt with his good looks and coach filled with grand people had all looked so very glamorous. Spender, in his book *The Comments of Bagshot*, wrote: 'A man's wealth lies in the fewness of his wants.' How true I have found this to be throughout my life, even in the darkest periods.

On 1s. 1d. per day, it was not easy to keep up the supply of books. I was hungry for knowledge and avid in my search. The more I read the more my ignorance was exposed. However, I set my course based on the realisation that only through reading could I offset my lack of education and deficiencies.

How right King Edward VII was when he said: 'A hundred break at billiards before you're twenty-one is a sign of a mis-spent youth.' Mine was not mis-spent—it was squandered.

My great favourite was John Masefield and I memorised 'The Everlasting Mercy' until word perfect.

In 1914 emerged a young poet who looked like a Greek god and who could draw a vivid word picture, whether it was the quiet of Grantchester or a mud-covered private soldier. This was Rupert Brooke. I could almost smell the muffins when reading:

> *'Stands the Church clock at ten to three?*
> *And is there honey still for tea?'*

And 'The Soldier'—romanticising war, if you will, but to me his sonnet was a spiritual cry from someone ill-equipped to fight life itself, let alone to resist death in action.

I am aware that the Great War touched me at a period when I was emotionally susceptible and my moral and spiritual values were somersaulting, but in retrospect the period represented an atmosphere and spirit that affected me profoundly. Coming as it did as a climax to the golden years, there was grace, elegance and chivalry in the 'war to end all wars'.

Rupert Brooke left a deep impression on my mind and—just as King Edward VII dozing in front of Queen Victoria's statue at Hove and my singing 'Boys of the Chelsea School' set up mental pictures of Queen Victoria and Nell Gwyn—he was my inspiration when I produced my very first silent film of *The Wonderful Story* by I. A. R. Wylie. Off stage a baby was born and its cries were heard. Over a cloudscape I superimposed a sub-title:

> *'But Winter's broken and earth has woken,*
> *And the small birds cry again;*
> *And the hawthorn hedge puts forth its buds,*
> *And my heart puts forth its pain.'*

When Nurse Edith Cavell, in my silent version *Dawn*, was shot and buried at the Tir National, Brussels, I concluded the film showing a mound of newly-turned turf over which a sub-title ran:

> *'. . . some corner of a foreign field . . .'*

And finally in *The Courtneys of Curzon Street*, during an episode showing the Great War, Michael Wilding, in the role of a man home on leave from France who takes his son, at school in Tunbridge Wells, to afternoon tea in a tuck shop, recited the sonnet of 'The Soldier' against a background of actual war scenes.

How obvious and 'corny' (whatever that word means) these sentiments appear in 1966, with kitchen sinks and off-stage flushing of toilets pushing the music of Tchaikovsky and Elgar off the soundtrack. However, at the time the films were shown, the scenes enriched by Rupert Brooke's quotations were profoundly moving.

I had been promoted to lance-corporal (unpaid) and to my own—and the C.O.'s—astonishment I found I could drill a battalion and be heard on the square.

The C.O. complimented me, saw I had Army Regulations in my

hand and asked what made me so interested in the Army. I told him of my early heroes of the Boer War—Roberts, Fighting Mac, Baden-Powell and Kitchener.

The following Sunday, I visited the home of my tent mate, David Dowling—the book-reader—and met his sisters, who ran a girls' school in Balham. Another turning-point in my life. They were wonderful, not only in hospitality, but because they thought I had something in me. And that hadn't happened since Douglas Hawkins at school. They lent me books, told me how to approach writing—from the heart, not the head. In addition they were influential, and talked to a friend at the War Office about me.

The C.O. sent for me a few days later.

'There's a shortage of officers. Would you take a commission if I recommended you?'

I could hardly stammer my acceptance and thanks. Apart from anything else, my pay rose from 1s. 1d. a day to 7s. 6d.!

Within a week came an order from the C.O. to see him at once. No commission, I thought. Much too soon.

The C.O. asked why I hadn't told him I was already on the priority list at the War Office. I confessed I didn't know. The C.O. had himself received word I was to be gazetted to The Buffs (East Kent Regiment); and the War Office advised him that I was gazetted to the Grenadier Guards (the smart regiment I had passed on my way to Victoria, led by the Prince of Wales!). My good Balham friends, the Dowlings, had been busy—and successful.

The C.O. saw my confusion. 'You can accept only one,' he told me.

'Whichever you say, sir.'

'Any private means?' he asked.

'No, sir.'

'You'd find life in the Guards difficult if you had to live on your pay.'

'Could I—in the Buffs?' I asked. He told me I could—so that was settled.

More farewells. To my brother, who was so much better qualified to take a commission than I. And, of course, to my sister; but this time I played it down and she understood.

I was now an officer, with hopes of becoming a gentleman.

I found it easy to master the manuals and also became an expert shot. Finally I was short-listed for France, and given overseas leave.

At Brighton, walking along the front in my new officer's uniform with brand new Sam Browne belt, I saw two girls. One was the most beautiful I had ever seen. She caught my eye and, I thought, smiled. I turned back.

Over tea in the Palm Court at the Metropole, she turned out to be the daughter of a ship's captain. She had no mother, and was working as a V.A.D. Whilst she was talking, I realised that here it was—not the cheap shoddy affairs of Dulwich and Camberwell, but the real thing. Certainly I had not thought about women since I left the little church in Gibraltar. Army life was full and disposed of any surplus energy. The faro-playing sex back-chat in the tent amused, but didn't intrigue me. Now I was up against real love for the first time in my life. I found it difficult to contain myself and not shout it aloud to the tea drinkers in the Palm Court.

I would have proposed there and then—having, to a certain extent, found myself. But, magnificent though it seemed at first, could it be done on 7s. 6d. a day? No, I must wait a bit—do some thinking. There was that writing bug in me, something might come out of it; something must.

I took her to the theatre to see *Tonight's the Night*. 'They didn't believe me' was the theme song. 'That from this great big world you've chosen me...' Of course she hasn't—yet, but unless I'm sadly mistaken, she has the same feelings for me as I for her. Yet not a word of this has been spoken.

I asked her to arrange for me to meet her father and I'd get leave and come back. A tender farewell. I kissed her hand. She offered her lips.

Back on a special overseas course, I could not settle down to work. 7s. 6d. a day and out of that a mess bill to meet. How could I expect her to wait? With her loveliness—I felt it was hopeless. However, the dilemma had to be put aside since the not unimportant matter of the war intervened and I found myself in France.

After an uneventful spell I was sent home on leave and appointed an instructor of cadets training to be officers in Kitchener's Army.

I reported at Fermoy, in County Cork, the territory of my mother's 'clan'—the Healys. It was spring 1916. My work embraced the passing-out training of cadets prior to their being commissioned. There were sixty in my company.

This was a tricky situation, since they were neither officers nor in the ranks. On Good Friday, my commanding officer sent for me.

'There's going to be trouble,' he said. 'Your cadets will be given rifles and ammunition and you will be in charge. For the time being they will be regarded as private soldiers and not cadets.'

'I don't understand, sir.'

'There's going to be trouble with the Irish and they must be regarded as our enemies until we get the situation under control.'

'You mean I have to fight the Irish?' I asked.

'Of course,' the C.O. told me.

'But I never joined the Army to do that, sir,' I protested.

'You joined the Army to do as you were bloody well told—and I've told you.'

The Irish Rebellion of Easter 1916 started in Dublin, then spread throughout the country. The first shot in Fermoy killed the great young hero of Cork County. He was their 'Michael Collins'.

The second bullet hit me.

We were both taken to Fermoy hospital. One Irishman dead—one Irish-cum-Englishman wounded.

A deputation called at the hospital.

'We want to hold a wake and we need "Mike's" body,' they said.

They were sent about their business by the officer in charge of the hospital. Within an hour they returned.

'We want his body by six o'clock tonight or we'll burn the hospital down to the ground, so we will,' they told the officer.

It was just after three, and here I was with a bullet in my leg and the important corpse in the next bed. The doctor came in, a small, wizened, elderly Irishman with a soft hat over his eyes and smoking a pipe. The sort of Irishman you find in any play or book, but never in Ireland. He removed his hat and stood in silent prayer a few minutes in front of 'Mike'. He then replaced his hat and turned to me

'And what can I do for you?' he asked.

'I've been shot, doctor.'

'And you expect me to minister to you—a bloody foreigner,' he replied.

'But doctor,' I protested, 'I was born in Cork.'

'Then you're a damned sight worse—you're a bloody traitor,' he said as he walked off.

My C.O. got a despatch-rider on a motor-cycle through the blockade set up with a message. Did I need anything?

'Some crutches,' I sent back, 'and quick! They've threatened to burn down the hospital at 6 o'clock.'

The hospital was surrounded and cut off by the rebels. But about 5 o'clock a party of soldiers came, carried me out and got me into a

1. Anna.

2. (*left*)   The statue of Queen Victoria at Hove.
3. (*centre*) King Edward VII walking on Hove front.
4. (*right*)   Harris's 'Sausage, Potatoes and Onions' shop in West Street, Brighton.
5. (*below*) A. G. Vanderbilt's London–Brighton coach outside the Hotel Metropole.

6. (*left*) Aged twelve, winning a five-mile walking match. (First prize: three Eton collars, India rubber and washable.)
7. (*right*) Myself (in light sweater) as goalkeeper of a cup-winning school team. (Played twelve; won twelve. Goals for, eighty-nine; goals against, nil.)
8. (*below*) Aged thirteen, as a page-boy in a Brighton hotel.
9. (*below right*) As a junior billiards champion.

10. (*left*) K. S. Ranjitsinhji, who showed me his 'leg glance'.
11. (*right*) Private Wilcox H. S., Royal Fusiliers, August 1914.
12. (*below*) As a pilot officer, Royal Flying Corps, France, 1916.

car. We ran the gauntlet of bricks, bottles and bullets but got back to the camp alive.

The regimental doctor took a look at my leg, found the entrance wound but not the exit. The bullet was still there.

It still is today. The only time I am aware of it is swimming, which I have had to give up, as cramp is always round the corner. I feel it dancing, too, which I have also had to forsake.

I miss swimming but not dancing. Let me digress to a sad little story about my dancing.

Lady Mountbatten, President of the Royal College of Nursing's Appeal Fund, which benefited from a unique series of *premières* of our film *The Lady with a Lamp* (with which I will deal later), gave a dinner party and dance at Broadlands, the home of the Mountbattens at Romsey. It was frequently visited by Florence Nightingale herself when Lord Palmerston was in residence there.

The Queen, Prince Philip and Princess Margaret were to be there. Although in active production at the time, Anna and I accepted the invitation. Then the thought struck Anna.

'Suppose the Queen expresses a wish to dance with you?'

'I can't explain about the bullet—I must dance,' I told her.

'But can you?' asked Anna. 'Any of the new dances, I mean?'

A good point, that.

'You must have some lessons,' said Anna.

An instructor came to the studio and my lunch hour was devoted to him for two weeks—after which I could at least go through the motions.

Within a few minutes of the commencement of the dancing at Broadlands, Prince Philip led Anna on to the floor, and both must have enjoyed it for they had dance after dance together. Meanwhile I looked on or found a friend at the bar.

Anna never stopped dancing throughout the evening—one partner after another. The Queen was also having a wonderful time. But still I waited.

About 2.30 a.m. I begged Edwina Mountbatten to excuse me as we had to be on the studio set at 9.00 a.m. She understood, and off to Shepperton we drove.

'All those lessons for nothing.' I said to Anna. We had quite a laugh about it.

The next day I heard from Lord Brabourne, son-in-law of the

Mountbattens, that just after 2.30 the Queen had expressed a wish to dance with me!

From selling the halfpenny *Evening Argus* in the Brighton streets and calling out 'Death of Queen Victoria', to dancing with Queen Elizabeth II as an honoured guest of Earl and Countess Mountbatten, was a giant stride indeed. And I only missed that dance by a whisker!

5

Back to 1916, Ireland and the bullet.

It was decided I should have an X-ray to locate the bullet and remove it. That meant Blighty—good!

Given the choice of a hospital, I chose Brighton. Apart from friends, there was also that lovely girl who, I was confident, when she saw me on crutches would fall into my arms. It would be so easy to propose and I would do it as soon as I met her. I decided not to write but take her by surprise.

I set out from Rosslare by boat with the vision of her face beaming a warm welcome. U-boats were reported in the vicinity, so we put back and went by train to Dublin and crossed to Holyhead.

Her face kept recurring and *en route* to Euston I kept working out my proposal speech. At Crewe, a Zeppelin was overhead and dropped bombs. After a wait, we pressed on. At Victoria, before the train pulled out, there was a daylight raid by a squadron of Fokkers. A near miss, but off we went on the last lap. Could anything else happen, I wondered?

It did.

Arriving at Brighton, I drove straight to the Metropole, then a Military H.Q. and Club. A clean-up before we met. I made for the phone to call her and was almost knocked over by a dashing Major, and waiting for him—yes, it was! She did not see me.

I watched them go off, and ordered a double brandy and soda. The 'Camberwell Casanova' was not doing so well.

The X-ray showed the bullet to be embedded in my calf muscle which might waste if an operation was performed. So it was decided to leave it, in the hope it would work itself out. I discarded my crutches and now hobbled with a strong stick.

I wandered along the front in the sunshine and was wondering how long it would be before I could get back to France, when suddenly there she was, walking towards me, arms outstretched, a glorious smile of welcome on her face.

'Why didn't you let me know?' she asked.

'Wanted to take you by surprise,' I told her.

'You certainly have,' she exclaimed, and oblivious of the passers-by she kissed me passionately and took my arm. 'Daddy wants to meet you. I'm taking you home,' she said.

Her father, a retired sea captain, approved of me but was concerned about my pay as a 2nd Lieutenant. 'I'm due for a second pip and an extra 3s. 6d. a day,' I told him.

'Let's talk again when you get it,' he replied. I went back to my station.

And then something out of the blue—and I mean blue—turned up the following day. Pilots were badly needed in the Royal Flying Corps. The pay was 21s. a day. I'm afraid *that* more than my love for King and Country settled it. 21s. a day in those days was being in the money, and as an officer in the R.F.C. I was sure my dream of the perfect marriage was 'in the bag'. I applied and was accepted.

Once again there was leave, before training at Reading and Netheravon. Back to Brighton—fully approved by her father, proposed, accepted and married during the leave period. Wedding at Reigate in my new R.F.C. uniform.

'Flying Corps pilot weds beautiful girl', the local paper headlined it. And she was. A short honeymoon in London. Lobster mayonnaise at Scott's. To the Alhambra to see George Robey and Vi Lorraine in *The Bing Boys*. 'If You were the only girl in the world,' George sang, and I grabbed her hand and squeezed it. She returned the squeeze and looked at me with a smile that made me forget all sense of time and place.

Then on to Maidenhead, to spend a few days at the home of our best man and his wife. Here absolute heaven was suddenly interrupted by an urgent call from Adastral House for all R.F.C. officers to return to duty at once.

My orders took me to Upavon, there to rush my training, get my wings and be off to France. I was given my pilot's wings when I had only been off the ground for dual instruction and solo flying for seventeen hours! I went to France with that same record. Not a good pilot, I'm afraid, and duck soup if I met an enemy plane too soon. But I could fly and experience would come if I survived. It should be recorded that the plane I flew—a BE2C—was capable of a maximum speed of 55 m.p.h. with the nose slightly down.

The bliss of marrying the girl I madly loved quickly gave way on my first confrontation of war. Novice, raw as a pilot, the thing was to survive. Conditions were also entirely different, with the whole of Flanders under a cloak of snow. The casualties were grim. Yes, this was war all right. Concentrate. Not even time to write to **her, but** she'd understand.

My greatest difficulty was reading the topography of a strange landscape with all identification marks obliterated by the snow.

I was doing a night reconnaissance up to the enemy lines but got hopelessly lost and decided to turn back. I had apparently made very little headway since our aerodrome lights were still almost below my plane. I started to come down and, in those days, we had only three instruments—altimeter, pilot tube and joystick. The altimeter, which indicated height, had to be set before each flight. Mine either had not been set or else was faulty, for it read 900 feet—whereas I found myself flying below treetop level and straight into a dense forest!

Only thirty feet up, I tried the unpardonable—a quick flat turn; otherwise I would have been nose on into the forest. Naturally I stalled and dived straight into the ground. It was fortunate the cockpit was an open one, since I was thrown clear of the plane on to a soft clump of bushes as the entire machine became enveloped in flames.

My C.O. and brother officers rushed from the Mess to pull me out. The C.O. stared at me. 'After that flat turn at tree-top level, Wilcox, you'll get out of hell.' Later, he gave me the 'boss' of the propeller, 'to remind you not to do it again. The nearest cemetery is thirty miles away, transport is short and—in case you don't know—planes cost money.'

No! I was not a good pilot.

A week later, over enemy lines still white with snow, I encountered a 60 m.p.h. head wind, which meant 5 m.p.h. retreat. Whether it was the cold or frustration I don't know, but I was gripped by appalling abdominal pains and hardly remember landing my plane. I had been shot at by ack-ack guns, so I thought it was merely the wind-up. I was helped out and rushed to the field hospital to discover I had acute appendicitis.

Within hours I was on my way back to Blighty and Guy's Hospital for an operation . . . and to her!

The Mess Orderly handed me a note before I left the station. 'Oh yes, the mess bill.' I said I would settle it with Cox's (the R.F.C. bankers).

But it was *not* my mess bill. It was a letter from my wife, telling me she had left me and gone off to live with our best man, who had left his wife and home. She realised she loved him more than she loved me, she was sorry and asked me to forgive her and divorce her.

The surgeon at Guy's took out my appendix. I prayed I would not come out of the anaesthetic, but I did—in good time for the divorce court to take away my love. I was awarded heavy damages, which I gave to Guy's Hospital for saving my miserable life. I had experienced ten days of heaven from which I was confident I would never recover.

My petty problems did not hold up the war that was to be 'over by Christmas' 1914 and which was still going strong. The battle of the Somme was a ghastly tragedy with 60,000 Allied troops killed on the first day. The French at Verdun, in spite of a solid phalanx of patriots, were suffering enormous casualties.

However, I was not yet fit to return to France and was selected to open a new R.F.C. aerodrome at Stamford, Lincolnshire, and take charge of a pilot training squadron. There I taught many to fly and get their wings, including the first of the American Eagle Squadron pilots.

Since Stamford, 1916, I have regarded my days as living on borrowed time; in the following manner.

It was my duty to make the first morning flight to test the air for turbulence and visibility, and the instructors usually gathered round an open brazier, drank tea brewed in dixies and ate breakfast cooked over the fire. Sausages were the favourites.

One morning, while we were biting into our sausages, my second-in-command told me he had a hell of a hangover, having been out until 4 a.m. It was now only 6.30 so I appreciated how he felt! 'Let *me* test the atmosphere,' he said. 'It will be a life saver.'

At that station we were flying D.H.6's, known as 'clutching hands', with open cockpits. I demurred but he persisted and, as I had the authority to decide, I told him to go ahead. He rushed off and got into the waiting plane with its propeller already ticking over. He took off in a matter of seconds.

I decided to cook another sausage, and I noticed he had left half of his—with the imprint of his teeth still upon it. I looked up and was just in time to see him collide with a plane from a nearby training squadron. He nose-dived into the ground and burst into flames. When we got him out there was not sufficient evidence even for identification.

For weeks I could not get that half-eaten sausage with teeth marks out of my mind, and realised that, but for the grace of God . . .

The news from France was bad, and I felt I could do more there than I could here in England. I applied for a transfer, and within a few days I was back. My wings were slightly singed; I could not shut out the hurt of my marriage on the rocks. But in France I was thrown into the company of men who had forgotten sentimental things like broken marriages, and were only interested in licking the enemy.

One of our instructors at Upavon was Captain H. H. Balfour, M.C., in the last war Under-Secretary for Air and now Lord Balfour of Inchrye. 'The Babe' we called him, since he was little more than seventeen when he was given his wings. And a brilliant pilot and leader he was: he was made a subaltern in the 60th Brigade in France when only seventeen. He was the perfect image of the new chivalry which the Royal Flying Corps epitomised. Handsome and loose-limbed, he was the pin-up boy of Upavon and we all sought to be his pupils. Unfortunately I was not one, but my closest friend, Rhys-Davis, who graduated with me, was, and he turned out to be the ace of aces. I cannot do better than quote the tribute paid to Rhys-Davis by Harold Balfour in his book *An Airman Marches:* 'There passed through my hands Rhys-Davis, an Eton scholar who was destined to earn a reputation throughout the whole of France for bravery, to be awarded many decorations (D.S.O. and bar, M.C. and bar) to bring down the German ace Voss, and finally to be killed in combat against impossible odds, fighting to the very last minute rather than breaking off the combat and returning to safety!'

And so ended the life of a very dear friend—a brilliant and gay young Englishman.

Billy Bishop, the outstanding ace of World War I, with whom I had the good fortune to serve, was not a great pilot but a magnificent shot, and this accounted for his seventy-three victims, a V.C., D.S.O. and two bars, M.C. and two bars and other medals. He was an amazing personality.

Billy had a crystal-clear mind. I remember once in France he addressed the officers in his squadron and asked if they had taken any snapshots lately. They mostly had done so.

'Burn them. Burn the bloody lot,' said Billy.

Before I burnt mine I looked at the group. All but myself and one other were missing or killed. I realised what Billy had in mind.

My meeting with Bishop many years later, in 1940 in Hollywood, was a strange one, for he had a different face, built up by plastic surgery, from the face I had known in France. A gay fellow, as his picture with Winston Churchill, reproduced in this book, will show.

'What was Winston saying to make you smile?' I asked Billy about this picture.

'He was looking at my ribbons,' said Billy, 'and his comment was: "Overdid it a bit, didn't you, Bishop?"'

The exploits of Billy Bishop in the Great War are legendary, his recognition unparalleled in the annals of the R.F.C. or R.A.F., but I do not believe that his record then equalled his fanatical war effort as Air Marshal Bishop, supreme head of the R.C.A.F., in the Second World War. Especially memorable were his beloved Commonwealth Training Plan, conceived and carried out in Canada, his Air Cadet Plan and his unique inspirational appeal to young Canadians, particularly as they regarded my generation of warriors as 'old fuddy-duddies' ('fuddy-duddies' was not the word they used) who gave battle in some remote antiquated aircraft.

Every man Bishop could rally for the European 'kill' became his personal responsibility. On a fund-raising tour for his air cadets he took precious time off to accompany us across Canada and he was received everywhere with wild enthusiasm by audiences when he appeared in his Air Marshal's uniform, heavy with ribbons. His cherubic, humorous smile and his telling address brought not only the dollars, but many desperately needed recruits.

At this time Billy was in his fifties and I doubt whether he had piloted a plane for twenty years or more, but when we met in Montreal, despite his record of seventy-three enemy planes in the Great War, he was still practising landings! I twitted him on this and he replied, 'Last week as Under-Secretary of State for Air, Harold Balfour inspected a fighter unit, saw a Spitfire ticking over, and although he had not flown for some time, jumped in and flew her for half an hour, then landed like a bird. Can't let him get away with that.'

He was a very lucky man, was Billy. In the first place, in being alive at all; and secondly, in being married to a most beautiful and lovely woman, Margaret Eaton—a member of one of the wealthiest families in Canada.

In France we had communiqués of the work of the R.F.C.—'comic-cuts', we called them. Frequently I saw the name of my younger brother, Lieut. P. W. Wilcox, mentioned. He was apparently a brilliant fighter pilot and had many 'kills' before he himself was killed. As pilots in the R.F.C. we never met.

My eldest brother, I heard, had emigrated from his racing stable to Australia, and was now secretary to Billy Hughes, the Premier, after having been a Professor of Economics at Sydney University. How he got there without any basic education I shall never know.

One day near Amiens, as I was on my way to Bertangles, I passed some Australian troops halted on a roadside. One Australian had a handful of hard biscuit and bully beef with jam on top, a three-course meal in one. I looked again. His face seemed familiar. I stopped my car and got out.

'What's your name?' I asked him.

'Wilcox,' he replied.

'Joseph Michael?' I asked.

He looked at me.

'I'm Herbert.'

Bang went the biscuit, bully and jam.

'Where are you stationed?' I asked him. 'We must meet.'

'We're on the move up to the front,' he told me.

'Can't we have a meal together?'

He looked down at his filthy uniform and boots. 'Like this?'

I sought his C.O. and told him my story. 'Get him back by nine. We're moving up,' he told me. What an extraordinary man my brother was. 'Best prisoner's friend ever, with a profound knowledge of King's Regulations,' his C.O. told me. 'Best vet in the division,' he went on.

'Why is he only a private soldier?' I asked.

'Offered him stripes, commission—everything. But he won't take it.'

A strange dinner. Two brothers—and total strangers. He was studying Homer in the front line! Taking Honours in Greek! When he saw my bewilderment he went on: 'Takes my mind off the job—don't want the responsibility of others—keeping myself alive is all I'm trying to do.'

My mind went back to 1914. The coincidence of meeting my younger brother in my own bell tent and out of thousands on the march, and then my eldest brother on his way to the front line. And to get Honours in Greek, a professorship in Political Economy and become secretary to a Prime Minister, all without any scholastic training! It was beyond me.

Back in England on leave—a morbid curiosity took me back to Brighton and to the very spot I first met my ex-wife. I wondered if she were happy. I hoped she was not!

Yes, this was about the spot. I stopped, looked and reflected—for how long I cannot say. Then I was suddenly aware of a woman smiling at me and holding out her hand. I took it and said, 'Hello.'

'We were so sorry about you and Dorothy.'

'Thanks,' I said, and then realised it was the other girl whom I had met with her.

'That's all forgotten,' I lied. 'And how are you?'

'Fine,' she said. 'This is a friend from Bedford.'

Hellos were said before I looked at her friend. We all had dinner together that night. I must have been in a receptive mood. Her friend from Bedford was no great beauty, but she had charm and personality. I proposed to her before we said 'Goodnight,' and she accepted me. What can you do with the Irish?

Before I could see her again, I got my orders for France. So I left her a note telling her that I would write. But things were so hectic at R.F.C. Headquarters that Brighton and women were pushed into the background. A letter arrived and asked if I was serious. If I were not she would understand, and no one would ever know I had proposed.

I replied at once. Of course I was serious. We would get married on my first leave. She was to arrange the details—if she was still of the same mind.

I was starting off on that leave when—history repeated itself. The mess orderly, sorting the mail, handed me a letter. I glanced at the writing on the envelope. It was hers!—my ex-wife's!

I decided not to open it, and put it in my pocket. I knew what was inside. She wanted to come back to me. Well—she was too late—I was not going through that hell again. Oh no—once was more than enough. In any event, I was on my way to Blighty to get married. I went to the bar and ordered a 'double'.

I must confess to an inner glow of satisfaction that she wanted to come back to me. Of course I had no intention of letting her do so. And yet—hadn't I? The memories of those ten heavenly days we spent together crowded back into my mind in one blinding flash. I knew then I could not resist the call.

But what of the girl who would be waiting for me at Victoria? She was a very understanding person, I told myself. And better for this to happen now and not after we were married. I decided I would meet her and explain. The die cast, I ordered another drink, took the letter from my pocket and opened it. She and our 'best man' were apparently having a very difficult time—financially. Would I let her have the damages, awarded by the court, which he had paid me?

I suppose I should have burst out laughing—but I am afraid my sense of humour failed me. How glad I was I had already given the money to Guy's Hospital. Otherwise... who knows?

I finished my drink, tore the letter into very small pieces and headed for Victoria.

As the leave train was pulling into the station, I tried to visualise her waiting for me. But, try as I might, I could not put a face to her. My ex-wife's face invariably blotted out all else.

Then the alarming thought: suppose I don't recognise her? I decided to walk very slowly and turn round constantly as though looking for someone. But no, she was not there. Ah, perhaps it was as well.

Suddenly my arm was grabbed and there she was—looking rather lovely, with a big bunch of Parma violets pinned to her black coat. I took her to lunch.

'Since you did not recognise me at the station,' she said, 'you still have time to change your mind.'

I laughed it off. 'Do you want me to?' I asked.

'No. I'd be very sad it you did.'

'Well, don't be sad—we're getting married. When did you fix it?'

'Friday,' she told me. 'The thirteenth.'

'Good! My lucky number. This is going to work,' I said. And it did.

I found her attractive and accomplished. A woman of many facets: painter—writer—singer. Often we entertained the officer's mess, when I accompanied her on the piano whilst she sang numbers from *The Maid of the Mountains* or some other musical comedy.

I cannot say I was as crazy about her as I had been about number one, but she was a very complete woman. She fitted into service life. She was a war widow, her husband having been killed in action in 1915.

Then another spell in France.

This time it was the most exciting of them all, with an outstanding event. The R.F.C. gained the supremacy of the air, and Baron von Richthofen, the greatest fighter the Germans produced, who led his famed circus from his blood-red plane, was brought down in a dogfight near Amiens.

Having been completely denied the air over our lines, the German Air Force, led by Richthofen, had determined to break the blockade. Without warning, squadrons of German planes crossed our lines. When this was reported to our H.Q., word was sent out by the O.C. for every plane to make a beeline for the 'battleground' and for each pilot to pick his own opponent.

The air was thick with planes of both sides, and an unprecedented air battle took place before the Germans were hurled back. One of the casualties was the red devil himself, von Richthofen. A manifesto to the entire German Air Corps was found in his pocket stating that no German planes had been allowed to cross the Allied lines for some time and exhorting everyone to break this black record.

The bringing-down of von Richthofen was the turning-point in the dogfight, the winning of which played so important a part in the warfare of the air and left the R.F.C. in control during a critical period. Had the fight ended otherwise the situation would have worsened considerably and the war would undoubtedly have been prolonged.

Reports of von Richthofen's fate poured in and the 'kill' was claimed by a B.E.2C pilot. 'Must have died of shame if it was,' said the O.C., the B.E.2C being a primitive training plane which really had no place in the front line, except for artillery observation.

The Australian Infantry claimed they shot him down from the trenches. The Royal Naval Air Service claimed one of their crack fighter pilots, Captain Brown, had done it. Two other claims came from the R.F.C. The plane was badly wrecked and was being guarded by Australian troops. Richthofen's body was in a French hospital outside Bertangles.

I was sent to inspect the plane and make a report. When I reached it, very little more than the engine was left (as can be seen from the photograph in this book). The rest had been disgracefully scrounged by souvenir hunters from all the services. I managed to tear off a piece of red fabric and a few inches of flying wire—as a souvenir! My rank did not impress the Australian privates guarding the wreckage. Trying to be friendly and democratic, I said: 'Hello—who did that?' One said: 'Search me! They've all claimed it, except the W.A.A.C.s.' (Women's Air Auxiliary Corps.)

Captain Roy Brown of 210 Squadron of the R.N.A.S. was later given credit for bringing down Richthofen. He was awarded the D.S.O.

When I told the O.C. of the caustic comment of the Australian soldier guarding the remains of the plane, he said he considered it a very civil answer to an unintelligent question! He told me of his one and only attempt to impose his own status on the Australian rank and file, which went like this:

O.C.: 'Put that cigarette out, stand to attention and salute me when I pass. I'm the O.C., R.F.C.'

Australian: 'You've got a bloody good job—you stick to it.'

Lest I appear, without good reason, obsessed or too romantic about 'my' war, may I relate two incidents to justify my attitude.

The first German gas attack near Ypres. That gas might be employed was accepted as a possibility but not seriously anticipated, since the retaliatory deterrent was as strong in 1916 as it is in these nuclear days.

The attack came without warning—silent and mysterious—to catch us totally unprepared. Our men went down like flies before Flit, not knowing what had struck them. One Irish regiment suffered heavily, and casualties were dragged out of the gas zone by rescuers using makeshift respirators of moistened handkerchiefs covering their nose and mouth.

One of the rescuers was a Jewish rabbi attached to the division. He brought in a young Irish boy of eighteen or so—a Connaught Ranger. The boy was blinded, and with lungs at bursting point he sensed his end. Being a Roman Catholic he begged for extreme unction—but no priest was available. The rabbi administered it!

This act of basic Christianity, carried out by a Jew, occurred just over fifty years before the wise men of the Christian churches established an Ecumenical Council in an endeavour to iron out the discord of man-made dogmas and compose their ideological differences. Because that compassionate rabbi jumped the gun by over half a century, a young Roman Catholic boy went on his way comforted because a man of God had administered the last sacrament.

When von Richthofen was brought down at Bertangles it was arranged to bury him near by, and word was sent through to the German Air H.Q. giving the exact location and time of the burial. The message also stated that for one hour no air opposition would be encountered if the German Air Corps wished to send Richthofen's comrades over to pay their last tribute.

As the body was being lowered into his grave by men of the R.F.C. Richthofen's 'circus' roared over, flying very low, dived at his grave in salute and dropped wreaths. Almost before the earth had covered the coffin, the 'armistice' having expired, both sides were at it again in a series of dogfights.

On a lesser note.

During the Great War the name of Cox's Bank was greatly respected and feared. In my situation, with no security and nothing but my monthly service cheque as income, not a penny overdraft was permitted. No doubt a wise directive in those fatalistic days; yet there were times . . . but then aren't there always?

Once when I was on leave, a fellow officer in the R.F.C., Keld

Fenwick, took me to the 'Cavendish' in Jermyn Street for a drink. I met the proprietress, Mrs Rosa Lewis. Keld was a young millionaire —I was cleaned right out; but the difference was a matter of small moment to Rosa Lewis. After a critical scrutiny that by comparison would have made a Guards' dress parade a pleasure, Rosa cashed my cheque for £5—which Cox's had refused to do. She also agreed to hold it until the end of the month before presentation.

On my next leave I again went to the 'Cavendish', saw Rosa and repeated the operation twice. Afterwards I had difficulty in reconciling my bank balance, but did not worry; banks don't make mistakes.

When Rosa died, they discovered a chest of drawers filled with unpresented cheques from service chaps like myself; amongst them must have been my own three, each for a 'fiver', since they were never presented. 'My war contribution,' Rosa called those cheques.

A great character, Rosa, in her unique old-world-style hotel, which she ruled like a benevolent dictator.

I suppose memories such as these do tend to make me emotional about 'my' war and deplore the fact that chivalry, so often encountered in those days, has given way to the indiscriminate bombing of open cities and the slaughter of countless innocent non-combatants.

At the beginning of November, 1918, I was back in England—a flying instructor at Hacknall in Nottinghamshire. One morning I was on the point of taking off with a pupil when I heard church bells ringing—bells that had been silent since 1914.

'That's peace,' I shouted, and shut off my engine, leaving my pupil to find his own way home. I went straight to my quarters, collected some money and was off to London, despite the protests of my C.O.

'Do what you like,' I told him. 'I swore that when the war was over I'd never fly again.'

I went, reaching London in time to see all the madness and near madness of Armistice night. I had been there for the 'off' at Buckingham Palace in 1914, and I was there at the winning post in Trafalgar Square in 1918. I was lucky to be alive, but I had come through it.

I refused the offer of a peace time commission in the R.A.F., and gave the bullet in my leg as an excuse. It was a valid one really, because cramp in the air would be risking not only my own skin but that of a pupil.

It was twenty years before I flew again. The world *première* of

Victoria the Great was set for Ottawa, and Anna and I were to be the guests of the Governor General, Lord Tweedsmuir, at dinner. It was short notice, so the only way to be there in time was to fly. Reluctantly, I agreed. The following year, 1938, Anna and I were made American Admirals of the Air—having flown over 100,000 miles during the year!

They were memorable days in the R.F.C. and R.A.F., for which I shall always be grateful. In 1920, I was able to repay in some small measure my debt of gratitude.

When Air Marshal Sir John Salmond—who was in command of the R.F.C. during my service in France—conceived the idea of an air pageant at Hendon, it included the bombing of an Arab village from the air. Since I was at this time firmly established as a film producer, Sir John sought my advice about the pageant and particularly the construction of the village, the contractors' estimate for which was some thousands of pounds and, therefore, out of the question.

'Grant me facilities to buy aeroplane parts at the disposal depot and, as a token of thanks for my time in the service, I will make you a present of the village,' I told Sir John.

He protested that it was too much and could not accept the offer.

'Grant me the facilities I've asked for—and I'll undertake it will not cost me £50,' I told him.

He gave the green light and I bought wings of Handley Pages for 2d., fuselages for 3d.—and then brought in my expert construction team who gave their services. The result was a magnificent village painted and completed for £24.

The bombing of the village was a highlight and, according to Sir John and his A.D.C., Lord Balfour of Inchrye, it set the seal of success on the many annual air pageants that followed at Hendon.

The contractor who lost the contract never spoke to me again!

6

The end of World War I found me with no fixed profession. I had a good, but not striking war record as a pilot in the R.F.C. and R.A.F., and a gratuity of £117 to keep a wife and myself. She had £100, so with £217 between us we faced a world to which I had been lost for over four years—and still felt lost.

What could I do?

As this thought was recurring, my brother Charles, who had been unfit for military service, 'phoned me from Leeds. Apparently he was a salesman in a new business called Films.

A strange world I found it. After life in the services, it was everything I disliked. Drinking with customers, no particular selling methods, and a strange jargon of new words—synopsis, serials, block booking, stars, features, distribution, exclusives, first runs, and territorial rights. Gibberish to me, but apparently understood by the tough Yorkshire exhibitors.

No! Not for me. But when my brother told me that in a good week his commission was £50, I decided it might be! After £1 a day as a pilot, out of which mess bills had to be paid, the financial prospect seemed like Lombard Street.

My first job in the British film industry was selling American films to Yorkshire exhibitors. Fifty-two 'Flying A' full-length feature films starring Mary Miles Minter, Margurita Fischer and William Russell, produced at the Santa Barbara studios, California; also the first serial of *Tarzan of the Apes* which ousted in popularity *The Perils of Pauline* featuring Pearl White.

As a film salesman my equipment was a briefcase full of highly-coloured 'synopses' of the product, which was 'block booked' fifty-two at a time, plus the 'serial'. One programme a week; therefore one booking and that cinema was full up for product for the whole year. So advanced were the bookings that it was impossible to secure any playing time less than two years ahead or more.

However, relief sometimes came to the exhibitor, who could not have cared less what he showed so long as it was cheap, because numerous films described in the lurid synopses never even reached the production line.

As the cinema owner could only be seen at night, it was tough work with no way of getting from town to village except on foot: Barnoldswick; Heckmondwyke; Slaithwaite (pronounced Slowitt); Shipley; Todmorden; Barnsley; Hunslet; and of course the cities. I certainly knew my Yorkshire before very long.

Wearisome waits to see the manager. I would sit in the smelly, smoky flea-pits waiting for the 'boss'; and it was there, with the flickering, ill-lit screen, and the interminable solo piano accompaniment, that I learned much about audience taste and reaction.

At one cinema in a mining community, the top price was 9d. for the stalls, 4d. for the gallery and—'bottles'! I was curious about the 'bottle' admission and found that the cinema was very long and narrow—too long for the projector throw—so the screen was suspended half-way down the hall and, being transparent, the film could be seen from behind, but of course in reverse.

The 'bottle' customers. mostly children, brought their admissions—a clean bottle was a condition—and all were armed with a small piece of mirror. They would sit with their backs to the screen and look in the mirror, thus reversing and correcting the view.

The 'bottle' cinema was always well patronised.

My brother's business associate was a man named Victor Saville, who has since moved on to do great things as a producer in the film world—both here and in Hollywood. *Good-bye, Mr Chips* was probably his finest film.

I was much impressed with Saville who, apart from being an ace film salesman, had a great sense of humour and loved music. After I had made the plunge into films, Victor and I would often trudge the Yorkshire moors together—where we found the hearts of the exhibitors as hard as the stone hedges which characterise the county. As we walked we would sing or whistle: Puccini, with the accent on 'La Bohème', or the musical comedy *The Lilac Domino* were our favourites, and particularly 'Your tiny hand is frozen'.

The toughest nut to crack in Yorkshire was an exhibitor named Joe Holmes of Keighley. He wore a large pearl stud, surrounded by diamonds, high up in his shirt front, and his cold stony stare made it a fascinating triangle. The stud, they said, was to hypnotise and distract film salesmen, and it was most effective.

My brother, Charles, was hailed as the super salesman of Yorkshire, and that was praise indeed. He once made a bet he would book Joe Holmes a certain film he had rejected. It was an early D. W. Griffith film. Bluff was called for. Expounding the film for several minutes to a cold, staring, dumb Joe Holmes, Charles finished up by saying:

'I know you never pay more than £4 for three days for a super film, Joe, but I am going to surprise you. For this film I am asking £100 for six days!'

Joe quietly replied: 'And I am going to surprise you, Charlie. My offer is 30s.'

'And I am going to surprise you, Joe,' replied Charles. 'I'm going to accept it.'

Victor Saville called on Joe one day to book him our output of fifty-two films. 'Did he sign on the dotted line?' I asked Victor when he returned to the office. Shaking his head, Victor paraphrased our song of the moors and replied, 'His tiny hand was frozen'.

Another day Victor's humour hit a high when, on our rounds, we started telling our war experiences. He had been invalided out.

'What were you in?' I asked him.

'I was the only Irishman in the London Irish,' he replied. Victor is Jewish!

Soon afterwards he left Yorkshire, met a lovely girl, married her, and they've lived happily ever since.

Suddenly the big idea hit me, and I told my brother and one of his colleagues: 'If you can make this sort of money as salesmen, why don't we set up in business on our own?'

My idea was readily accepted. But what about the capital? I offered my gratuity of £117; my brother and his colleague, Jack Smart, made it up to £500—and off we started as Astra Films Ltd., 5 Queen Victoria Street, Leeds.

From this humble beginning, and on £500, we launched our attack on the film industry. Owing to the war, there were practically no British productions. They were almost all American films.

From the start Astra Films flourished. Big profits—paper ones—were being made, and then I suggested to my colleagues: 'Yorkshire is only 10%. Let's expand.'

Yorkshire to London, which added $37\frac{1}{2}$% of the British market. So to Wardour Street, 89/91, in 1919—and the rat race!

After four years of service life with a minimum of chicanery to cope with, I was soon hopelessly out of my depth with some of the adventurers who had swarmed into this new Klondyke. Contracts for thousands of pounds were being secured on which commission was paid, but the gap until the 'play off' and payment was considerable.

On paper we were making a fortune; but at the bank our capital dwindled and our credit suffered. The squeeze started and increased. Why hadn't I been content with Yorkshire?

Since I was looked upon as the guiding light of the company, and we had barely two weeks' salaries left, I had to do something. I sought out an exhibitor who was booking our films and was reputedly wealthy, and requested a short-term loan.

'My wife takes care of all financial matters. I have nothing to do with them,' he told me.

'Can I meet your wife?' I asked him.

'No good. She doesn't believe in lending money—says you lose your money and lose your friends.'

'Can I meet her?' I asked again.

'If you like. Come and have a cup of tea—but it won't be any good.'

So off to Stamford Hill I went, with my briefcase containing contracts worth several hundred pounds. I explained my case to his wife, a charming little Jewish lady.

'How much do you want?' she said.

'£100 will see us through until the contracts start maturing,' I told her.

'You don't know much about business, do you, son?' she said.

I confessed that my experience was very short.

'You've got to toughen up. You're in a hard business,' she told me. 'Those contracts may never mature—and you've paid commission to the salesmen?'

I admitted that was so.

'Have you got any security?'

I told her I had not.

'And do you expect me to lend you £100 without security?'

I agreed it was asking a lot—but yes, I had hoped she would.

She paused and shrugged her shoulders as she looked at her husband, who was over busily engaged in reading a newspaper. She went to a cupboard and unlocked it.

I watched and realised that what she decided either meant I would go forward in the film business, or beat a hasty retreat to Yorkshire and shut up shop in London.

She came towards me holding some money.

'I'm lending it to him,' she said to her husband, whose face was a study. 'On one condition,' she told me. 'And that is you cut your weekly costs right down and pay no more commission to salesmen except on matured contracts. The other condition is, you never over-trade as you have done now.'

I agreed I would follow her advice which, of course, was unchallengeable.

'As interest, I want no money, but your promise to do what I've told you.'

I protested, but she said: 'I'm lending you the money, and I'm telling you the terms.' I thanked her. She held out her hand which I took and shook.

I followed her advice. The £100 was repaid within a very short period, and our entire fortunes seemed to have changed overnight as our bank balance grew. Our business flourished and new films were offered to the company to distribute. And, all because a total stranger felt I had something and could be trusted, I went on to become one of the leading figures in the British Film Industry. Had she decided otherwise I should undoubtedly have sunk without trace in the film world, for no bank in those days would lend money to any branch of the industry—certainly not without security.

If Lady Wolfson, wife of Sir Isaac, should read this, she will appreciate that but for her mother, my benefactress and wise counsellor, in those early days of my film career, I might not be writing this book—since that generous gesture to a stranger resulted in my emerging as a somebody instead of a nobody.

The strangest thing about this episode in my life, and the reason I have gone into so much detail over it, is that some forty years later I broke my promise. I over-traded to such an extent that I found myself in the hands of the official receiver and was declared bankrupt!

In 1919, we distributed a British film, *A Peep Behind the Scenes*, and it was so successful I decided I would produce a British film myself.

But how? We had distributed, amongst other films, a magnificent epic called *Intolerance*. It was produced and directed by D. W. Griffith, without doubt the greatest pioneer of film technique of all time. I would study *Intolerance*, see it several times and chart on paper the method Griffith used.

That part of it was easy, but he used thousands of actors and actresses and horses which must have cost enormous sums. And all I could raise for my first film was £1,400!

So the story had to be simple, with the minimum of actors. In *The Wonderful Story* by I. A. R. Wylie, I found the ideal subject. It was an old country cottage setting—two actors and one actress.

I knew an exhibitor in Newcastle who was employed by the late George Black. He confided in me that he would leave his job, which was permanent since he was regarded as the master showman of the North, if I would let him direct the film. Furthermore, his idol was D. W. Griffith, so we were in harmony.

His name was Graham Cutts. He not only directed *The Wonderful Story*, which I produced, but went on to become one of the top British directors of his time.

The statistics of *The Wonderful Story* are worth recording. The production unit consisted of the director and cameraman, a boy to carry the camera (Emile Littler, straight from school), a continuity girl, one property man, and myself. Six all told.

My production crew on *Yangtse Incident* (the escape of H.M.S. *Amethyst*)—made in 1957—was 92!

The production cost of *The Wonderful Story*—£1,400—represented 10% of the cost of hiring the props, furniture and carpets for my production *The Courtneys of Curzon Street*.

The cost of the artists was £78—Elizabeth Taylor is reputed to get a million dollars per film, plus a percentage of the box office!

The overall shooting time of *The Wonderful Story* was eight days. Epics these days take from one to three years.

The first showing of *The Wonderful Story* at the old Alhambra, Leicester Square, was sensational. Hardened critics like E. W. Fredman of the *Film Renter* and W. G. Faulkner of the *Evening News* came out wet-eyed.

The three stars, Herbert Langley, Lillian Hall Davies and Olaf Hytten, were established. Graham Cutts was likened to D. W. Griffith and myself to Sam Goldwyn. The reviews were almost embarrassing in their fulsome praise. A leading article appeared in *The Times*. Cartoonists predicted that American films had met their Waterloo.

All very much overdone—I thought. I was offered £4,000 to sell the film, a profit of £2,600. I accepted. It was the financial foundation stone of all my films that followed; and how fortunate for me that I *did* sell, for *The Wonderful Story* emptied every cinema at which it was shown! A ghastly failure with the public. Never again have I had, or expect to get, such magnificent critical acclaim. Never again can I produce a greater box office flop!

It was fortunate that a gap of some months separated the critical triumph and the box office failure, for I was able to obtain considerable financial backing on the strength of the reviews and to line up a number of subjects, whilst basking in the glory of a phantom success. Had the box office reaction been exposed at the time of the trade and press showings, I should once again have been sunk without trace and said a sad farewell to Wardour Street and films.

I now turned to a bigger field and developed grandiose ideas. American film stars in the silent picture days were merely attractive shadows flitting and fluttering across the screen. Despite enormous world followings, they were not regarded as real people. So for my second film, a melodrama called *Flames of Passion*, I decided to bring to England an American film star. I chose Mae Marsh, the D. W. Griffith star of *Intolerance* and *The White Rose*. Astonishing publicity followed my announcement, and I sent a special envoy to New York to negotiate the contract and to bring her to England.

The crowds and scenes at Waterloo on the arrival of Mae Marsh in 1922 would make a Beatles welcome appear modest. 100,000 people, the police estimated. They gazed in wonder and cheered as they realised a shadow had come to life.

A wonderful artist was Mae Marsh. She knew her job from every angle and could bring a tear to the hardest-hearted. I had the same *The Wonderful Story* star, Herbert Langley, opposite her. And it was in *Flames of Passion* that dear Aubrey Smith, well established on the stage, made his film début.

By this time, with the 'success' of *The Wonderful Story* and the Mae Marsh episode, I had made something of a reputation for myself as a showman. This was heightened at the *première* of *Flames of Passion* at the old Oxford Music-Hall in Oxford Street.

In these days, stage prologues were the big picture symbol, and I had erected on the stage, in solid rocks and wooden structure, a set which I called 'Dante's Inferno'. Trick lighting with imitation flames and a red filter, plus a wind machine, made something which I considered was a reasonable impression of Hell.

That, and the picture itself, already created a sensation. After the performance, the press swarmed into the bar for the usual drink and a news story.

They certainly got the news story. At about 1 a.m. I went down to see if the car taking Mae Marsh to catch her boat at Southampton had arrived. As I passed through the auditorium, I saw a fireman on the stage—obviously more than a little the worse for drink—trying to put out a fire on the Dante set. I rushed over and questioned him.

'It's on fire,' he mumbled in a beery voice.

'Bring down the safety curtain,' I ordered. Eventually he understood and did so. I telephoned the fire brigade.

There was still the problem of a bar full of pressmen and artists who would have to come through a smoke-filled theatre. So I went up and asked for 'quiet'. Then I asked everyone to follow me and ask no questions. They could obviously sense something was wrong and I led them down a back staircase into the street. When all were safely out, I told them about the fire. With my announcement the fire engines arrived. And what a laugh went up.

But the damage was considerable and the London County Council ordered the theatre to be closed, which it was for a week, and the prologue on which I had spent two thousand pounds was stopped.

Flames of Passion: and that had to happen! 'What a coincidence!' said the press boys. 'What a title!' It was too costly for me to see the joke; but I did appreciate a telegram from C. B. Cochran, which read: 'Dear Herbert—my congratulations—and admiration—Cocky.'

As a film, *Flames of Passion* survived the fire and publicity, went on to make a substantial profit and did much to re-establish me after the box office failure of *The Wonderful Story*. No doubt because of Mae Marsh, I sold it to America; and I believe it was the first British film to be sold to the U.S.A. after the First World War.

Then I held an inquest.

My production record at that point was one flop, one hit. The flop had been a realistic short story with a humble cottage setting, and with ordinary country people. The hit was a florid melodrama, with the Old Bailey reconstructed and a murder scene, plus a finale in which the black and white film burst into Kinemacolor.

My thoughts went back to the time when I had gone from one Yorkshire town or village to another, sitting in the ill-ventilated cinemas and being compelled to sit through innumerable films while waiting to see the booking manager, of the dreary uniform Lowry-like tenements with their outside water closets.

I struck my flag.

No more stark realism. Audiences have enough of that, and rationing and shortages were still with us. My objective now was escape entertainment of pleasant people in pleasant surroundings doing pleasant things, or highly coloured musical romance.

Remembering the promise I made to the little lady in Stamford Hill I saw my bankers and sought their support before proceeding to my next move—once again a matter of showmanship.

I wanted to buy the film rights of *Chu Chin Chow*, the theatre record-breaker. I needed £20,000—in those days a vast amount, and record sum for any British producer to pay. The bank agreed to advance the purchase price plus preliminary costs.

I started the script and production preparations. Once again, I would import an American star—and the ideal was Betty Blythe, who had broken cinema box office records as 'The Queen of Sheba'.

The war being only just over, Anglo-German relations were not at their warmest. But I felt that a German production of *Chu Chin Chow*, with the imagination and facilities of the Universum Film Company (U.F.A.) under the direction of Erich Pommer, would be perfect for this type of musical fantasy.

A deal was made whereby I would undertake distribution of *Die Nibelungen* in England, and U.F.A. would lay on facilities for me at their Berlin Studios to produce *Chu Chin Chow*.

The climate of Berlin at that time of the year was perfect for exteriors, I was told—eight to ten hours of sunshine a day. And the studios on Kurfürstendamm were the finest in the world, having turned out films such as *The Dubarry*, *The Cabinet of Dr Caligari*, *Die Nibelungen*, *Metropolis* and *Dr Mabuse*, with great directors—Ernst Lubitsch, F. W. Murnau, Fritz Lang—and stars like Pola Negri, Emil Jannings, Werner Kraus, Conrad Veidt and Brigitte Helm.

Apart from the price of the rights, the production would cost £20,000, which included massive sets and crowd scenes with thousands of extras.

The interior scenes were completed on schedule and we moved out to Steglitz—an enormous outdoor studio lot with magnificent sets which we could use. There we awaited the alleged eight to ten hours sunshine a day.

For thirty days we never saw the sun until I called the lunch break. It shone whilst we ate and drank, and went in again as soon as we returned to the set.

There were rumours of a German revolution and the collapse of the Mark. I cabled our bank in London and gave instructions to sell Marks for the credit balance in our account. Each day the cost of production was covered this way, and the absence of sunshine compensated so that we came out slightly under budget, having spent twice as long on location as budgeted.

As an illustration of the immediate effects of inflation, I saw a baby grand piano in a store. It had once belonged to the Crown Prince

(Little Willie) and had the most beautiful tone. I asked the price.

'Marks or pounds?' the salesman said.

'Marks,' I told him. 'I'll pay on delivery—if you can deliver today at the Eden Hotel.'

The store was in the Unter den Linden; the Eden Hotel in Kurfürstendamm—about a mile apart. I walked to the hotel and before I had finished lunch the piano arrived.

At 12 o'clock it was to cost me the equivalent of £330 sterling. At 2.30 p.m., when I inquired of the exchange, it cost me £12 10s. The piano was mine, and the next day the old Mark was valueless!

As I watched the beautiful triple-strung Ibach grand being taken into the most fashionable hotel in Berlin, my mind flashed back to the cheap upright piano taken out of our modest terraced house at Brighton. Seized for debt under the prying eyes of our neighbours, it had accelerated—even if it did not actually cause—the death of my mother.

Chu Chin Chow as a film was only a moderate success. But in Newcastle, with the help of George Black, I fixed up loudspeakers at the side of the screen and had live singers synchronising with the lip movements of the artists. A success, but ahead of its time, I fear.

Mention of George Black automatically brings C. B. Cochran and Albert de Courville into mental focus. Great showmen—with impeccably good taste. Where are their counterparts today? All three were great friends of mine and 'Cocky' dedicated one of his books to me.

George Black was my partner in some early film ventures and I owe him a good deal since I had the opportunity of studying his methods and showmanship approach right from his early days as a cinema owner in Newcastle, when he used blaring 'loud speakers' (in their infancy) to 'get 'em in' and synchronised records to silent films when he 'got 'em in.'

It was George Black, with his native instinct for spotting unique talent, who brought Flanagan and Allen and Sid Field from the provinces to blossom in London's West End. He it was who pioneered the establishing of the London Palladium as the showpiece of the variety world. Val Parnell, of course, raised it to the dizzy heights of the last decade or so, but Val would be the first to give George Black credit for having started the ball rolling.

Apart from his showmanship, George was blessed with an incomparable sense of dry humour, and one of his stories I would like to pass on, although in the telling here it will lose the value of George's timing and blunt North Country language.

'The thing that's wrong with show business, Herbert,' he said to me one day, 'is too many "flipping" accountants—adding machines with no imagination, no souls and very little body, and all living on comparisons.'

'For instance?' I asked.

'Well, the Gillespies. We're running *Lisbon Story* at the Hippodrome. The war's on—anything goes—packed every performance. The only imponderable—are there three or seven standees at five bob a time?'

But every night in all weathers, Colonel Gillespie, deeply conscious of his duty to his shareholders, presented himself at the box office window.

'How's business tonight, my dear?' he would inquire of the girl.

'Sold out as usual, Colonel,' she would reply, 'and seven standees.'

'Seven standees—excellent, my dear—excellent. Four up on last year.'

Come Christmas Eve—blinding snow and freezing hard—but still the colonel called. Making his way into the theatre, a little old man shivering with the cold greeted him.

'Happy Christmas, Colonel.'

'Happy Christmas, my man,' replied the colonel.

'Oh, Colonel,' said the little old man, offering a box of matches. 'Buy a box, Colonel. I'm hungry and I'm frozen and I've been here since four o'clock and only sold three boxes. Please buy a box.'

'Been here since four o'clock and only sold three boxes?' the colonel inquired.

'That's right,' said the little old man hopefully.

'How does that compare with last year?' asked the colonel.

One has only to look into any branch of the British entertainment field to discover George Black's inspiration for this story.

I suppose a sense of humour such as George Black's is vital to a top showman, having to deal with the imponderables and changeable temperaments of show business. C. B. Cochran certainly had it. When Lee Ephraim was enthusiastically discussing new seating for the theatre where he was proudly presenting Cocky's new show, he waxed eloquent.

'Now Cocky, I would like your opinion, would you like to see the seats covered in leather, plush or some bright animal skin?' he asked.

'Backsides,' answered Cocky! Although that was not precisely the word he used.

However, the production and near success of *Chu Chin Chow* furthered my reputation as a producer and showman, and I was approached by almost every important continental production company to join them in co-production. England was a closed market to them, and here was their way in. The Viennese were most persuasive. I believed every word, and started out with a skeleton crew to produce a story they had provided but which was not made available to me until I boarded the boat train at Calais. It was melodramatic and cinematically impossible: so on the train I wrote another story and decided to back out of the deal if it were not accepted.

It *was* accepted.

The studios turned out to be the melon house in the gardens of Schönbrunn, and the time was August. The heat was such that the grease-paint on the artists' faces melted as it was applied.

Lighting was out of the question as there was blazing white light from dawn to dusk. I shifted the interiors to the exterior. The wonderful lighting I had been promised was non-existent, and our scene at the Vienna Opera-house, filled with thousands of extras and a big stage show, could not be shot without imported lamps from Berlin.

When these were fixed, I was visited by the authorities and advised that, if I used all the lamps at one time, Vienna would be plunged into darkness. By this time I believed nothing the Viennese told me. So I called the extras, hitched up the lights and shot the scene; but only once.

The authorities were right! The technicians must never have seen a film produced, because they crowded round and invariably applauded. In believing the very charming Viennese gents, I had bought a large-sized pup. No one was in a hurry to get on with the production except me, since I had a limited amount of finance arranged and this envisaged no delays.

I became the most unpopular man in Vienna as I drove through relentlessly and completed the film on schedule; I then fell into the Orient Express and did not wake up until I reached Calais.

I had the negative—such as it was—with me, and after recovering my reason would look and see what I had shot. I could only hope against hope it was not a complete disaster. I had American, British and Viennese stars in it so there was hope of a patched-up job.

I edited *Southern Love* and, to my amazement and relief, it made sense. Now to sell it! It was a story set in Spain, and no more of a story than one could expect from twenty-four hours' writing on the Orient Express.

I had an idea. The Albert Hall was a round building; so was a Spanish bull-ring!

I hired the Albert Hall for one night and turned it into a bull-ring.

To do this, a new hardwood floor was needed and had to be laid in the twenty-four hours for which I had hired the hall. The contractors agreed to do it on time on pain of a heavy forfeit. They succeeded. The entire floor was covered with sand and sawdust, and the boxes were camouflaged to look like bull-ring boxes.

A chorus emerged from the tunnels singing the 'Toreador' song from *Carmen*, supported by an orchestra of eighty. Spanish dances took place, and mock bull-fights.

12,000 accepted invitations for the *première*—for which I should explain that there was no charge! After forty minutes of the prologue, a big screen was lowered. The projectors I had specially installed behaved perfectly, and the film was shown. The ballyhoo took everyone by surprise—so much so that the shortcomings of my film were scarcely discussed.

It was quite a success and made a handsome profit in this country. The great American showman, Al Woods, heard about the *première* of *Southern Love* and offered 250,000 dollars for the American rights. Since it had cost only £12,000 I was indeed in the money.

... Until Al Woods viewed the film! His offer was astutely protected by 'subject to viewing'.

That was the end of that mirage. Not an offer did I get for it from America. Not that it deserved one, but it was hard to have 250,000 dollars almost in my grasp and see it disappear entirely.

Erich Pommer, chief of the U.F.A. organisation in Germany, had heard about my near disaster in Vienna and also about the denigrating remarks of the Viennese on the technical facilities in Berlin. He was at once on the warpath, since he saw my unhappy experience reacting against co-production in Germany.

He invited me to make another film in Berlin; and U.F.A. would provide the story, screenplay, the greatest cast of German artists ever assembled in one picture, plus 50% of the finance required. For my part, I was to produce and direct, and bring in British and American stars to create an international attraction, plus providing the remaining 50% of the finance.

I accepted—signed up Ivy Duke, at that time top of the British glamour girls, and Lionel Barrymore from the U.S.A. The subject was Boccachio's *Decameron Nights*, with its unlimited international appeal. With my production team and artists, I arrived in Berlin a few days before shooting was to commence to find magnificent sets including the Doge's Palace and St Mark's Square, Venice, already erected, and thousands of costumes ready for fitting.

The Germans were all out to score off the Viennese after my disastrous experience with *Southern Love*.

The original story, with its overtones of sex, could not miss—but the film-script presented to me stank to high heaven, and Pommer agreed with my opinion. To have proceeded with that script would have been disastrous, at all events in the markets I understood; but to abandon the film would have been equally disastrous.

I made a proposal to Pommer, the real architect of the great German films of the time, and without hesitation he accepted my offer. I would produce and direct without a script and write the scenes from day to day.

Pommer had lined up a great cast, all in the tradition and class of Emil Jannings: Werner Kraus, Hannah Ralph (Jannings' wife), Bernard Goetake, Albert Steinruch. When they asked to see the script, Pommer—without batting an eyelid—said, '*Er hat es im Kopf!*'—in English—'It's all in his head!' Without exception they walked out, but Pommer's persuasive powers prevailed. He must have sold me sky-high as a writer, producer and director.

Lionel Barrymore looked rather surprised when I broke the news to him, but with a smile said: 'O.K.—but do me a great favour—before we start, tell me my first and last scene!'

I got through the film on schedule, and whatever faults could be found with *Decameron Nights* they were not in the screenplay or continuity. The critical acclaim was extraordinary and in my view out of proportion to the merits of the film.

I personally took *Decameron Nights* to New York and showed it to the trade press journals. As a result, I met one of the legendary figures of the American film industry—Dr Giannini, who, with his brother, A. P. Giannini, founded the Bank of America, now the largest bank in the world.

A story is told that, during the San Francisco earthquake in 1906, the two Italian banker brothers dug holes in the ground themselves and carried the bullion and valuables from the bank's vaults and buried them.

Dr Giannini—'the Doctor', as he was known to all—was a colourful character. Swarthy and as strong as an ox, he was erudite and a master of most of the arts.

As a banker, he relied more on the man than he did on the security, and his pioneering of film financing was largely responsible for the birth and emergence of Hollywood's world dominance. He lent billions of dollars to film producers, and often boasted in public and in the press that he had never lost a cent doing so. He also refused to charge high interest rates and spurned a share of the profits. 'Hell,' the Doctor would say, 'you made the picture—you keep the profits. I'm a banker.'

Our first meeting in New York was startling. He was being shaved by a barber with a cut-throat razor. He asked me my business; I told him.

'Joe Dannenberg sent you to me—did he?' he asked.

I assured him he had.

'How much money do you want?' he went on.

I told him I needed £40,000.

'Any security?' he queried.

When I told him I had none save the U.S. income from the film, I still marvel at the manner in which the barber missed his windpipe.

'Didn't Joe tell you I was a banker—and bankers need security before they make advances?' he literally shouted.

'No,' I replied. 'Joe saw my picture and liked it, and said if you need money to make another picture, go and see Dr Giannini, he'll let you have it.'

'Oh, he did, did he?' he stormed. 'Did you say you want £40,000?'

He was now drying his face and the barber looked relieved. 'How long do you want it for?' was the next question.

'Six months,' I replied.

He looked me over, and then: 'This is the first time I've set eyes on you and I want you to know that in my world six months is six months, and a day over is a default—understand?'

I answered him I did.

'This picture Danny saw—is it good?'

'Joe thinks so, and is going to say so in his paper,' I told him.

The barber left, and the Doctor picked up the phone.

'Get me Joe Schenck,' he demanded.

Whilst waiting for the call, he turned to me.

'No one has ever let me down yet and do you know why?'

I confessed I didn't.

'Because I'd beat the living daylights out of 'em and destroy them—they'd never make another film anywhere.' From the way he looked, I had no doubt he would have done so.

Schenck came on the line.

'Joe,' said the Doctor, 'I've got a very old friend of mine with me (it was our first meeting) and he's made a great picture—the best I've seen in a long time (he hadn't seen a foot of it). He's a goddam Britisher and he needs £40,000. I'm lending it to him but I'm insisting on United Artists distribution—now go ahead and sell it and get my money back quick. What's that?' He held his hand over the mouthpiece. 'What's your name?' I told him, 'He's Herb Wilcox—yes, he's all right. Have lunch with me, Joe—the Astor at half-past twelve.'

I was astounded, as for years American distribution had been a will o' the wisp. And also an advance of £40,000! I felt I was dreaming.

'Now, Herb,' said the Doctor, 'I like you and you can draw the dough right away—but if you let me down you let Danny down— and you know what to expect.'

I assured him I did and thanked him.

'And it's six months less a day!' was his parting shot. I rushed out of the bank, and but for prohibition would have knocked back a couple of stiff doubles.

The advance was repaid before the date it was due. And subsequently my borrowings from the Bank of America totalled £7,000,000, mostly during the period when the British joint-stock banks would not look at the financing of British films.

Having at this time established quite a reputation in England, I thought a visit to Hollywood was called for.

A quaint experience. Armed with the blessing of Dr Giannini and the New York press, who must have oversold my importance, the red carpet was run out everywhere and visits to all the studios laid on, including Cecil B. de Mille's whilst he was making *The Ten Commandments*.

De Mille was a great showman—the legend of Hollywood—the 'Barnum' of motion pictures. Dressed in his proverbial breeches and top boots, he was directing, through an enormous megaphone, an open-air scene of a vast procession of biblical humans and animals, elephants both real and fakes, with ears and legs that moved mechanically like Christmas toys. Never had I witnessed such production value. His organisation was superb.

Whilst the procession was in progress his publicity chief whispered in his ear, and de Mille, as if by magic, stopped everything and in a stentorian voice announced through his megaphone that a great British film producer had arrived on the set. He eulogised my immortal contribution to motion pictures and pointed his index finger at me. Charming of him, since prior to that moment I doubt if he even knew my name.

The thousands of extras applauded me as de Mille shook me by the hand and then, horror of horrors, the great brass band in the procession struck up 'Tipperary' and, as though taking up their cue, the elephants, real and fake, started off again and the gargantuan procession followed. It was certainly a long way to Tipperary! The musical background of 'Tipperary' to such a period scene was too much for me and I burst out laughing—though not as loud as Cecil B. de Mille!

Later, at a private dinner party in Beverly Hills given by the British consul and his wife, Francis and Mary Evans, Anna and I had the opportunity of meeting de Mille and we found him a profound thinker and scholar. His love was the Bible, which he regarded as the greatest literature of all time; its highlight, the Sermon on the Mount.

One other point that impressed me enormously was the fact that de Mille completely financed all his own productions, and would not permit the distributors to contribute a cent. 'If I did,' he told me, 'they would tell me how to produce and I know more about creating entertainment than they do.'

On the domestic side, my second marriage—entered into so suddenly and on an emotional rebound—was working out very well indeed. Not the searing passion of 'number one' but a deep attachment and a friendship that became firmer every year.

At this time we had two children—Pamela, born in Yorkshire, and John, born in Hampstead—and another on the way. A wonderfully calm background to my rather restless and unpredictable way of life in films.

Then followed a period of unimpressive films, until I bought the rights of *The Only Way*, the stage play based on *A Tale of Two Cities*, and signed Sir John Martin Harvey to play his greatest role of Sydney Carton. It was a unique experience, since Martin Harvey was the finest actor I had directed up to that time.

I was given critical praise for my direction of the kind one reads only in a pipe-dream—or an obituary. E. A. Baughan of the *Daily News*, whom I rated as the top critic of his time (he taught me much), wound up his review by saying: 'At this point the film ceased to be great—it became sublime,' referring to the scene where Sydney Carton mounts the steps of the guillotine and speaks the words: 'It is a far, far better thing I do now than I have ever done.'

I was inundated with congratulations and praise for my direction. But, remembering the hard lesson of the praise lavished on *The Wonderful Story*, I took no risks and put all my knowledge of showmanship into presenting it.

13. *(left)* The German First World War ace, Baron von Richthofen.

14. *(right)* The end of Richthofen's 'Red Devil'.

15. *(below)* Air Marshal W. A. Bishop, V.C., D.S.O., M.C. with Winston Churchill. Churchill, looking at the ribbons, is saying, 'Overdid it a bit, didn't you, Bishop?'

16. (*left*) Mae Marsh—the first American star to play in a British film—with C. Aubrey Smith in *Flames of Passion*, 1921.
17. (*right*) With Werner Kraus, Lionel Barrymore and Emil Jannings at Neubabelsburg studios, Berlin, for my production of *Decameron Nights*, 1922.
18. (*below*) With Betty Blythe for my production of *Chu Chin Chow* in Berlin, 1923. This was the actual caption used.

Below: *Herbert Wilcox teaching Betty Blythe how to hate.*

20. One of the bills for *The Only Way*.

21. An extract from the *Sphere*, 3rd October, 1925.

19. Sir John Martin Harvey as Sydney Carton in the final scene of *The Only Way*, 1925.

22. With J. D. Williams, founder of Elstree studios.

23. Nelson Keys, Dorothy Gish and Will Rogers in Gershwin's *Tip - Toes*, 1928.

The Home Secretary, Sir William Joynson-Hicks, accepted my invitation and presented it personally at the London Hippodrome. A highlight in my life was hearing the Home Secretary and Martin Harvey, on the stage of the London Hippodrome, refer to *The Only Way* as the banner-bearer of British films throughout the world.

A lucky stage for me was the London Hippodrome. Many years later, it was on this same stage that I saw a lovely young English girl dancing in a musical comedy with Jack Buchanan. Her name was Anna Neagle.

Stating that Martin Harvey was the finest actor I had directed up to that time poses a question. Who now, forty years later?

Rex Harrison; without a doubt. I should add that I have produced, but never directed, Laurence Olivier.

Rex's repose is second to none. With a glance he can convey more than most actors applying every trick in the book. He has figure and clothes sense, and an effortless technique which hides technique but which can blaze into anger and fury at the drop of a hat, coupled with the most engaging smile.

All this I say after only one experience. This was *I Live in Grosvenor Square*, in which he played opposite Anna with Robert Morley and Dean Jagger. Both Anna and I enjoyed the experience and so did Rex. We arranged to make many more pictures together. Rex agreed to buy my farmhouse in Chalfont as a present for his wife Lilli Palmer and the search for subjects began.

Meanwhile I took my film to New York and showed it to Spyros Skouras of Twentieth Century Fox, who immediately took it into their American programme. When I got back to England, Rex met me and told me Twentieth Century Fox had offered him a Hollywood contract!

'What about our deal?' I asked.

'Nothing signed,' he replied.

'But we agreed on a deal—and I sold you my house.'

'This is my first Hollywood nibble, Herbert, and I must take it. You can easily get rid of your farm,' he told me.

I decided that was the end of a short but pleasant association. I would never speak to him again.

Rex couldn't have cared less. To Hollywood he went and made *Anna and the King of Siam* and, from there, film after film.

One comforting thought—as Rex predicted—I did sell my house and for three times as much as Rex had agreed to pay!

Many years later I went to New York with Trevor Howard, who knew my story. My lawyer, who always has theatre house seats for the big shows, had reserved two seats for *My Fair Lady*. I could not refuse since he had gone to such trouble to get them, and they were selling 'on the kerb' for sixty dollars each. So Trevor and I went; and started off like two stiff-lipped Englishmen.

'He'd better be good.' said Trevor.

'It couldn't matter less if he is,' I replied. And were we grim as the curtain went up!

Within five minutes of Rex's opening scene I glanced at Trevor. He was grinning from ear to ear and chuckling. In another five minutes I was laughing and applauding madly. Never had either of us seen a better performance.

I buried all past grievances and went round rather reluctantly to tell Rex. I was ridiculously fulsome but he loved it. He poured out a drink and all was forgiven on my side. I'm sure it was forgotten years before on his.

"You're both coming out to supper with me," said Trevor.

We dined under the ever watchful eye of Bob Kriendler at "21." There is nothing like it anywhere, and it is run on lines of dignity and service. This compulsive hospitality brings to mind a fundamental difference between American and British hospitality. After an absence (for any reason) the British greeting invariably is, "Where have you been?" "Why haven't you written?" "Thought you were dead," somewhat demanding and possessive. Whereas with Americans, they start where the last conversation left off—be it a day, a month, a year. As an extreme example. Anna and I were unable to secure accommodation in our favourite New York hotel.

"Come and stay with us," said Yvonne Mills. Yvonne's husband, Harry C. Mills, "Buster" to his friends, is in the millionaire class and at the time was head of one of the biggest chain of stores in the U.S.A. Through her father, Jules Brulator, one of the founders of the film industry, Yvonne is a woman of considerable wealth in her own right. We demurred . . . with all their money and friends it would mean being on hand at all times.

But thank heavens we accepted. We were allotted our own suite in the Mills' elegant Park Avenue apartment—even a separate telephone —and we did not see our hosts for 24 hours. Then came a phone call from Yvonne. "Hello—How are you? What are you doing tonight?"

"Theatre and supper afterwards," she was told.

"Come and have cocktails before the theatre," said Yvonne, "Buster would like to say 'Hallo!' "

And when we were in the mood later, New York was an open oyster —and the town was painted red in our honor.

Anna and I have voted Yvonne and "Buster" Mills the perfect hosts!

7

The day I completed *The Only Way* with Martin Harvey, I was driving from Twickenham to my home at Elstree at about 3 a.m. (we worked in those days) and was wondering what would be my next subject.

Gazing drowsily out of the car window, I saw a theatre bill, underneath a street lamp. At the top of the bill was a name in big letters—'Dolly Elsworthy'. My mind flashed back to Camberwell Palace where I saw her do her famous 'Orange Girl' sketch.

That's it, I thought. The film of *Nell Gwyn* was born at that moment. A perfect story, but needing a great vivacious actress. Before I reached home, I had drafted out a cable to my lawyer in New York. 'Is Dorothy Gish available for British film of *Nell Gwyn*—wonderful part, cable reply.'

My lawyer passed my cable to her agent, who opened it and promptly threw it into his waste-paper-basket. Dorothy was expected that morning to discuss a Hollywood film. Casually her agent told her about the British offer.

'What sort of a part?' asked Dorothy.

'Something that sounded like a shoe polish—Nell Gwyn.'

Dorothy sprang to her feet.

'Where's the cable?' she demanded.

He indicated the waste-paper-basket. Dorothy started searching.

'What's all this about?' her agent asked.

'You can forget Hollywood,' said Dorothy. 'I'm going to England.'

'Without knowing the terms or seeing the script?'

'If it's Nell Gwyn, and it is, I don't want to see a script, and I'll accept whatever they offer.'

Well, Dorothy arrived—I met her at Southampton. What a girl! She knew more about Nell than the scriptwriter, and couldn't wait to get to work.

For some years she had appeared in films with her sister Lillian, and D. W. Griffith had decreed that Dorothy would always be a brunette so as to avoid any collision of looks with Lillian.

I turned her into the blonde which the part called for—and Dorothy was born again. Fundamentally she is extremely intelligent and wildly humorous—never bitchy, but biting to a degree. And dead right to play 'Pretty Witty Nellie'. How she revelled in it, and how I loved every minute!

Restricted and frustrated as she must have been as a brunette, and possibly overshadowed by the acting of her sister Lillian—probably the greatest silent film actress of all time—in Nell Gwyn she found scope for uninhibited expression and she positively radiated with the joy of life. It was humour out of the top drawer and sex appeal galore. George John Nathan, when he saw the film, said: 'It took an Englishman to discover that Dorothy Gish has legs and extremely beautiful breasts.'

Nell Gwyn brought me for the first time in contact with City finance. On the point of commencing shooting, a well-known chartered accountant, in the running for Lord Mayor of London, told me he wanted to meet me at once on a matter that might uncover mutually beneficial common ground.

We met and made a deal on *Nell Gwyn*: fifty-fifty on the cost of production, fifty-fifty share of profits. This meant a real saving in interest charges and my friend assured me it was merely the prelude to much bigger things. So I advised my bank I would require only half of the amount requested, and started production.

Even before the contract was signed my City friend, for some reason which he could not explain, wished to withdraw from the project. Furthermore, the money he had advanced up to that time must be refunded.

What a pickle! I could not go back to my bank without giving them a reason for the City withdrawal, and all I could get out of him was: 'We've changed our mind.' Could any reason be more deadly to a bank?

I somehow found the money, paid him back and set off on my own. The period was late November and the 'enemy' fog had a merry time. It delayed the crew and cast getting to the studio in Islington, and some fog which invaded the studio itself was picked up by the cameras, so that certain scenes had to be re-shot.

With Dorothy Gish receiving £1,000 per week—a top figure in those days—I soon found myself in trouble with *Nell Gwyn*. However, by scraping the barrel and keeping everyone waiting for payment—including the electricity company supplying my Kensington flat—I finished the film with literally my last penny.

With insufficient money left to pay for cutting rooms or an editor, I decided to edit the film myself—at home. Borrowing a fire extinguisher (all films in those days contained nitrate and were not only inflammable but explosive), I used an electric light behind the film—and had almost completed the job when our electricity supply was cut off pending payment of the account!

My children were highly amused—I was not. The editing had to be completed, so I went out and bought some candles and, with the film held against the naked flame, I finished editing. The very thought of the risk I took, not only for myself but for others, now horrifies me.

Christmas was approaching and the children wanted toys and we wanted our Christmas fare. We had to forgo both.

On 15 December, I sought out an American film man, J. D. Williams, who was just forming a new British film company. He agreed to see *Nell Gwyn* with a view to buying it.

I was at lunch at Ciro's (where my credit was good) with my bank manager (where my credit was *not* good), trying to raise enough to meet Christmas. I did not enjoy my lunch. 'Wanted on the phone, Mr Wilcox,' Louis, the manager, told me.

It was J. D. Williams. He and his colleagues had just viewed *Nell Gwyn*. Would I take 50% profit, plus the production cost? That meant £14,000 production cost plus £7,000 profit. And at that moment I could not have paid for my lunch in hard cash. I almost fainted.

'I'll accept it on one condition,' I said.

'What is it?' asked J.D.

'That you send the profit, banker's draft, not cheque, for £7,000 to Ciro's within half an hour—the production cost can be paid over when the amount is checked.'

Within the half-hour Louis delivered an envelope to me. I peeped inside, saw a banker's draft. I took out my cheque book and made one out to Ciro's for £100. Without a glance at my bank manager, who I knew would be on the point of apoplexy, I called Louis.

'Take your bill up to date out of that Louis,' I told him, 'and a fiver for yourself.' Louis smiled and left.

'You don't expect me to meet that cheque, do you?' my 'friend' asked.

'If you don't, I shall sue your bank for heavy damages and you'll get fired,' I told him. 'And I would also ask you to recall all the things you have said today, and to remember they were famous last words.'

I pulled out the banker's draft and handed it to him, saying: 'Let me know by tomorrow my precise credit. I am transferring it to another bank.'

I left him and phoned my wife.

'I'm not mad or drunk. Take the kids out and buy them anything they want for Christmas and have the bills sent in—and buy yourself a fur coat.'

'You're not well,' she answered.

I told her the facts and asked her to be ready for dinner at the Embassy.

The film of *Nell Gwyn* was a riotous success throughout the world. It broke the record at the 'B and K' Chicago theatre, taking 59,000 dollars. In 1925 that was a lot of dollars.

Nell Gwyn also represented the foundation stone of the Associated British studios at Elstree. It had the distinction of being chosen to open the first American-owned cinema in Great Britain—the Plaza, London, operated by the handsomest young American I had ever seen, Earl St John, who until his recent retirement was head of production for Rank at Pinewood.

To digress—but for a reason—it was through Earl St John that I met a young American lawyer not well known at the time. In fact I was one of his first clients, but now in New York if you want to make a deal with top entertainment talent anywhere in the world, it would be extremely difficult to avoid meeting him.

Dedicated, with a brilliant legal and business mind, he is ruthless when watching the interests of his clients, but compassionate to a degree. Coming from a humble origin and having struggled to get through law school, this man has emerged as a legal giant to whose ability many great artists would have good reason to testify.

My reason for introducing William (Bill) Fitelson in my book is that he is inextricably coupled in my mind with my benefactress of Stamford Hill, in those far-off pioneer days of 1918, whose sage advice helped keep me on the top of my profession for over forty years. When I ignored it—disaster followed.

Throughout my entire film career Bill Fitelson has been similarly Anna's and my good friend and wise counsellor and the solitary instance, due to circumstances beyond my control, on which I did not seek his advice, initiated the slide downhill that ultimately ended in bankruptcy.

Returning to Elstree and the *Nell Gwyn* story, J. D. Williams, one of the top American film pioneers, formed a company to purchase the world rights. The company was called British National Films and, on the success of *Nell Gwyn*, J.D. signed Dorothy up to make three films which I was to direct. He also invited me into the company and we bought forty acres of land at Elstree with a view to building studios comparable with Hollywood. The price of the land was £100 per acre, which we considered too high. Today the same land would cost £15,000 per acre!

J. D. Williams' wife and right hand 'man' was a wonderful woman named Hope—'Hopie' to everyone.

The studios were built, and I produced and directed the first film to be made there—*Madame Pompadour*—with Dorothy Gish playing the name part.

I have a warm recollection of being called for one Sunday morning in 1925 and with J. D. Williams, Hopie and Dorothy driving out to inspect the plot of land we had bought at Boreham Wood (Elstree).

When we got there the first stanchion was ready to be lowered into the earth. J.D. took the shovel from one of the workmen, handed it to Hopie and invited her to turn the soil. An historic occasion, when one views the present magnificent studios of Associated British Picture Corporation, comparable to any in the world, and realises that every brick and every piece of steel work stemmed from that one stanchion helped into position by a spadeful of Hertfordshire soil dug by Hopie.

I would like to tell you more about Hopie—although it means a brief move forward from 1925 through to 1966.

She was born in Yorkshire, but when I first met her she was already married to J. D. Williams, and played a big part in J.D.'s life as hostess in their Park Avenue, New York, apartment. Gay, witty, generous and beautiful, she was quite a force in New York society and the film world. Mary Pickford, Charlie Chaplin, Rudolph Valentino, Douglas Fairbanks, Lillian and Dorothy Gish all idolised Hopie and respected her considerable judgment.

There came a battle of the American film giants and J.D. lost. He and Hopie came to England—they would do for British films what J.D. had done for Hollywood. They set up house in Portland Place and that was where our paths met. 'J.D.' and I became business associates and Hopie was always on hand, her judgment and help of enormous value.

Again there was a battle of the giants, British this time, and again

J.D. lost, plus considerable money of his own and Hopie's. So they went back to New York—in the dog days of finance. Hopie sold her jewellery, but somehow they couldn't get going again.

Then J.D. died. Hopie was penniless. But she didn't weep or seek charity; she could still type and make herself useful. So she became secretary to the fabulous 'Roxy', and when he died Martin Quigley, publisher of the *Motion Picture Herald*, asked her to take over his London office. And a grand job she did. For twenty-seven years. She met Peter Burnup, for years film critic of the *News of the World*, married him, and all seemed set fair again for Hopie.

Then came the word Hopie dreaded: 'Cancer'. Her first impulse was to throw herself out of the hospital window, but her strength of character came through.

'If I've got cancer, I'll live with it,' she said.

And she did. Operation followed operation. She became the idol of the Middlesex Hospital. She carried on her work between whiles, and endured pain and constant discomfort with the same humour and wit as of old.

When I first heard the word 'bankruptcy', Hopie was number one on the phone with words of comfort.

But twelve years of suffering took its toll, and she had to give in at last. Once queen on the New York film scene, she entered the Benevolent Home of the British Film Industry at Morecambe and, with Peter Burnup, decided to enjoy a well-merited retirement.

Then Peter died, and fearful of the effect—he had been everything to her, nursing her through her operations, and he loved her dearly—I phoned her.

A cheerful Hopie answered: 'Yes, Peter's gone, but he's left behind twenty-five years of wonderful memories. I shall live on with them.'

Dear Hopie. She has now joined her beloved Peter.

Now let us get back to 1925 and Elstree.

Adolf Zukor of Paramount, who bought the U.S.A. rights of *Nell Gwyn*, had given J. D. Williams a contract for three films starring Dorothy Gish with myself as director which were budgeted to cost a million dollars; Paramount were to put up the entire million.

I was now well and truly home and in the big money class.

My family had increased to four by this time and I decided they should have everything money could buy. My own early life of poverty and hunger was not to be for my children.

A lovely house at Elstree with seven acres of garden and grounds; two cars, new stables and horses for all; servants; and a doting mother. That was the plan by which I sought to bring them happiness. A plan which I deliberately set and carried out.

On the film side, as a director of British National Pictures, I had the pleasure of approving an unheard-of contract of £13,000 a year—and that was money forty years ago—to a brilliant young director, Alfred Hitchcock ('Hitch').

It was J. D. Williams who signed 'Hitch', without doubt the greatest director the British film industry has produced, and in off-studio life a *bon viveur* as well as the most entertaining man I have met.

But soon discord sounded in British National between J. D. Williams and I. W. Schlesinger from South Africa, who had provided finance. Whilst the conflict between them was at its height, John Maxwell, the founder of Associated British Picture Corporation as we know it now, was called in. He provided a modest amount of finance and secured control of the company and the studio.

After a short time I broke away, and with Nelson Keys, a top musical comedy stage star of the twenties, founded the British and Dominions Film Corporation.

Knowing of Lord Beaverbrook's interest in the film industry through his company, Standard Films, which controlled Pathé Pictures and also Provincial Cinematograph Theatres, the first major country-wide circuit, I asked if I might see him and seek his advice.

'Come at once,' I was told.

It was the first time I had met Beaverbrook and he was most helpful and charming. He gave me the advice I sought and, as I was leaving his office, called out:

'Have you got important shareholders?'

'Not yet,' I told him.

'Go and see Jimmy Dunn—and Harry McGowan and Hugo Hirst—and Melchett. They've all got plenty—get some of it.'

I thanked him and asked: 'May I say you suggested I saw them?'

'No—prove your own case. If they don't respond your case is not a good one.'

They all came in, so my first group of shareholders was indeed impressive: Sir Harry (Lord) McGowan, Head of Imperial Chemical Industries; Sir Hugo (afterwards Lord) Hirst, Head of the General Electric Company Limited; Sir James Dunn, Canadian industrialist; Lord Melchett, Chairman of Brunner Mond; Jack Solomons, stock exchange broker; Otto and Ernest Schiff, bankers. In this company

I travelled in the *Aquitania* from New York.

Have you ever noticed how very wealthy business men, having made their fortunes, enjoy the simplest pleasures? Many of them play the piano—not very well, but well enough to strum out mostly nostalgic or sentimental songs of the old music-hall brand. On the *Aquitania*, Jack Solomons at the piano led the chorus as they sang their favourite song (believe it or not): 'The Best Things in Life are Free'!

Millionaires, every one, and within a year each made 800% profit on their film investments when my company British & Dominions went public. Today the capital of British & Dominions runs into millions and controls Denham and Pinewood studios, an important part of the Rank empire.

Harley Drayton, one of the legendary City financiers and head of a trust company, also loved the old songs, and when Anna and I gave him a guinea album of 1910 music-hall ballads as a Christmas present, he was overwhelming in his thanks.

Isaac Wolfson also loves the 'oldies', particularly Leslie Stuart. I can still picture him with a friend outside the London Pavilion, after seeing our film *Lilacs in the Spring*, singing and dancing a few steps to 'Lily of Laguna'.

Perhaps the most memorable thing that happened to me in the silent film days was, once again, an accidental glance at something in the street.

Nell Gwyn had emerged from a music-hall poster. This time it was a statue.

I had produced and directed a film from the play *Mumsie* by Edward Knoblock, for which I brought from Hollywood a great dramatic star, Pauline Frederick. In *Mumsie*, Herbert Marshall made his film début—and outstanding he was.

To make another film with Pauline Frederick, I secured an option from Noel Coward on the film rights of *The Vortex*. But Miss Frederick did not like the story. And since she had a firm contract with me with a fixed starting date, it was up to me to find a subject she would accept. I was unsuccessful.

Living at Bedford, I came up to London one Sunday to meet her and crave her co-operation. She was living at the Hyde Park Hotel and, as I arrived at St Pancras with an hour to spare before our meeting, I decided to walk.

I must have taken the wrong turning at Charing Cross Station for

I found myself approaching St Martin's Lane from the Strand. And I glanced up as a shaft of sunlight lit up the word 'Dawn' on the statue of Edith Cavell.

My brain whirled—the perfect subject which Pauline Frederick *must* accept. I almost ran to her hotel and breathlessly told her of my suggestion.

She was wildly enthusiastic and asked: 'When do we start work?'

'Monday week,' I told her and, since she wanted to spend a few days in Paris, arranged to meet her in Brussels for the exteriors.

Reginald Berkeley was to write the script and we went over to Brussels with my entire production team. I booked in at the hotel in which I had reserved a suite for Miss Frederick. The reception clerk gave me a note. It was from Pauline.

'Sorry Herbert dear—I can't do it—on my way back to California—Love Polly.'

I was shattered. A production crew and equipment in Brussels, and no star. I made inquiries and discovered the German embassy had sent a deputation to her. They told her very politely that if she played Nurse Cavell, no film of hers would ever be shown again in Germany, and furthermore, pickets would be placed on important cinemas in the States. Under that threat, I realised it would be futile making a further appeal to her.

Desperately I scanned the theatre columns of the London theatres to find a substitute. Manna from heaven—Sybil Thorndike was playing at the Lyric Theatre, Hammersmith.

I gave instructions for atmospheric shots to be taken with a double for Nurse Cavell, and rushed back to London.

Sybil listened but said nothing. She searched and brought out a small black book. 'Do you see this?' she said. It was Thomas à Kempis' *The Imitation of Christ*. When Sybil and Lewis Casson were married, she was given the book. When Edith Cavell was executed, she left her copy of the same book to her cousin Eddie. She had annotated certain pages with comments reflecting her last thoughts. Eddie Cavell lent it to Sybil and gave her permission to annotate her own book in the same manner.

Sybil told me how much she would like to play the film part and I knew, by the way she reacted, that the Pauline Frederick disaster was really a blessing.

The making of the film *Dawn* with Sybil Thorndike was a joy and an inspiration. The look in her eyes when being led out to the firing squad, in which she half-smiled at her grief-stricken jailer, is to me one of the great moments, conveying compassion and forgiveness, that only the cinema can achieve.

I have admired and loved Sybil since that unforgettable experience, and you can imagine how I rejoiced to hear Alec Guinness sum her up: 'If everyone loved someone as much as Sybil loves everyone—what a wonderful world it would be!' A sincere tribute from a great fellow artist that requires no comment from me.

The picture *Dawn* completed on schedule, our early troubles were forgotten. But many, many more lay ahead.

My first showing was to my distributor, C. M. Woolf, one of the giants of the film industry and a champion of British films when so many of his contemporaries 'didn't want to know'; his colleague, Colonel Bromhead; and the sales and publicity staff of Woolf's distribution company.

The effect was overwhelming and disturbing. The woman in charge of publicity had hysterics and affected all the other women, and even the tough salesmen found it hard to take. C. M. Woolf, an emotional man himself, was very affected.

'Herbert,' he said, 'it's wonderful. Too wonderful. You've created a Frankenstein monster—I can't distribute it.'

This of course spelt financial disaster but, in a gathering overcharged with emotion, Colonel Bromhead told 'C.M.': 'It's a great picture of a great Englishwoman, and even if we lost every penny I feel it should be shown—and as widely as possible.'

C.M. quickly accepted the point and gave instructions that everyone must get behind it. What a relief—no more troubles.

Did I say 'no more'? Why, we hadn't even started!

The censor at that time was an old friend of mine—T. P. O'Connor, M.P. Sir Austen Chamberlain was the Foreign Minister of the Conservative government. A meeting took place between them. The Foreign Minister had been approached by the German ambassador and informed that the showing of the film of Nurse Cavell would do irreparable harm to relations between the two countries. Chamberlain suggested to 'T.P.' that the film be banned—and he agreed.

Then the storm broke which not only threatened Austen Chamberlain's office, but according to informed opinion almost brought down the government. The mistake was to ban the film without seeing it. Pages in all the newspapers were devoted to my defence.

Lord Beaverbrook sent for me and advised me in the strongest terms to say nothing in my own behalf. 'Leave it to the press. You stand apart as the innocent victim.' Good advice.

Many years previously, I also received good advice from another press baron—Lord Northcliffe.

I was very young, impetuous and sensitive. I had produced a film which the *Daily Mail* film critic tore to pieces. I was furious. He had exceeded his province as critic, I felt confident.

I told my solicitor to consult counsel. I was right and, according to counsel, bound to win. The writ was issued and I was licking my chops.

Sir George Sutton (Northcliffe's right-hand man) asked me to come and see him. I did—but remained firm.

'Come and have a word with the chief,' he suggested.

I found myself feeling a midget facing a man who appeared to be ten feet tall. He turned to me.

'I'm told you've taken action against the *Daily Mail*.'

'Yes, sir—I have, and I'm assured I shall win,' I replied.

'You're very young and new to your job. I'm old in mine—I'm giving you some advice. Never reply to criticism, never.'

That was the end. I left. I was incensed and, with my solicitor, saw our counsel, Mr Jowitt, later Lord Jowitt. He listened and smiled. 'Can I also give you some advice?'

'Why—of course.'

'Never litigate.'

I telephoned Sir George Sutton telling him of my decision and asked him to pass information on to Lord Northcliffe that I had dropped the case.

'That won't be necessary,' replied Sir George. 'Lord Northcliffe told me when you left him there would be no lawsuit!'

Whenever I have ignored Northcliffe's advice, it has always been to my detriment. But I have *never* ignored Jowitt's.

I have been fortunate in personally meeting the press Barons—Northcliffe, Beaverbrook, Rothermere, Roy Thomson, Cecil King; and had the die been cast otherwise I would have chosen, not to be a baron, with all the financial operations of a press empire, but an editor of a national daily newspaper in much the same spirit as some young hopefuls yearn to be engine-drivers.

Of all editors I have known, and they are many, I rate Tom Innes and Arthur Christiansen ('Chris'), both for many years shining lights of the *Express* group, as the Daddies of them all.

An extraordinary man was Chris—as simple as a child in some aspects, with the sharpest nose for news in Fleet Street.

Unsophisticated, as when we showed *Victoria the Great* representing British films at the Paris Exposition, and his telling comment at the end of the viewing was: 'Herbert—it's great—you've made a Victorian newsreel!'

And afterwards our drive around Paris after midnight in a taxi with a sliding roof! Chris would stand up and with his head outside the top of the taxi would shout: 'They like it, they like it!' His delight at the reception given our film could not have been greater had it been his own.

One outstanding moment with Arthur Christiansen comes to mind. I had returned from showing *Victoria the Great* in the States and called on him to bring him into the picture. He was singularly interested as though he had nothing else on his mind.

A sub-editor came in and put a note in front of him. In a flash he became a man of action. On the 'phone he summoned one after another of his top staff. Suddenly, seeing me as though for the first time: 'Get out, Herbert,' he said, 'See you some other time.'

I caught sight of the note and wondered why such a routine message should trigger off such a transformation. The note ran: 'Mr. Baldwin had an audience of the King.'

That was all.

The first member of his staff came in. 'He's going to abdicate,' said Chris.

He was right. The abdication of Edward VIII was announced the next day.

The 'Quiet Man' of Fleet Street, Cecil King, I had only met at cocktail parties or at his business office, but one night I visited his home on the Chelsea waterfront to discuss with his wife, Ruth, details of a programme by her beloved National Youth Orchestra to be included in a film. Ruth greeted me warmly but Cecil, who was seated in an easy chair, merely gave me a nod and went on reading his book throughout our discussion, which was at times quite heated since Ruth did not wish the orchestral programme to be vulgarised to meet film requirements. I sometimes glanced at Cecil, who looked remarkably like Northcliffe; but he was apparently taking no interest in us at all. He did not even seem to hear us. Our interview over, I said 'good night', and glanced at the book he was reading—a remote classic. He looked the picture of severe, scholarly detachment from the Fleet Street rat race. No big business problem on *his* mind, that was certain.

The next morning's papers announced he had secured control of the Reed paper group, a deal involving many millions!

The editor and newspaper Anna and I will always remember with a warm glow are Herbert Agar and the *Louisville Courier*.

We were in Kentucky the day France capitulated and it seemed the end. An inspiring leading article appeared in the *Courier* which rallied our spirits enormously and this was long before Pearl Harbor. It was to the effect that: 'Tragic as the fall of France was, trust England to stand full square—she will never capitulate!'

Anna was appearing on the stage in Louisville and we asked to meet the editor and thank him personally. Herbert Agar was the writer of the leader. He had just left for New York, but the publisher, Barry Bingham, would be delighted if we would come and take a glass of sherry.

Barry was young—incredibly handsome—and a raging anglophile.

We met him next in Falmouth, Cornwall, whilst we were on our honeymoon. Barry was then a 'high-up' in the American Navy. We talked of England and promised to show him round when we met in London: Westminster Abbey, the Tower and other historical spots. Barry said he would appreciate this as he was vitally interested in British history.

On our way back from Falmouth we stopped at Salisbury and wandered into the lovely cathedral. Almost the first effigy was Bishop Bingham who was buried there in the 11th century—he was Barry Bingham's forebear! We had been preaching British tradition—whilst Barry listened patiently and never smiled. We cabled him—'Just been to Salisbury Cathedral and met the bishop—You parvenu!'

We learned afterwards that Barry Bingham's father was American ambassador at the Court of St James's.

My meeting with William Randolph Hearst is worth recording since, once again, I was given good advice. It was in the *Queen Mary*. I told him the object of my American visit. He replied: 'That's a first-class news story.'

I thanked him and said I was meeting the press when we berthed.

'Tell them the story,' Hearst said, 'But tell them to hold it,' he said with a smile.

I did—and made it clear it was not 'off the record,' but that I would appreciate their holding it for forty-eight hours. It made every newspaper in an important way within the next twenty-four hours!

In my opinion the most exciting combination of news instinct and the big business of journalism is Hugh Cudlipp. His instinct particularly affects my story since he made a suggestion for a subject for Anna which I turned down flat, as it involved Anna, at the time of her romantic peak with Michael Wilding, having a seventeen-year-old daughter.

Hugh met me one day and said: 'Herbert, if you want to make a smash hit, put Anna in a picture with a seventeen-year-old daughter.'

I thought he was mad and told him so, but when I told Anna she said: 'I am old enough, you know.'

I contacted Hugh Cudlipp and asked why he felt so strongly about the subject. He told me that there would be sympathy and communion between hundreds and thousands of mothers with seventeen-year-old daughters and the attendant problems. I immediately saw his point and we went ahead and made *My Teenage Daughter* which was not only an outstanding success for Anna and financially, but also started Sylvia Syms on the road to stardom and caused John Osborne to pick Kenneth Haigh for his play *Look Back in Anger*.

Hugh Cudlipp's instinct emerged from his constant study of every-day problems and although I have asked several times since for more ideas—nothing has happened.

The wittiest and sharpest mind I have met in the editorial field is Abel Green—editor of the entertainment bible, *Variety*.

Abel is the alleged butcher of English who used phonetic ungrammatical headlines such as 'HIX NIX BRIT PIX' to indicate that the wide open spaces of the United States did not like British films! He also initiated the 'fractured French' vogue to send up the abuse of journalistic quotations in French.

The actual Abel is an erudite scholar of English and bi-lingual—and his wit!

Two examples.

He took Anna and me on a tour around the New York night-spots to report on the cabaret scene. At the Savoy Plaza Jacques Pils was the attraction.

Anna's invariable rule is not to talk or eat when a fellow artist is performing, so we were listening quietly when a young woman saw Abel and rushed to our table. It was Ella Logan, currently starring on Broadway in the smash hit, *Finian's Rainbow*. For ten minutes or so it seemed, Ella poured out her woes. Billing—orchestration—casting—the lot. She never let up and not a word could we say, even had we been so disposed.

Abel, sensing Anna's embarrassment, turned to her and summed up Ella's thousand-word tirade in two words: 'Management trouble!'

On another occasion two enormously wealthy and very sick elderly brothers were offered several million dollars for their business—but the offer was refused.

Seeking Abel's support, the man acting for the purchasers bellowed in desperation: 'Why the hell doesn't someone tell them they can't take it with 'em?'

'Don't tell them that,' cut in Abel, 'they won't go!'

I invited the entire House of Commons and Press to see *Dawn*. The showings (twelve in all) were successful beyond my wildest expectations. The film critics went overboard in their praise. E. A. Baughan of the *Daily News* wrote a brilliant review which diametrically differed from the policy of his paper—the only remaining one to support the ban. Leading articles appeared on all sides and it was generally conceded at the time that the uproar was without parallel.

Beaverbrook again asked me to visit him—at Cherkley this time.

I got there in time to hear F. E. Smith (later Lord Birkenhead) say to Beaverbrook: 'I'm going to write a letter to the editor of the *Daily Telegraph* which will smash Wilcox and expose him for exploiting the death of Cavell.'

'You can't do it, F.E.,' said Beaverbrook. 'He's got public opinion with him. He's been condemned without a hearing.'

Beaverbrook then stressed to me: 'However much you are tempted, say nothing. Remain the helpless injured party; and if the censor asks to see the film—don't make it too easy.'

At the height of the uproar, I had an offer for the U.S.A. rights from Archie Selwyn, including an offer to play New York at his theatre on 42nd street. I accepted the offer, which covered the production costs many times over.

Sybil Thorndike then stepped into the battle and asked me to arrange a strictly private showing for her friend, George Bernard Shaw. She would like his view, she explained. I made arrangements, assuring her that no one would hear about the private showing and that I would not cash in on Shaw's opinion.

A Saturday morning was the only time he could see it. The censor's office then telephoned to say *they* wished to see the film—on the same Saturday morning.

I remembered Beaverbrook's advice and told them the only print was being used for an important private showing in our own theatre at precisely the same time as they wished to see it—so it was impossible. The secretary of the British Board of Film Censors told me that as they were opposite our Wardour Street private theatre they would have the film collected reel by reel after we had seen them. I was cornered and had to agree, so reel by reel during the showing the film was picked up and viewed by the censor and his examiners.

I sat with Sybil and Bernard Shaw. It was a silent showing if ever there was one. There was no reaction of any kind on which I could form an opinion. I concluded that Shaw did not like it, particularly in view of his political opinions and as a professed pacifist.

The showing was over, Shaw turned to me and said: 'My boy, you have created a masterpiece which must be shown—not only here, but in Germany and throughout the world.'

At that moment, from behind a curtain, a stranger emerged and made for the exit. I was horrified and grabbed him by the lapels of his coat.

'What the devil are you doing here?' I asked him.

'I'm from the *Sunday Express*,' he replied.

I was furious, turned to Shaw and assured him I knew nothing about the presence of the reporter, who rushed out of the theatre.

'Let him go,' said Shaw, 'he's doing his job in his own fashion.'

I turned to Sybil to apologise.

'You've no need, Herbert—I know very well . . .'

Shaw cut in—'Where's your telephone?' he asked.

I took him to it and he asked for a number.

'Is that the Press Association? This is George Bernard Shaw. I want to speak to your editor.'

Shaw then gave his opinion of the film. He did the same with Reuters.

He smiled as he turned to Sybil.

'I'm afraid that young man will be late with his scoop.'

I thanked Shaw, and asked if he would repeat the passage wherein he advised all Germans to see the film.

He laughed, turned to Sybil and said: 'Bless the boy, he wants to hear it twice.' He did not repeat it, but here it is, as it appeared in the *Sunday Times*:

> The only thing to be considered is to know if this picture is a masterpiece, worthy of her (Miss Cavell) and you may take my word for it, it is, for you have here the living reincarnation of the heroine.
>
> This picture has been conceived and executed by a poet of the screen enthralled by a magnificent theme: a woman sacrificing her life to create, in the storms of European hatred, a refuge of goodwill and forgiveness.
>
> There is not a single note in this theme of weakness or brooding,

nor the trivialities of a sterile imagination. The actress and the director have felt, and have made us feel, that the law of Miss Cavell was far above any military code—a law infinitely higher than war and the idea of patriotism.

This picture may go to Germany as an English product without any fear that a German may remind us: 'People that live in glass houses should not cast stones.' This film casts the blame, with impartiality, on all of us, as well as enlightens us 'sans parti pris', and I hope that it shall be a lesson throughout the world.

George Bernard Shaw.

The censor! I went over to see them. If necessary, I would tell them about Bernard Shaw. His opinion, plus all the publicity, would, I was confident, leave me with their certificate.

It did. But not the one I wanted. A total ban—with the additional words: 'Not fit for showing to British audiences.' I could not believe it, and told the secretary, Brooke Wilkinson, of Shaw's opinion. 'I'm sorry, Herbert,' he said, 'but that is the opinion of our viewers and it's irrevocable.'

Eulogised by G.B.S. and totally banned by the censor within ten minutes of each other! I was confused and bewildered.

I announced the official banning of the censor, and this appeared in the same editions as Shaw's statement. Then the roar of the crowd—the entire press this time came down on my side.

But the censor was adamant.

However, even without a certificate, I could still show the film if approved by the London County Council and local Watch Committees.

I started with the L.C.C., who viewed the film as a body. I was invited to the debate—and to hear their decision. It started at 9.0 p.m. and went on to the small hours. The film's champion was Thelma Cazalet—afterwards Mrs Cazalet-Keir, M.P. She delivered a magnificent address.

Many were opposed. I was exhausted, but hung on for a division since a 'No' would have repercussions throughout the country, whereas a 'Yes' would be a precedent any Watch Committee would follow.

The division took place and all filed out of the chamber except one . . . who was fast asleep.

The result was announced—a dead heat.

Ramsay MacDonald's daughter went to the sleeping man and told him the division was on. He got up and I held my breath—which lobby would he favour?

He had apparently decided before his nap. Straight to the 'Ayes' he went, and once again I could breathe.

'What a bit of luck!' said C. M. Woolf—his favourite expression.

This close result meant even more publicity, so much so that Archie Selwyn cabled me from New York begging me to stop it if possible—it was defeating itself. There was also a New York cable from C. B. Cochran: 'Live and let live—don't make it too tough—Cocky.' But I could do nothing to stem the publicity.

With the L.C.C. in our favour, C. M. Woolf got busy; and when he got busy—he got busy! He appointed an exploitation expert, Castleton Knight, and eventually—of all unlikely theatres—the Palladium was chosen for the film's first showing in London.

An orchestra of fifty was engaged with the usual status-symbol prologue and a packed house. The prologue was called 'The shot that echoed round the world'—the climax being a fusillade which rocked the theatre and startled the audience as the screen was revealed.

I felt that Nurse Cavell might have approved the film of her later life produced on a modest budget and sincerely and superbly played by Sybil Thorndike. But she would strongly have disapproved of its public début at the Palladium with a concert orchestra and a full house shocked by a volley of rifle fire; also by two large offices of ours filled to the ceiling with press cuttings.

Much as I like showmanship and exploitation, I must say the whole affair was now overdone, and the fact that cabinet ministers' heads almost rolled because an independent British film producer had been condemned without a hearing was allowing the affair to assume a significance far beyond its proper proportion.

However, the film went on and was extremely successful. I quote an article by R. Lebreton in *Comoedia*, dated 11 November 1928.

> Yesterday morning at the theatre of l'avenue de Wagram, *Dawn* was presented for one man alone: *Georges Clemenceau*. At the end of the presentation we asked: 'Monsieur le Président, would it be indiscreet to ask you your impressions?'
>
> 'No. Why?' Through his moustache came a smile. 'I never refuse an interview, *voyons!*'
>
> 'Then, Monsieur le Président?'
>
> '*Eh bien!* I find the picture extremely beautiful and moving.'
>
> 'Did you find any scene to be offending?'
>
> 'Certainly not; it is very good.'
>
> R. Lebreton.

My company was now prospering and a series of unimportant but profitable films followed. But everything was too equable after the struggle with Nurse Cavell. I wanted something I could get my teeth into, and create the right sort of stir. In fact, it was expected of me.

It came in a message from Dorothy Gish in New York. Something was developing, I should come out and investigate.

In New York, I saw my first talkie—*The Sidewalks of New York*. There was a scratching sound throughout, but nevertheless artists were talking in synchronisation with their lips and movement.

I caught the next train to Hollywood.

8

Yes, indeed! Talkies had come and were drawing the crowds.
I cabled England to stop all silent production pending my return. Charles and Al Christie had sound-proofed an independent studio. I jumped the queue and rented it at £1,000 a day for five days.

I got hold of a story, *Black Waters*, with Marshall Neilan to direct. We finished in five days and I had produced my first talkie, which was the fifth ever to be made. Furthermore, I obtained a licence from Western Electric to equip the first sound studio in Europe.

It was during the production of *Black Waters* that I met the fabulous Howard Hughes—tall, young, slight, good-looking and a millionaire several times over, they told me. He was extremely charming when we met. An artist, Louis Wolheim, who had made a big impression in *All Quiet on the Western Front*, was under contract to Hughes and I considered him perfect casting for my film. I asked Hughes if I could borrow Wolheim for three days, and he agreed.

'He will cost you twenty thousand dollars,' he said—in such a tone that bargaining was out. It was very steep, but I considered Wolheim worth it, so I accepted and hurried off to tell Marshall Neilan, the director of the picture, of my scoop.

But Micky refused to have Wolheim in the part at any price! No contract had been signed, so back I went to Hughes less than an hour after our talk and explained the difficulty and expressed my regrets at having troubled him.

Hughes replied: 'You made a deal with me for twenty thousand dollars.' I tried to explain, but no good. Very quietly, he got up to go and, as he went out, turned to me: 'Wolheim will report on your set on Monday and be available for three days, and I want that twenty thousand before he starts work!'

I paid. Probably one of the many reasons why Hughes is a multi-millionaire—and I am not!

Then back to England—to find that only two theatres in London were wired for sound, the Piccadilly and the Tivoli. So under my arm I had a talkie costing £45,000 and nowhere to show it! Ironically I found a cinema in Coventry wired for sound. To produce the fifth talkie ever made and be sent to Coventry!

But I was ahead of my competitors. We started to build and equip sound studios adjoining the British International Pictures studios, which we bought from John Maxwell. I signed up the top stage artists, Jack Buchanan, Tom Walls and Ralph Lynn and Sydney Howard—with C. B. Cochran and Albert de Courville as producers.

For some time I had the field to myself, although Hitchcock next door had converted a silent picture called *Blackmail* into a talkie.

Meanwhile, at the Rock Studios, Elstree, I directed and produced the first British all-talkie ever made. It was called *Wolves* and starred Dorothy Gish and Charles Laughton in his first full-length film.

An extraordinary man, was Laughton. He despised all the conventions, and although he came from a fairly wealthy family of hoteliers in Scarborough, he appeared to be very hard up. I remember how he stepped in and made a test when another actor walked out of *Wolves* saying the part was not good enough.

I went to Laughton's dressing-room to talk about the character. He was changing and his underpants were literally in rags. When I told him he'd got the job, he chuckled and said: 'Good! I'll be able to buy some new drawers!'

An astonishing actor, he despised words and regarded them as an appendage to acting. But when it came to *using* words, he had no peer.

He startled his director, Leo McCary, and the whole of the studio in his early Hollywood film *Ruggles of Red Gap*, in which he played a manservant, when, from out of the blue, he suddenly reeled off the Gettysburg address as no one has ever delivered it—save perhaps Lincoln himself. Whenever he went out afterwards, he was asked to do it again, and seldom did.

Many years later, I met him in Madison Avenue, New York. Under his arm he had a priceless Renoir, and with his free fingers whistled for a taxi. He was enormously successful and very wealthy. We greeted each other.

'How are the underpants?' I asked him.

'If you mean my drawers, they're silk and in gorgeous Technicolor,' he cracked.

Laughton was a most amiable fellow in real life, but he could convey sadism and cruelty to a frightening extent in his portrayals in plays and films like *The Man with Red Hair*, *The Barretts of Wimpole Street*, *Mutiny on the Bounty* and *On the Spot*.

He had the good fortune to fall in love with and marry Elsa Lanchester, whose humour alone would make most marriages work. They made an eccentric couple, perfectly matched and both touched with the brush of genius.

After *Wolves*, I moved into the same studios at Elstree which I had originally opened with *Madame Pompadour*, having equipped them with Western Electric sound at a cost of £250,000. It was the first sound studio in Europe!

One story about the sound-proofing of the B. & D. Studios is amusing to look back on, although not so funny at the time.

The sound-proofing process involved double walls and the aperture was packed with special wool. Whilst under construction some local sparrows discovered the wool was warm and an excellent nesting-place and passed the word on to their friends, so that when we finally tested the studios for sound hundreds of sparrows chirped their approval and until we got rid of them shooting was impossible.

The main doors were left open and shots fired at random scared a great many who took flight; but in the end I had to call in a rat-catcher who in a few nights persuaded the sparrows to come out and eat, and whilst they did so caught them and set them free. We never found out what bait he used, but his bill of £10 a night was gladly paid.

Being passionately fond of music myself and aware of its universal appeal, my next move in 'talkies' was to enter into an association with His Master's Voice gramophone company, which gave me access to their celebrity recording stars—Chaliapin, John McCormick, Galli-Curci, Heifetz, Yehudi Menuhin, Mark Hambourg and others.

Our first joint production was *Robert Burns*, with Joseph Hislop, the Scottish tenor, playing the name part. A good film, I thought, but not commercially successful—and this relative failure blunted the appetite of the gramophone bosses who, like myself, had expected an enormous initial success of our venture. Almost at once they withdrew from the operation.

Had I chosen a less indigenous subject and a greater name star, the story might have been vastly different. A great pity, since I had interesting plans for this tie-up—not the least of which was Chaliapin playing Sancho Panza in *Don Quixote*—without singing a note!

That he had a remarkable voice was common knowledge, but I regarded him as a really great actor. Chaliapin was not the least interested in making 'talkies' of his voice, and when I put my idea of Sancho Panza to his advisers they reluctantly passed it on to him.

'He wants me to play in a film and I am not to sing?' he inquired. Nervously they confirmed this.

'I must meet this man Wilcox—he is very intelligent and I will act Sancho Panza for him and it will be my joy not to sing,' he told them. The link between the top artists and H.M.V. at that time was a famous character named Freddie Guisberg. He was not unlike Groucho Marx in appearance. His knowledge of music was profound. His psychology when handling stars never failed, but was sometimes startling. I introduce him here because I was to meet him with Chaliapin at the Savoy Hotel and discuss my project of Sancho Panza.

I was announced from the front desk and a page boy deputed to escort me to Chaliapin's apartment. As we approached, the glorious voice of Chaliapin could be heard coming from his suite, singing an unaccompanied aria by one of the great Russian composers. We arrived outside his door and I stopped the pageboy from knocking, dismissed him, and told him I would wait until the singing finished.

But it went on and on—and since I did not wish to be late on my appointment, I eventually rang the bell—twice. After the second time the door opened, and someone looking like something between a giant and a lion greeted me and put his arm around my shoulder. He was going through the motions of singing, but the voice was way back in his suite. Not a word of greeting from Chaliapin as he led me into his room, and still mouthing and gesturing he sat me down opposite the instrument.

The aria finished and Chaliapin glowed with satisfaction—five minutes of unaccompanied music is no mean achievement.

From behind the door, unseen by me up to this moment, was Freddie Guisberg, who had been listening. He had his hat on and took no notice of me as he crossed to the piano and struck the last note of the aria.

Chaliapin's voice was still in our ears and Guisberg, again defiantly hitting the note, looked at him.

'Flat,' was all he said. And he was right. Chaliapin *was* flat!

Chaliapin glanced at Guisberg—and his look was such that Guisberg should have died on the spot. He crossed to the telephone and picked it up.

'Here is Chaliapin,' he said. 'I wish to speak to the manager.'

I felt terribly embarrassed by the whole situation, and would have been even more so if I had had to witness the beloved and revered Freddie Guisberg being escorted from Chaliapin's suite. Before I could think of an excuse for leaving, the manager was on the line.

'Here is Chaliapin. I want you to send at once—a piano-tuner. The piano is sharp!'

He put down the receiver, looked at Guisberg and burst out laughing! and Chaliapin's laugh was a cross between *Boris Godunov* and 'The Song of the Flea'.

Guisberg, grinning, held out his hand: 'Very good joke.'

Chaliapin grabbed his hand and shook it warmly.

'Shall I lay on orchestra and studio tomorrow morning?' asked Guisberg.

'No, Freddie dear—not tomorrow morning,' Chaliapin replied. 'In the afternoon I visit a beautiful lady—and I need all my strength!'

My Sancho Panza idea was warmly received and agreed by both; but the distributors of the proposed film thought I had gone out of my mind to make a film with Chaliapin in which he did not sing. They turned it down flat.

Maybe they were right. But I was very angry.

In looking back to the early days of talkies, I certainly did not lack courage or imagination.

When I made the life story of Irving Berlin, starring the then B.B.C. top band attraction Jack Payne, partly opened curtains in one scene revealed Jack at a white grand piano playing and singing his theme song, 'Say It With Music'. The curtains, opening slowly, revealed two more white grand pianos, then four more until on the screen were thirty-two pianists playing the theme song on thirty-two white grand pianos.

The result was a splendid sound both on the screen and in the audience. That was in 1932. I am flattered that since then some of my contemporaries have borrowed the same idea in 'super' films costing forty times that of *Say It With Music*. What it would cost to produce such a scene nowadays would tax the resources of Onassis.

For over a year I had the 'talkie' field to myself and quickly made *Rookery Nook* and other Aldwych farces with Tom Walls and Ralph Lynn; *Up for the Cup* with Sydney Howard; and then the film that changed my entire life, *Good Night, Vienna*.

I can say without fear of contradiction that these films, with cinemas installing sound as fast as they could get the equipment, truly represented the box office renaissance of British films. Records were broken everywhere and, since the cost of production was low, our profits soared sufficiently for our private company to be floated as a public one. I produced these films in from ten to twenty-one days and had no 'talkie' competitor in the field. *Rookery Nook* cost £14,000, and in England alone yielded £150,000.

Tom Walls was a 'corker'. Never was there anyone like Tom, who could swear like a trooper and make it sound lyrical. He and Ralph Lynn established a comedy partnership record by running continuously at the Aldwych Theatre for over ten years.

Racehorse owner and trainer, and possibly the greatest *farceur* of the century, Tom loved the flesh-pots and the good things of life. He must have made a quarter of a million pounds out of the pictures we made together but with fourteen horses in training and several lovely women adoring him—he needed half a million. On the slightest pretext Tom would play truant from the studios to see his horses win—or lose. And I had to take a firm line, because an absent star costs a lot of money.

So Tom promised to reform. But one day he said to me: 'Herbert! I'm not feeling too good—if I'm not better tomorrow I think I'll have a day in bed.'

'Where's the racing tomorrow, Tom?' I asked.

'What are you, a bloody hermit, don't you know it's Derby Day and I'm going to win it?'

I made arrangements to shoot without Tom the following day, but at 3 p.m. the production crew moved towards the radio set and work stopped whilst the Derby was run.

Tom Walls won it with April the Fifth!

The entire studio went mad—all had backed it on Tom's strong tip. Tom turned up at the studios the next day with twelve cases of champagne, and very little work was in sight. What with champagne all round and all backing the winner—bang went our schedule!

The next day was gloom. The entire studio had been welshed—the bookmaker having gone leaving no address!

Tom left me to make more money with another company. But he never made another success and always bitterly regretted having left me.

Some years later he came to see me. He was broke.

'Give me a small part, Herbert—I really need the money.'

I wrote in a part for him in *Spring in Park Lane*. As always he was brilliant, and the money was a life-saver; well, not exactly—because Tom died soon afterwards.

He told his son, a fine boy: 'Cremate me and sprinkle my ashes on the course at Epsom.'

'Which part?' asked Tom Junior.

'At the winning post!' said the irrepressible Tom Senior, 'that's where they pay out.'

At that time I was producing some thirty films a year (twelve to fulfil the 'quota' needs of Paramount) but directing only a few.

Domestically, all was set fair. My four children were all at school, and my wife was wholly absorbed in her stables and garden.

One morning came a 'phone call at the studios. Eric Maschwitz and George Posford had written a musical score they wanted me to hear and were on their way with a vocalist and pianist.

I heard the score. It was *Good Night, Vienna*, I liked it and secured the rights. Within a week I had persuaded Jack Buchanan to play the lead, but the leading lady could not be found, despite a search embracing the continent as well as England. I wanted Lea Seidl, who had starred in *White Horse Inn*, or Evelyn Laye. Both were heavily booked up.

I went round to the London Hippodrome to tell Jack Buchanan and to suggest a postponement. *Stand Up and Sing* was the show and it was moving out for a provincial tour. I stood at the back of the stalls with Frank Boor, the manager, and suddenly saw a lovely young English girl dancing with Jack.

But let Caroline Lejeune (then film critic of the *Observer*, and surely the finest within memory) tell the story as she did on her B.B.C. series. Herewith the text of the illuminated excerpt presented to me.

A Year to Remember—1932
C. A. Lejeune

'And something historic's just happened in a London Theatre, The Hippodrome, where Jack Buchanan's playing in "Stand Up and Sing". It's a matinée and a little Irishman with a quiet voice stands at the back of a box for the last act. He doesn't care about the show. He wants just to talk to Jack about a continental star for their new film "Good Night Vienna". Jack's dancing with a girl with reddish hair, and the little Irishman suddenly has a brainwave. Why bother with a continental star? What's wrong with this girl, Anna Neagle? No experience? Never mind—he'll give her plenty, or his name isn't Herbert Wilcox. I needn't tell you the rest of the story, but it all began in 1932—the greatest husband, wife partnership the film industry has known.'

We had just three weeks to shoot *Good Night, Vienna* before Jack opened with *Stand Up and Sing* in Liverpool. Anna was to be paid £150 for the film, unlimited working hours and a seven-day week!

Since I had started directing films more than one leading lady had shown a personal interest in me—but I was interested only in my work and my home life was tranquil. So I dismissed the thought of affairs, seemingly the accepted thing between artist and director. A not unnatural outcome of personalising the constant submission of the artist to the artistic demands of the director.

I decided—not for me. In any event, with my strenuous activities as director and producer, I guess I had no spare energy to dissipate. I adored Dorothy Gish, with whom I worked for two years, and I'm sure she was terribly fond of me. Had circumstances been different I'm pretty certain we would have got together. However, we were both married.

One particular star, and a beautiful Viennese at that, burst out one day with: 'Don't you ever?'

'Quite a question,' I told her, 'but since you ask it—I don't!'

That first marriage of mine had not entirely burnt itself out and I was determined never again to experience such emotional turbulence.

The object of explaining my attitude towards women is to record that I was not promiscuous and would not permit anything to upset the even tenor of my private life. That was my big idea. But at the end of the very first day of shooting *Good Night, Vienna*, I knew it. I had fallen deeply in love with Anna Neagle!

Incredible! Or perhaps even naïve—call it what you will but there it was. As deeply as I had fallen in love in those far-off Brighton days of the First World War. And every day the production went on my love for her was intensified.

I did not, of course, say anything to her.

The production of *Good Night, Vienna* was completed and Anna passed out of my life. As I thought, for good. It had been a wonder-dream while it lasted and no one was hurt. How I hated saying 'Good-bye' and thanking her for the show she had put up.

Good Night, Vienna was my greatest success up to that time. It cost £23,000 and Australia alone yielded £150,000. It played for thirteen weeks at the Capitol (now Gaumont) Theatre in the Haymarket, and broke records throughout the country.

Jack Buchanan, already a great musical comedy star in the theatre, now became the top box office star in films. He was the perfect professional and the perfect gentleman.

Since we had a very tight schedule on *Good Night, Vienna* of three weeks and two days, it meant a sixteen-hour day—sometimes longer. Towards the end of one long and heavy day and a difficult scene Jack said: 'I'll have to cry off for a while, old boy.'

'But Jack, we'll get it next time,' I replied.

'Sorry, Herbert, but I must go to my dressing-room—and be sick,' said Jack.

'How long will it take?' I asked anxiously.

'Twenty minutes at the most,' he replied and dashed off apparently only just in time.

In ten minutes he was back, smiling and ready for action, and we got the scene next time.

The last day of production was a nightmare, as we had to get through before *Stand Up and Sing* opened at Liverpool the next day.

The scene was a gay drinking party in a Viennese open-air cafe. After ten takes the cast was exhausted and not helped by the lashings of ginger ale, alias champagne.

I called a halt and whispered to 'Props' to fill up next time with real champagne. The result was totally unexpected. As soon as the cast sipped it they stopped—burst out laughing and downed it in one gulp.

But the next take, again with real champagne, the scene was in the bag.

There is no one like Jack Buchanan in the film world today, as his picture shown here will bear out. Charming, handsome beyond description, and masculinely virile to a degree, I doubt if we shall see his like again. For elegance and charm he stood alone, and his own unadorned personality filled any theatre or cinema in the country. I endeavoured to develop this to the full—but Jack had different ideas. He always wanted to play down his charm and elegance.

'I love to hear them laugh, old boy,' he told me so often, and his main prop to get the maximum laughs was a funny hat. I could not talk him out of it since the laughter of an audience was food and drink to Jack. To hear them chuckle was not enough. Belly laughs he wanted and he invariably got them.

I doubt if any member of the theatrical profession ever did as much for the down-and-out troupers as Jack. They would line up on Saturday night and seldom go away without something for a meal and a drink.

Jack's weakness was his desire to engage in big business—theatres, management and, above all, television.

When the medals for pioneering world-wide television are handed out, the first should go to Jack Buchanan, for his financial and personal support of his boyhood friend John Logie Baird made it possible for Baird and Britain to be the world's technical leaders of TV. How sad it is that, with so many fortunes being made out of his brain child, Baird's widow needed assistance which was not available until her predicament gained wide publicity.

For seven years Jack and I worked together on films, and all were successful. He also supported me financially in the making of *Victoria the Great* but I was able to reciprocate later when, at a time that he needed finance, I sold his Leicester Square Theatre to my film colleagues.

Jack's courage in his closing days, when in the grip of the most painful cancer, I hope I may match if ever I am put to the test.

One spot of prestige in a spate of popular box office successes was *Escape Me Never*, which introduced Elisabeth Bergner to British films. The play, presented by C. B. Cochran, had established a theatrical record by selling out for the entire run (including *matinées*) before it opened. 'Cocky' had several offers for the film rights but he apparently wanted me to do it. I've since heard that one of the other offers—from an American company—was considerably higher than mine.

I engaged Bergner's husband, Paul Czinner, to direct; William Walton (now Sir William) to compose the music for the ballet: and George Perinal as cameraman.

Bergner, great artist as she was, was mercurial and her moods differed from day to day. Her husband understood her perfectly and knew how to meet every changing mood. He finished the film on schedule—and it then went out to beat the records set up by my 'commercial box office' pictures.

The scenes outside the London Pavilion, where it played for eight weeks, thereby recovering its cost from this one engagement, were comparable to recent scenes with the James Bond films. I suggested to Cochran and Margaret Kennedy, the author, that an extra payment for the rights should be made. Dear 'Cocky', who never personally made the money his genius warranted, said: 'You've made the picture as we hoped to see it. Margaret doesn't need the money and I wouldn't take it if you offered it.'

Bergner, of course, was the ideal 'Constant Nymph' and her elfinlike personality had in it much of Peter Pan. I'm confident that J. M. Barrie, who saw *The Constant Nymph* in Germany and *Escape Me Never* in London, recognised his beloved Peter in Bergner and fell in love with her. He decided to write *The Boy David* for her, but unfortunately it was not successful.

Escape Me Never gave me the heaven-sent opportunity of meeting

Barrie several times. I asked Elisabeth to invite him to the studios. She laughed as only Bergner could laugh. I was puzzled. She told me: 'He asked me last week how I could bring myself to act in "talkies". "They fix a microphone under some ornament on a table. You and your lover are playing a scene together when he rushes you from the table, shouts into the microphone: 'I love you.' When he comes back, you do the same—Elisabeth how can you?" Barrie asked.'

But I persisted.

'Ask him down to the studios for lunch, darling. He will have a surprise, I promise you.'

Barrie came down and after lunch was taken on to the studio floor. I had a few minutes with Paul Czinner, who turned to the principals.

'I want to try a new scene which Margaret has written. Would you both—Elisabeth and Hugh (Sinclair)—come over here?' said Paul.

A few whispered instructions from Paul whilst I engaged Barrie in conversation. Apparently he did not hear me, for from out of the blue he asked:

'Do you like Americans?'

'Most of them,' I replied, not knowing what else to say. But then it dawned on me how his works had been travestied beyond recognition in Hollywood. 'I didn't like what the Hollywood producers did to *Peter Pan*, if that's what you mean.' I told Barrie.

'No, I meant just what I said. You like most of the Americans—do you like Paramount Pictures?' he next asked.

I told him I did—but by now was completely foxed.

'I found them charming, both Americans and Paramount,' he went on, 'and very generous they are, too.'

'In what way?' I asked, now hopelessly out of my depth.

'Well, they pay me a lot of money for my plays, but never use the material. It is all new stuff and ideas—some very original.'

'Don't you resent that?' I asked him.

'Oh no, not at all. You see, they not only change the play—they change the title!'

His dry Scottish humour was too much and I rocked with laughter. I should mention that the title of *The Admirable Crichton* was changed in Hollywood to *Male and Female*!

My laughter died as Paul Czinner called for 'Quiet' and the new scene was rehearsed. It went exactly as Barrie had described it to Bergner—Hugh Sinclair leaving her and leaning over the table microphone box and shouting at the top of his voice 'I love you', then back to Bergner who then did the same.

24. With Dorothy Gish, star of *Nell Gwyn*.

25. With Tom Walls in 1930.

26. Anna, with Jack Buchanan in our first film together, *Good Night, Vienna*, 1931.

27. Directing Brigitte Helm in *The Blue Danube*, 1932.

28. Anna in *The Little Damozel*, 1932. This was the dress which shocked the critics into acclaiming her, and her brother cabled from South Africa: 'What are they doing to you?'

29. The famous 'cleavage' picture of Anna as Nell Gwyn, 1934. This was the first film banned under the U.S. Purity Code.

30. Two cartoons by Low depicting the ban.

That was my Irish humour which Barrie appreciated. Bergner roared with laughter and rolled on the ground. Barrie and I became good friends from then on.

My work has given me the opportunity of meeting many authors. Besides Barrie, there were John Galsworthy, H. G. Wells, George Bernard Shaw, Conan Doyle, Noel Coward, Frederick Lonsdale, Somerset Maugham, Terrence Rattigan and others; dramatic craftsmen all, dedicated since apprenticeship to their craft, who believed a play should have a beginning, a middle and an end—as well as something worth while to say.

I've also met most of the new cult of angry young men who scorn the play construction that made both sense and entertainment, and endeavour to substitute, by means of off-beat themes, four-letter words and other methods, a series of shocks in reaching the same objective. In each succeeding play the angry youngsters appear to get angrier.

About what, it is difficult to imagine. With ridiculous figures being paid for the film rights of their material, pushing their incomes up to many times that of the Prime Minister, it cannot be their fear of finding themselves on the bread line.

Ah, well—I've no doubt they've written me off long ago as all 'square'; and since I regard the preponderance of their output as all 'spherical', we must geometrically and spiritually disagree.

When I told Galsworthy that my ambition was to write, he gave me golden advice which I now pass on in the hope that it will catch the eye of any aspiring writer:

'If you have to write, the first rule is discipline and routine. Never say or think "I must wait until the spirit moves me". The spirit may never move you. Sit down at your desk every morning, blank paper and pen ready, stay there and write for a number of hours every day. If it is rubbish, throw it away and start again. Rhythm is as important in writing as it is in tennis or dancing.'

My association with Galsworthy was a bitter-sweet affair. On several Saturday evenings during the late twenties I had witnessed the intense feeling aroused amongst the audience by his play *Loyalties*, which without being anti-Semitic showed the wide ideological gulf between Jew and Gentile on a specific principle.

I bought the film rights for, in those days, the fantastically high figure of £9,000. Even with that amount offered Galsworthy would not close the deal until he had met me and ascertained my approach to the subject. We met, and achieved complete agreement on the screen version since, like Galsworthy, I intended to balance the conflicting views and values honestly and objectively. Had my approach been even slanted towards anti-Semitism I would not have got to first base. After our meeting Galsworthy paid me the compliment of saying that, subject to my personally directing the film, he did not wish to approve the screenplay, although that condition was stipulated in his agreement. In the subject we both saw a highly controversial entertainment without racial bias or prejudice.

That's what *we* saw—but every distributor I approached must have seen something else and regarded the film prospect as dynamite. I therefore found myself with an excellent screenplay which cost £2,000 plus film rights £9,000, with no one interested. £11,000 at that time represented almost my entire pre-production working capital. Then a miracle. William ('Bill') Fox, founder of Fox Films, the parent of Twentieth Century Fox—made me an offer. £20,000 cash! Needless to say I accepted at once—but recalled I had to secure Galsworthy's consent if I did not produce the film myself, but assigned or re-sold the rights.

Before I could see Galsworthy, Bill Fox arrived from New York with his cheque book. He did not like the screenplay approval clause which, since it embodied Galsworthy's comments, I regarded as an asset.

Fox's reason was that he intended to make the main character, De Levis, a Scotsman and not a Jew! I told him he was destroying the fundamental argument and missing the conflict and contest. Since Fox was a strict orthodox Jew himself, I made no impression and he insisted on the elimination of the approval clause as a prerequisite to the deal.

With grave misgivings, I called on Galsworthy and told him of my problem. His reply was very much to the point.

'I will not agree and furthermore I will stipulate in my will that my executors have no power to agree.' That was not definite enough for Bill Fox who suggested a meeting between all parties and our lawyers.

Graciously, Galsworthy agreed to the meeting, but at it there was not the slightest unbending on his part. In order to save some of my money I suggested that another Galsworthy story, *The Stoic* (a favourite of mine on which I had an option), be substituted.

Fox's 'bodyguard' representative, a true product of Brooklyn of the twenties whom Dorothy Gish would have described as a 'Dis-Dat-Dees and Doos Man', piped up and asked:

'*The Stoic?* Ain't dat der boid Limeys bull their kids about bringing der babies?' (which, literally interpreted, means: 'The Stork? isn't that the bird the English tell their kids delivers babies?').

John Galsworthy left.

Bill Fox sat slumped in his chair but after a moment or two came and walked over and shook me warmly by the hand. Then, addressing his lawyer, he said, 'We complete the purchase of *Loyalties* today and Galsworthy approves script.'

And they did.

I've always followed Galsworthy's advice about the necessity for discipline and have invariably found it works.

Monckton Hoffe once advised me: 'Never write an informative line of dialogue.'

Gene Fowler's advice was: 'Hit them hard with your first sentence.' In writing *Above the Timber Line*, which dealt with two disreputable newspaper publishers in the Middle West, he started his book by introducing one of them thus . . . 'He had one thing in common with his father. They never married!'

Noel Coward's advice to would-be authors was short and to the point. 'Entertain.' A warm and sentimental person, Noel, but as a director a martinet. For those who fail him in the slightest degree there is no second chance. They are out on their ear, irrespective of status or reputation.

There has always been a sympathetic link between Noel and myself, and he adores Anna.

I was at the first night of *Bitter Sweet* at Her Majesty's Theatre, and Noel said: 'I'm dying to know what you think, Herbert. I'm sure it's the best thing I have ever done and will ensure that my family will never want.'

I bought the rights and produced the film version. *I* did not provide for my family from the profits—there were none! It must have been my fault, for surely a better musical play has never been written. I never hear 'I'll see you again' without a thrill going up my spine. Perhaps, however, the story is rather too sad for a film.

Anna Neagle had not, as I thought, passed out of my life for good. On 5 April, 1932, after the trade show of *Good Night, Vienna* in Birmingham, I signed her up on a long-term contract.

In the film she had been hailed by the press as the typical English rose. That was good up to a point, but it would be fatal if she were to be labelled as such, or type-cast. So I decided her next picture must shock the critics into noticing the actress in her, and also shock audiences out of the English rose image.

When I was young I loved the theatre and, if I could raise the money, would go and sit in the gallery on the first night of new plays. One of these was *The Little Damozel* by Monckton Hoffe at the Haymarket Theatre, London.

One evening in 1932—wondering how I could kill Anna's English rose label—I wandered into the Savoy, ordered a drink, and went to wash my hands. Standing next to me in the cloakroom was a man I knew but had never met.

'Aren't you Monckton Hoffe?' I asked him.

Despite the strange location and situation to exchange introductions, 'Pat' Hoffe—dignity and elegance personified (as his friends will vouch)—replied: 'I am. Should I know you?'

I explained who I was and how much I had enjoyed *The Little Damozel* and *The Faithful Heart*.

Before we left the lavatory I had negotiated the film rights of *The Little Damozel*, and Hoffe became one of Anna's and my greatest friends up to the time of his death.

The Little Damozel produced, I arranged for Anna to sing and dance a prologue on the stage, going right back to the first night of the play at the Haymarket.

The film opened in London at the Plaza, and broke the record for the theatre. Anna made a personal appearance in, at that time, an outrageously daring diaphanous dress designed by Doris Zinkeisen, and a great gasp went up when the audience saw her. She wore the same dress in the film. I certainly succeeded with the shock method.

Anna repeated her success with personal appearances at all the big provincial centres, and the national press went overboard. So did her brother, Alan—who saw the film in South Africa and walked out in disgust. He cabled her: 'What are they doing to you?'

I found Anna a joy to direct. A perfectionist, she never objected to going on and on until we felt the scene was right. On many occasions some members of the press, watching me directing Anna and repeating a scene many times, have queried my motive.

'I go on,' I told them, 'until I cannot recognise Anna Neagle or her own voice. Then I know she's lost in the character.'

Anna herself is a hard taskmaster. Even when I have a scene to my own satisfaction, she often says: 'Just once more. I can do better.'

By this time my love for Anna was overwhelming. But I didn't tell her how I felt until I had no need to—and I knew she felt the same about me.

One day I asked why we had not met before.

'You weren't very interested,' replied Anna, with a twinkle.

'In what way?' I asked.

'Nelson Keys asked you to keep a blind date with me at the Charleston Ball at the Albert Hall, but you turned me down.'

'I didn't know you,' I protested.

'Oh yes you did—Bunch (Nelson Keys) described my short scene with him in *Rose Marie*. And then again at the Stoll studios I came for crowd work in a film. You were good enough to see me—but it was the usual 'Send me a photo'... I didn't—but wrote in my diary that night: 'Saw Herbert Wilcox about film work—think I'll stick to the chorus."'

'Third time lucky,' was all I could think of to answer.

Life now became difficult for I had a wife and children, and Anna was not the girl to break up a marriage—even if it were unsatisfactory. Time after time we met and said:' It's no good—this must be the last time.' But we couldn't say 'Good-bye'. We had everything when we were together; nothing when we were apart.

My wife was also attracted to an old friend of hers—so it was altogether a sorry mess.

Since nothing could be done about our situation, Anna and I decided the only antidote was to get back to work. It was fortunate that the subject I had chosen needed a vast amount of research. For Anna loves nothing better than digging down and finding out everything about the character she is to portray.

It was Nell Gwyn!

9

I had produced *Nell Gwyn* as a silent film with Dorothy Gish. But Anna as the big-hearted Cockney mistress of Charles II made an enormous appeal to me.

'Do you think I can play Nell Gwyn?' asked Anna.

'Why not?' I replied.

'She was a bit of a wild one, wasn't she?' said Anna.

'And aren't you a bit of an actress?' I asked.

She threw herself into intensive research and study, and within two weeks knew as much about Nell as Dorothy Gish. Cedric Hardwicke was perfect casting as Charles II, and off we started on time.

Anna groped and groped, endeavouring to find the character. And after a few days I began to wonder if this was just one too many dips in the well.

Then, without warning, in one scene Anna got the lot—accent, voice, laugh, lack of inhibition. She virtually became Nell Gwyn—not merely acting her. And she never let go. She held her tight throughout the production from then on. It was a delight to direct her and full of surprises, I never knew what to expect next.

I had no need to wait and see what the film was like. I knew I had a gem.

Meanwhile, off I went to New York—tail well up!

United Artists were to distribute it in America. And after seeing it, their distribution chief, Al Lichtman, told me I had struck gold! 'You can count on 900,000 dollars as your share and perhaps much more,' he said.

I was asked to arrange the first New York showing for the trade and critics. Expense was no object. I took over the Astor Hotel ballroom, installed projectors and made arrangements for a supper for 500, giving them a meal—as served in the film at Whitehall Palace—of pigs' trotters and umbles washed down with firkins of sack!

What a success! So great was the enthusiasm, I had to repeat the showing of the film at midnight!

'Does 900,000 dollars still stand?' I facetiously asked Al Lichtman.

'And as much more,' he replied.

For some time afterwards if you asked any film man in New York to have a drink, his reply was: 'Thanks, I'll have a firkin of sack!'

After the Astor showings, I telephoned Anna, who was pacing the promenade at Broadstairs, anxiously awaiting the result which would make her a world star. I told her of the wildly enthusiastic reception and particularly the verdict of D. W. Griffith, who voted it one of the most beautiful films he had ever seen and Anna the greatest foreign star ever to streak across the American film firmament.

I was staying as the house guest of a very old friend, Martin Quigley, publisher of all the combined trade papers and one of the founders of the Production Code, 'popularly' known as the Purity League. Martin, strangely enough, was rather less demonstrative about the film than the other newspaper-men and I taxed him about it. He looked at me for a few seconds before answering:

'As a good Catholic you should know the reason.'

I confessed I did not.

'It's not pornographic,' he replied, 'but it's as near as it can be to being so.'

I was astounded. But Martin was a man of broad outlook and the story of Nell Gwyn and Charles II was, of course, a bawdy one. I told Quigley of D. W. Griffith's opinion, but it fell on stony ground. Next day, Lichtman asked me to come and see him.

'We're in trouble. We may not get the seal.'

That meant the film could not be shown in the States. When I recovered I asked for information.

I was given it. The story was immoral, and the girl got away with it! The King must marry Nell; and I should have to shoot a scene showing this!

Too much 'cleavage' (this was how and when the word originated); in answer to my query, cleavage was 'a valley between two mountains'.

Next objection? Nell should not be 'passed on' to James II when Charles died!

There were thirty-three other objections which, if met, would emasculate the film to such an extent that it would be unprofitable to show at all.

For days I argued with the censors. It was *history* that Charles and Nell were lovers. To marry them would be dishonest and immoral. As for the 'cleavage', that was as God made Anna, and how could anyone see anything but beauty in those lovely shoulders and breasts? To interpret the famous last words of Charles to James II—'Let not poor Nellie starve'—as 'passing her on', was beyond my comprehension, as were most of the other objections.

However, I had to be temperate and conciliatory. Nearly one million dollars were at stake.

Eventually one suggestion was made and, a million dollars or nothing, I stuck my toes in. Would I shoot a new scene showing Nell's body in rags huddled in the gutter of a street, with the caption: 'Nell Gwyn lived as she must and died as she must—in the gutter.'

I would rather have done without American distribution altogether than perpetrate such an insult to the memory of one who still enjoys a warm place in the hearts of most Londoners. But the American distributors, who had a small financial stake in the picture, were not so sentimental or squeamish. They made most of the cuts and, after I left, shot the shocking epilogue—but not with Anna, of course.

The film duly made its appearance on the American screen and, not surprisingly, was a failure. However, I made a very handsome profit indeed from the rest of the world, and Anna's stock as an actress of stature grew enormously. When *Nell Gwyn* opened in London the critics went wild. Audiences went wild. At the Leicester Square Theatre it was more like a football match than a cinema. Endless crowds waited to get in. The takings (and in those days it was 10s. 6d. top) exceeded £1,000 per day. And there it stayed for months.

In this year of grace 1966, *Nell Gwyn* is still shown in the United Kingdom on TV (and how well it stands up). It is shown in its original form on TV in the United States without a murmur of protest from viewers! But there are plenty of squawks from me about that million or so I lost in those early days of American censorship.

Having recently seen *Who's Afraid of Virginia Woolf?* I can well imagine Martin Quigley, rest his soul, doing nip-ups in his grave.

The world press was indignant about the fate of Nell in America, as some of the cartoons I have reproduced show. Altogether a tragic and unhappy experience. But one bright spot that brought Anna infinite pleasure was the opinion of D. W. Griffith. He was so enthusiastic that I wanted him to have a word with Anna on the telephone —the word that would have transported her with happiness and pleasure.

'No,' said Griffith, 'I might be disappointed. Tell her I am cabling.'

His cable to Anna is one of her most treasured possessions. It read: 'Once in a while a star shoots across the film horizon and lights up the sky. That's what you have done with *Nell Gwyn*. May you shine brighter every night. D. W. Griffith.'

'When she next comes to New York,' I told him, 'I would like you to meet her.'

'Fine,' said Griffith. 'Do that. But bring a chaperone. I have been known to steal 'em—and boy, she's a peach. And she can act!'

It was some time before Anna went to New York with me. After a theatre or cinema, we invariably walked back to the St Regis Hotel. One night, almost abreast of the 55th Street Playhouse, I saw a dark figure, felt hat pulled well down over his nose, coat collar turned up to his ears—an actor, I guessed.

As he passed, I stopped dead. 'Griffith,' I told Anna, and rushed after him. Anna followed me. He heard me coming and quickened his steps. I touched his arm and he spun round.

'Why the hell can't you leave me alone?' he demanded.

'D.W. . . .' I said, 'I'm Herbert Wilcox, and here is the girl you threatened to steal—Anna Neagle.'

He looked at her, and after a moment muttered: 'For God's sake, Anna Neagle!—and I had to meet you like this.'

He refused to come and have a drink or a meal but in a few minutes, with furtive looks over his shoulder, he told us his story. Pursued by process-servers—he thought I was one—the only time he could get out for a walk was after 11 p.m. and then only through battalions of garbage bins at his hotel's tradesmen's entrance. He had no money. The hotel bill was 'on the house', owned by an old actor who had been in several of D.W.'s pictures.

Griffith died shortly afterwards. Universal tributes echoed from everywhere motion pictures had been seen.

Perhaps that of Eric Von Stroheim over the radio made the greatest impact. Towards the end of his tribute Stroheim broke down—emotionally overwhelmed. He apologised to listeners, saying 'You must excuse me—I was going to say—I don't remember—I can't go on. All I can think of at this time is that Mr Griffith, the creator of the art of motion pictures and the man who taught all we film-makers our craft—who made millions of dollars for others—died—PENNILESS—in the heart of the most heartless city in the world.'

The partnership of Anna and Cedric Hardwicke received such critical acclaim and was so profitable (despite the U.S.A.) that I decided on another historical film—this time with Anna as the Drury Lane actress, Peg Woffington, and with Cedric Hardwicke playing David Garrick.

It was uneventful in production, so I will pass over this period. But it was enormously successful both here and in the States, artistically as well as at the box office. It also introduced to British films a young actor who played Orlando to Anna's Rosalind in *As You Like It* at the Open Air Theatre—Jack Hawkins.

Peg of Old Drury was also to prove a monumental factor in my career. For while it was showing at the Leicester Square Theatre, where it equalled the business of *Nell Gwyn*, it was seen by someone entirely unconnected with the British film industry, but who subsequently became the greatest commercial and financial factor in establishing what is now known as the Rank empire. Afterwards he asked to meet Anna and me.

He was Lord Portal of Laverstoke ('Wyndham' to his friends) and, after our meeting, he brought into our film operation Arthur Rank, Lord Luke and Leslie Farrow, a colleague of Portal on the board of Wiggins Teape Ltd., the paper firm. Portal became a very close friend of Anna's and mine and, through his influence and enthusiasm, our group went full steam ahead.

Having been pushed into the background by my American distributors to the detriment of my own company, I decided to defy their threats, withdraw my productions from their distribution, and resign my own position as managing director of British and Dominions—for which I was paid £9,000 per annum plus a share of the company's profits.

I was no match for the Americans. I knew it, and asked C. M. Woolf to accept the managing directorship and my £9,000 per annum, plus profits, in my stead. I knew they would have a very different proposition to face with C.M. They threatened to sue me and get an injunction against the company. I gave them the name of my solicitors who would accept service.

C.M. asked to be joined in the battle. They decided to call it a day, and I made a fresh start in a new company with the full support of Lord Portal and Arthur Rank. In this C. M. Woolf joined us. And that is how Rank came into the film industry. Before this he had financed only some short religious films.

Portal, having made a great success of his paper operations— Portals Ltd. and Wiggins Teape—was determined to do the same in British films. He raised a large sum of money and was always available for advice. C. M. Woolf, having had a rough experience in Gaumont British, bloomed and flourished in his association with Portal and Rank.

I lined up a programme of films and bought the Leicester Square Theatre from Jack Buchanan as a West End shop window.

I was exhausted by my battles with the Americans and, after preparing a six-film programme, I went to Switzerland for a brief holiday. Arriving about 10 p.m. I went straight to bed and left instructions not to be disturbed. I felt like sleeping for a week, but it seemed only a matter of minutes before the telephone rang. Would I take a call from New York?

'Hello,' said a voice. 'This is John Bullock speaking from New York.'

I knew no one of that name and presumed it was a writer or artist seeking work. So I hung up and went back to sleep.

Again that darned phone . . .

'Hello!' I shouted irritably. 'You've got the wrong number.'

'Are you Herbert Wilcox?' said the voice at the other end.

'Yes.'

'The British film producer?'

'I am—and I'm on a holiday, so would you please contact my London office for anything you want.'

Before I could ring off again, the voice went on:

'Would you like to buy Universal Pictures for England?' (Universal was one of the top and most flourishing companies. I now realised I was being hoaxed.)

'Yes,' I replied. 'And M.G.M. and Paramount, too!' And down went my phone again.

Once more it started ringing and I was furious. 'Would you please try your jokes on someone else—I'm giving instructions that no more calls . . .'

'Before you do that, have a word with an old friend of yours—my father . . .'

'Hello, Herbert, this is William Bullock of the *Daily Mail*. You remember?'

Of course. F. W. Bullock was one of the great international journalists and a personal friend of Lord Northcliffe.

'Just wanted to confirm my son John is talking to you and can implement any deal he discusses with you.'

'Thanks—put him on.'

The fact that I had broken with United Artists and had formed an association with a powerful financial group had been published in New York. At once the head of Universal Pictures, Cheever Cowdin, had approached Bullock to negotiate the sale of the English side.

Since the Universal American output was some fifty films a year, plus an excellent newsreel, it struck me at once that here was a solid foundation on which to build.

'How much?' I asked.

'Five million dollars,' replied Bullock.

'Can I have a seven-day option?'

I could.

No sleep now. No exhaustion. My imagination was going at top speed.

I phoned C. M. Woolf in London. He was not there. I tried Paris. There I reached him.

'Meet me at the Gare du Nord tomorrow evening,' I told him.

'I thought you were tired and wanted a rest,' he replied.

'Too important to sleep on this. Sure you'll agree.'

We met at the station. C.M. had with him his son, John—now the guiding light of Anglia Television and Romulus Films. I recounted the phone calls.

'What do we use for money and where do we get it?' C.M. asked.

'First of all—is the deal all right?' I inquired.

'So good that it can't happen,' he replied. 'With what we've got lined up and Universal and the newsreel—don't be silly!'

'Then you recommend it?' I asked.

C.M. smiled.

'I'm booked through to London, and I'll phone you when it's in the bag. I'm seeing Wyndham Portal in the morning.'

'Now, I'll tell you something, Herbert,' said C.M. 'I believe you'll pull it off with him. If you don't, no one else will.'

'Thanks,' I said, and we parted. I fancied I could hear him laugh as he walked away with John.

My meeting with Portal was proof—if proof was needed—of the methods by which he had made such a success of his business life. At once he saw the potentialities and the solid base for all other activities. A holding company must be formed, separate from British & Dominions. In a few minutes he had described a financial structure which even I, in my ignorance of such matters, could readily visualise.

'What about the five million dollars?' I asked.

'Securing finance is never a problem if the operation is sound,' said Portal. 'I'm lunching with the governor of the Bank of England tomorrow—I'd like you to join us.'

At lunch I met Montagu Norman, who succeeded in embarrassing me as never before.

Portal's firm supplied all the paper for banknotes—not only in

England but in every part of the world. Portal, although not on the board of directors of the Bank of England, was invited to board meetings on matters of importance. He and Montagu Norman were very close friends.

Introductions over, Portal started to outline the Universal deal when Norman broke in with: 'Wyndham, you're surely not going to interest yourself in that awful film industry?'

Portal caught my eye, and tried to make out a case, but Norman was adamant. 'It's no good, Wyndham! It's unsound. And those dreadful people are not your class. Keep out of it.'

Seeing that a request like this could mean a directive, I did not enjoy the lunch that followed. Neither was I flattered that Norman completely ignored me after the formal introduction and must have known the effect of his remarks on me. He mentioned several top names in the industry—some of whom I knew very well—and he was devastating about their ethics and methods.

We walked back to Portal's office at Wiggins Teape. During the walk not a word was spoken. In his office, he ordered coffee.

'Where is C.M.?' asked Portal.

'Paris,' I told him.

'And he recommends the deal—without qualification?'

'Could not have been more enthusiastic, but of course he was doubtful—'

'About what?' he cut in.

'Raising the five million dollars.'

'Phone C.M. and tell him the deal is going through and I am the first subscriber—and ask him to get back as soon as possible.'

What a courageous decision!

'Don't take the governor too seriously. He has a bee in his bonnet about the British film industry.' he went on.

'And about the people in it,' I replied, as I recalled the vitriolic references to the businessmen engaged in the industry at that time.

'There's only one way to meet his prejudice,' said Portal, 'and that is by successful operating. With C.M. at the helm and you on production, we'll do it—and the governor will be the first to say "Well done".'

Well! We did it, but if Montagu Norman said 'Well done'—I never heard it.

Cheever Cowdin, president of Universal, and his advisers came from New York, accompanied by John Bullock, to meet Portal, Rank, C. M. Woolf and Leslie Farrow. We all assembled in my suite at Claridges.

A solid week of negotiations and the deal was closed. A deal that has proved to be the very corner-stone of the Rank empire. My assertion is based upon the fact that a regular supply of product plus a newsreel represents the hard core of any film organisation. The follow-up of acquiring cinemas and the establishment of studio and home production automatically follows. Without so stable a foundation survival would have been difficult, if not impossible.

However, little did I dream that in the 1960s we were to see Universal, revitalised under the guidance of Lew Wasserman, the one man who can justifiably be put into the Irving Thalberg class, emerge as the leading producers of quality film and television in the world, and owners of Hollywood's largest and most modern studios.

And this vitally important association stemmed from an overseas call from New York to Switzerland—between strangers!

A holding company called General Cinema Finance was formed. And it was typical of Wyndham Portal that, for my part in having initiated and furthered the deal, he stipulated I should be offered £20,000 cash, or 20,000 shares in the company. I chose the shares, which delighted Portal since it indicated my confidence and encouraged my active association with the project. I was also appointed to the board of directors of the Universal English company and the Universal American parent company. G.C.F. would control the distribution and production of films and acquire cinemas.

Then followed the absorption of Gaumont British with its production, distribution and studio operations—a triumph for C. M. Woolf after his bitter quarrel with his co-directors before he dropped out of Gaumont British. The control of the Odeon circuit from Oscar Deutsch was also completed.

Then Arthur Rank decided to build studios as they should be built—and run on efficient lines. He bought a Buckinghamshire estate from Colonel Grant Morden, M.P., with a lovely house and grounds. He took me to see the nearly completed studios and I was scared when I saw the endless number of offices, all of which I felt would house secretaries and office boys. Up would go the overheads and the costs of film production. At Elstree I had the minimum staff in an effort to hold down production costs. I decided to stay out—at all events for the time being.

Arthur Rank was very disappointed, and C. M. Woolf tried to persuade me, saying: 'Stay where the money is, Herbert.' But I stood firm.

However, I was disturbed at not going in with Rank. And that night at my home in Elstree, which stood high on a hill, I could not sleep. I got up and wandered over to the window. A red glow filled the sky. I looked at the source.

It was a huge fire at the studios—*my* studios!

The phone rang and warned me. In minutes I was on my way, clad only in pyjamas and an overcoat. I arrived in time to save the films in the vault, but my lucky studios where I had made the Walls-Lynn, Jack Buchanan, Anna Neagle and Elisabeth Bergner films—plus a million pounds—were destroyed. The damage amounted to over £250,000.

At about 6 a.m. Lord Portal, Arthur Rank and C. M. Woolf arrived and, after viewing the ruins, we adjourned to my house for breakfast.

The die was cast. Whether I liked it or not. I was bound for Arthur Rank's studios at 'Pinewood', as they were to be called.

So once again I opened a new British film studio, when I made *London Melody* with Anna Neagle and Tullio Carminatti, and my colleague, the Hon. Richard Norton, in charge of the new studios, presented Anna with a silk picture of herself as Peg Woffington.

Rank's partner was a builder of considerable status, a Mr Henry Boot of Nottingham. An extraordinary character, this Mr Boot, with a white Van Dyke beard. His voice seemed to escape through the gap where his lips might be.

The opening ceremony was unique in the history of British films. Dr Leslie Burgin, President of the Board of Trade, declared the studios open and received a golden souvenir key. Portal, Rank, Farrow, Luke, were all present plus two thousand guests including the greatest stars of British films and theatre at the time.

Mr Boot made his speech and was very fulsome in his praise—not for Dr Burgin or the great stars present, but for the plumbers! The gathering rocked, and although I am sure the plumbers had done yeoman work, it was not exactly the occasion for such a sanitary salute!

The plumbers' tribute apart, perhaps the most amusing story of the early days of Pinewood studios was when C. M. Woolf was being proudly shown round, in the V.I.P. tradition, by the Hon. Richard Norton, son and heir of Lord Grantley.

Richard, one of my co-directors in British and Dominions, was a stern disciplinarian and this—plus his old Etonian manner and his title, the Honourable (how the workmen outrageously over-emphasised the aitch)—did not enhance his popularity with the plasterers and the carpenters in the workshops.

Whether he was expected or not will never be determined, but when he and C.M. arrived at the plasterers' shop, they came face to face with a legend chalked on the wall in illiterate lettering: 'The Honourable Richard Norton is a s . . t!'

They stopped dead. C.M. saw the funny side and rocked with laughter.

But Richard was not taking that from anyone. Like a true old Etonian and without turning a hair, he picked up a piece of hessian and dipped it in a water butt, then obliterated the words 'The Honourable Richard Norton' and, in the same illiterate style, substituted 'Lord Grantley'!

Richard's father had passed away the previous week, and he had inherited the title!

The outcome? Richard became the pin-up boy of Pinewood. When later he was badly injured in a car accident, amongst the first batch of goodwill messages and flowers was one from the carpenters and plasterers with a card in the same illiterate handwriting: 'Best wishes for a speedy recovery and respectful regards to Lord Grantley!'

Meanwhile, the film distribution operation headed by C. M. Woolf flourished and blossomed forth in many directions.

But then came an unexpected shock.

10

My own production company, which contracted to produce films for the distributing company, General Film Distributors Ltd., was Herbert Wilcox Productions Ltd. I, as chairman and managing director, controlled the shareholding. The only other shareholders were C. M. Woolf and his brother Maurice.

The Universal deal was working out according to plan and I produced what and when I liked. My friendship with C.M. and our mutual confidence was reflected in the fact that I never questioned anything he did on the distribution side, and he never questioned anything I did on the production side.

This amicable arrangement lasted until 1937, when I was able to visualise the dream of my career—a film of Queen Victoria. This was made possible during the reign of King Edward VIII. But for this brief reign I might never have produced *Victoria the Great* and Anna Neagle might never have played the Queen. And if it hadn't been for the woman who later became the Duchess of Windsor, I don't suppose Edward VIII would have given it a thought.

It was during his 325 days as King that Mrs Simpson said to him: 'If it's all right to do a play about Queen Victoria, why can't they make a film about her?' (The Duchess was referring to Laurence Housman's *Victoria Regina*.

King Edward knew me because I had 'starred' him years before in a silent picture called *A Day in the Life of the Prince of Wales*, and had been at parties given in his honour in the twenties. *He* couldn't understand this ban either; so he looked into it.

And suddenly I got a message: 'Go ahead.' Without wasting a minute, and feeling confident of securing valuable facilities, I announced in the film papers: *Victoria the Great*—production immediately. As was the custom in those days, that established my claim to the subject. It also pipped Alexander Korda by a few hours, and how badly Alex wanted to make it.

This was the one film I had always wanted to make. I suppose the ambition was there, deep down, before I even dreamed I would make pictures; when I was the hungry young boy scrounging stale sandwiches from Brighton restaurants, and had seen Edward VII dozing on a seat on the Hove sea-front with his back to the statue of Queen

Victoria. And stuck in my mind for ever were the words I shouted as a Brighton newsboy the day she died: 'Death of Queen Victoria.'

So when Korda asked, 'Couldn't we join forces?', I told him, 'Not this time, Alex,' and landed myself with the biggest gamble I had ever taken.

I told Anna I wanted her to play the Queen.

'Queen Victoria?' she gasped. 'But she was a very old lady.'

'Not always,' I told her. 'And we can always make you older. The reverse is not so easy.'

'If you think I can play her, I'll do my best.'

And a wonderful best it turned out to be.

But from the moment I announced that Anna was to play the Queen, the sniping began. In and around Wardour Street—and then the press came into the open. The leading fan magazine of those days devoted a leading article to an attack on my casting of the Queen. 'What can Anna Neagle know about playing a Queen?' they asked. 'Why, she was a chorus girl.' And so on.

Anna was hurt but I was not unduly worried. They had said the same about *Nell Gwyn*.

If I had my doubts about Anna, these criticisms strengthened my resolution. I didn't remind the critics that Anna had already made profitable pictures out of characters such as Nell Gwyn, Peg Woffington and a torch-singer. I didn't think there should be any need to do so.

They probably thought my being in love with Anna, which most film folk knew, was the heart of the matter. But it wasn't. I knew in my considered judgment that Anna, being the actress I believed she was, could do as well—if not better—than anyone else.

I raised the matter with the only man who would have the right to question my judgment—my distributor, C. M. Woolf. I knew that in him I could count on a vote of absolute confidence.

I was wrong. To my amazement, C.M. agreed with the doubters. I was badly shaken and went to great lengths to support my casting. I could not convince him. He was as strong as those who had come out into the open.

'Herbert,' he said. 'Your friends' money is in this company and they expect me to protect it. You must trust me and have confidence in my judgment.'

'Why not have confidence in mine?' I countered. 'This, I am sure, is going to be my biggest success.'

'I wish I could think so,' replied a sad C.M., 'but I can't—and Maurice (his brother) agrees with me. Now, Herbert—do me a favour, will you? Forget Queen Victoria and find something else.'

We argued—until I realised it was of no avail.

'I'm going to make *Victoria the Great*,' I told C.M. 'and Anna is going to play the Queen. If you don't go along with me, I will buy you and Maurice out and find another distributor.'

A moment of quiet, and then...

'I'm sorry, Herbert,' said C.M., 'but if that's the way you feel—maybe that is the only answer.'

And so it was. I bought them both out. A sad story, which meant not only that I severed my connection with an organisation I had done much to establish, but also that I broke with someone for whom I had so much respect and affection. And all because of the production by which Anna and I will always be remembered in the annals of film history.

Wyndham Portal was so affected by the break that he seriously considered following Montagu Norman's advice and pulling out of the industry. But he did see C. M. Woolf's point of view—in refusing to finance a film in which he had no confidence, and which might result in a heavy loss.

Alone now, with no backing, I found a new distributor, R.K.O., and raised—including much of my own—£100,000 out of the £150,000 the film was budgeted to cost. Korda, who had me to thank for his being able to produce *The Private Life of Henry VIII*—which I deal with later—gave me a studio credit for £50,000 at Denham studios. I should explain that a studio credit enables a producer to have studio space, build sets and use facilities up to the figure limit, and not pay until the film is released. This system has ensured the completion of many films, and but for it their production would never have commenced.

This applied to *Victoria the Great*. But unforeseen circumstances caused me to over-spend. As all my money was sunk in the production I sought out Anna's father, who was taking care of her finances and tax problems.

A very fine man was Captain Robertson, and a Scot. He was sympathetic and suggested he ask Anna to use her savings in order to complete the film. She not only agreed but—unknown to her father—pawned her jewellery which, with her savings of £3,000, enabled me to complete my gamble.

I made the film in the incredibly short period of five weeks, sometimes working twenty hours a day. In one day Anna played the old Queen Victoria, the young Queen at her wedding, and the middle-aged

Queen with Gladstone. The old Queen's make-up was created by the greatest of all make-up artists, Guy Pearce. It took four hours to put on.

The last day of shooting was high drama. It was an open-air scene of the old Queen at St Paul's Cathedral on the occasion of her Diamond Jubilee. We needed thousands of extras but the money was just not in the bank. So the studio experts made hundreds of perspective toy figures and I managed with two hundred live extras. Even with so small a number I needed a sunny day. Without the sun I could not afford another day's shooting.

Anna was as worried as I was, and also had to endure the ordeal of the old Queen's make-up. When she did arrive on the set, an unprecedented thing happened. The extras and technicians broke out into spontaneous applause and cheers in appreciation of her wonderful make-up. I had a lump that seemed as big as a football in my throat, as no greater compliment could be paid any artist.

And then I looked up. The grey skies were breaking up and blue patches were visible. Suddenly the sky was all blue and the sun shone. And it went on shining for six hours. *Victoria the Great* was, to use a film expression, in the can.

And what a film. There were no jibes or doubts about the chorus girl meeting the challenge—only wonderment.

Any reference to Guy Pearce and his unique artistry in the world of make-up must include his wife, Pat Pearce, who on period wigs was the supreme artist. Whilst making *Victoria* I decided at short notice to introduce Disraeli into the House of Commons scene attacking the repeal of the Corn Laws. I chose Derek de Marney, then in his twenties, to portray Disraeli in his fifties! Guy Pearce dealt with the problem by creating a false nose and wrinkled make-up; but Pat had no wig ready, except one made for another actor twice de Marney's age and twice his head measurement.

In desperation Pat Pearce did the only thing possible to get him to the set on time. She slit the wig at the back and drew it tightly together and stitched it. The improvisation survived Disraeli's vehement speech but, as he sat down, no doubt due to the force of his oration, the wig slowly gaped wide open and the entire House shook with laughter and ruined the take!

Charles Laughton had implicit confidence in Pat Pearce, not only as a wig expert but as a judge of character acting, and he often sought her advice. Whilst making the ill-fated and unfinished *I, Claudius* for Korda, Laughton found himself completely out of harmony with the director Josef von Sternberg and as a result was very difficult and unco-operative.

Came the big speech scene. Laughton was having his wig attended when suddenly he turned to Pat Pearce.

'Pat—I can't do it—and I'm not going to do it!'

'Buster,' said Pat (Laughton was always 'Buster' to her) 'You can do it—and you're going to do it!'

'I can't—and I'm not' shouted Laughton, and retired to his caravan dressing-room and locked himself in.

All attempts to get him to open the door and come out failed. Pat was sent for. He shouted to her through the door and asked for a certain gramophone record. They secured one and it was passed through the window of the caravan.

After a few minutes Laughton came out, went straight on to the set which was already lit for the scene and at the first attempt delivered the *I, Claudius* speech word-perfect and in magnificent style.

'The record which did the trick for Buster,' Pat told me, 'was the abdication speech of Edward VIII!'

'The shock method', Laughton called it; and I know exactly what he meant. On 10th December 1936 I was in Waring and Gillow's, selecting materials for the decor of *Victoria the Great*, when suddenly the noise gave way to an ominous quiet as the B.B.C. announcement came over as clear as a bell: 'I, Edward VIII, King of Great Britain and the Dominions beyond the seas, Emperor of India...' I sat down sharply and listened up to the word 'abdicate'. I heard no more. I only knew that the King who, during a short reign in which he was never crowned, had made it possible for me to produce the film of his great-grandmother, was no longer a King and had gone into exile.

Nevertheless since I had official sanction I went ahead and on 13th April, 1937 I commenced shooting *Victoria the Great*.

No royal locations were made available nor details of the royal household off duty. I decided I would treat Victoria and Albert as an ordinary married couple in rather good circumstances.

That I did not make howling mistakes is a miracle. No members of the royal family saw the film publicly, but whilst Anna was on holiday in Madeira she was asked to join a family party for after-dinner coffee. It was Lord and Lady Elphinstone—sister of Queen Elizabeth, the Queen Mother. I was not there, but they told Anna the film had been privately shown at Balmoral and much enjoyed.

Anna asked if any serious mistakes of etiquette or behaviour had been made in presenting the private scenes of royalty.

'Only one,' said Lady Elphinstone, 'and that was when the servants or gentlemen-in-waiting bowed as Queen Victoria or Prince Albert passed them in the palace, whereas they would take absolutely no notice!'

I was surprised and relieved to hear that was the only 'black' I put up.

The world *première* of *Victoria the Great* was at Ottawa where Anna and I were guests at a banquet given by the Governor General, Lord Tweedsmuir. And we had an escort of the Royal Canadian Mounted Police (Mounties) from Government House to the cinema.

At the Venice Festival, our film was awarded the Gold Cup of All Nations. In Paris, at the Exhibition, it represented the British film industry. In New York, at the mammoth Radio City Music Hall, it played to packed houses, and I was made an honorary member of the American Institute of Cinematography sponsored by the University of Southern California.

Even in Harlem it was a riot—or at least, nearly caused one. They took off a Cagney gangster film to permit a preview of *Victoria the Great*. The customers who had paid to see Cagney were not amused. We got the bird—boos and catcalls.

Anna sat it out, but I couldn't. I walked round the block time after time, and glanced in so see how much longer it would be before the ordeal was over. The first time it was pandemonium; the second time, less noise; the third time, silence. At the end, they stood up and cheered. We had conquered Harlem.

I asked the manager if he did not think we had made a mistake in not telling the audience something of Queen Victoria before the film began.

'Hell no,' he said. 'Most of them don't even know where England is—and they paid to see Cagney!'

The showings away from England which I have described were part of a deliberate policy on my part. With world acclaim, not only for the film but for Anna, I felt that the British press and trade would be that much more receptive.

I was right. When we opened at the Leicester Square Theatre, the critical praise both for me as director, and Anna as star, was overwhelming. Not only from the national press, but from foreign correspondents representing every corner of the globe. Lavish and bountiful they were in full measure, but of the mass I would select the reviews of Sydney W. Carroll of the *Sunday Times*, Stephen Watts of the *Sunday Express*, Kate Cameron of the *New York Daily News*—who gave the film the coveted four stars, the top rating, universally accepted as the accolade of film acclaim—and Morgan Powell (of the *Montreal Star*) who, as a young reporter had covered the Diamond Jubilee of Queen Victoria from the steps of St Paul's. These were the ones which gave me the greatest pleasure and satisfaction. Here are some excerpts.

Sydney Carroll wrote: 'September the sixteenth may be counted a red letter day for British films, for on that evening a truly British film, directed by a truly British director and headed by a truly British actresss, achieved a complete and irrefutable triumph.

'Directed brilliantly with rare humour by Herbert Wilcox, whose Irish blood was never better or more conscientiously employed, the film's principal figure is portrayed by a London girl, whose rise from a chorus girl in the back row to a film star of the first magnitude is one of those romances, almost incredible but stirring and stimulating.

'Anna Neagle's performance as Queen Victoria is the most skilful and definite bit of genuine portraiture ever brought off by any actress since the talking screen made its first appearance. The artiste does appear actually to grow old before our very eyes. It is impossible to avoid eulogy tending to the extravagant in commenting on such a characterisation.'

Since Sydney Carroll, in his time regarded as the doyen of the critical field, had during his career passed judgment on Bernhardt, Réjane, Duse and Garbo, his praise of Anna's performance was praise indeed.

Stephen Watts, in the *Sunday Express* (Watts moved on to become London correspondent on the *New York Times*) headed his whole-page review with a banner line: 'VICTORIA IS "GREAT"!'

He wrote of Anna: 'Her performance is a personal triumph; to say it is the greatest piece of dramatic artistry ever presented in a British film is not to over-praise it. I do not see how anyone can fail to be amazed by the mature sincere persuasion she exercises in a role so fraught with opportunities for that one false step which would have ruined the whole picture. It was greatness or nothing; and greatness it was.'

Unnecessary to say I was delighted the *élite* of the critical profession had endorsed the film and my work as director, but even more delighted that they had gone overboard for the chorus girl who had made the grade, and who had so magnificently silenced the hoots of derision that followed my casting announcement. It was difficult enough for Anna to face up to portraying Queen Victoria, but made immeasurably more difficult by the snipers and doubters.

Anna herself nursed no grudge; I was less charitable! 'He's so in love with her', I often heard, 'he can't see or think straight.' My personal feelings for Anna were entirely beside the point and in no way interfered with my judgment as her director, and I could think and see straight enough to know, when casting her, that she was a dedicated student of any character she was called upon to portray, and also a very fine actress who only needed the challenge to become a great one.

Victoria was the challenge which Anna accepted and not until fifteen years later in *Odette* did she surpass it.

A good story of the London *première* was when Lord Beaverbrook, in his car heading for Fleet Street, was held up. Leicester Square was filled with crowds on all sides so the police diverted the traffic. Told by his chauffeur it was a Hollywood film *première*, and the star was attending, Beaverbrook was furious. Arriving at his office, he sent for the editor (Chris) of the *Express*.

'All traffic held up in Leicester Square for some damned Hollywood star; do something about it!' Angrily he added, 'and give it the full treatment!'

'That is no Hollywood star,' replied Chris, 'but a young London girl, born at Forest Gate; a chorus girl and a Cochran Young Lady who's playing Queen Victoria in tonight's film.'

'A chorus girl playing Queen Victoria,' replied Beaverbrook. Chris nodded. A moment's pause.

'Send Holt to see her,' with a grin, 'and give it full treatment!'

They did! The whole of the leader page. I have reproduced the headline and picture.

The fan magazine whose leading article of attack I mentioned came out with a handsome open letter addressed to Anna, hailing her performance—and I was given their Award for the Best British Film of the Year.

The first person to whom I showed the film privately was our friend, Lord Portal. My rift with the distributor had not damned our personal relationship and, when the viewing ended, Portal was unashamedly sobbing. He embraced Anna and shook me warmly by the hand. As he was not usually demonstrative, I was glad we were alone. The patriotic theme had struck him very hard indeed, which was understandable, for he was a great Englishman.

He made me promise that it must play at the Leicester Square Theatre, which I had bought for the group from Jack Buchanan.

It played there for months before being transferred elsewhere for another three months.

It was ironic and sad to know that C. M. Woolf's signature was on the weekly film rental cheque for the Leicester Square Theatre. It ran into thousands of pounds for each week of the run and—saddest of all—it was made out to an American distributor.

To digress for a moment, the story of Lord Portal and of our last meeting is worthy of record.

Some generations ago, his ancestors came to England in barrels—refugees from the Huguenot risings. They brought with them the secret of the watermark in bank-notes, and set up a fine paper factory at Laverstoke in Hampshire.

They were industrious and good citizens. By the time Wyndham Portal became head of the family, the factory had flourished; a magnificent house, Laverstoke, with its private chapel, had been built; and hundreds were employed in the unique paper process.

Wyndham Portal joined the Life Guards and served with distinction as a captain in the Great War. In the Second War, he did outstanding work under Lord Beaverbrook at the Ministry of Supply. He was chairman of the Olympic Games in both Berlin and London, and was one of the finest business brains in the City of London.

Imagine then, with that past record, my meeting him at Claridges during World War II.

'Where are you living, Herbert? I want to see you.'

'Here, at Claridges,' I told him.

'How can you afford it?' he asked. An unusual question from someone I knew to be a millionaire. Apparently he found it a little difficult himself—hence his question. We met, and he told me his problem.

'Herbert, I can't afford to die.'

I'd heard of many who could not afford to live—but to die? Astounding. Here was a man of exceptional character and ability, with an outstanding record of services as a citizen. And he could not afford to die! A bewildering thought.

'I've been having meetings with the governor of the Bank of England to seek permission to sell some of my holdings so as to take care of death duties.' he explained.

'Surely no problem?' I ventured.

'Full of difficulties,' he answered.

I had no doubt, however, that he would deal with them effectively as he did with all things. He confided to me he was worth between two and a half and two and three-quarter million pounds. Surely enough for all and to spare.

It wasn't. In less than three months Wyndham Portal was dead, and his millions melted almost to vanishing point. His widow had to move out of her lovely Laverstoke and go to live in a flat in London, with just about enough income to keep her in comfort, but not remotely in the comfort warranted by the industry and service of Wyndham Portal and five generations of his forebears.

After *Victoria the Great* it seemed that anything I did could be nothing but an anti-climax. But I found a way to overcome this. The Victoria story had been only lightly touched on. I would make a sequel in colour and call it *Sixty Glorious Years*.

Again the sniping started. Would I ever do anything that did not raise storms of protest? 'Leave well alone!' ... 'You can't better it!' ... 'Can only be inferior!' ... and so on—*ad nauseam*.

Well, I went ahead, and at a time critical to our national history. Hitler was making threatening noises and in London appeasement was in the air.

I sought out Sir Robert Vansittart of the Foreign Office, who for years had advocated a strong line of policy towards Germany. He was also a writer of distinction. Would he write my script? When I told him the title, *Sixty Glorious Years*, he leapt at the idea.

'Just the thing we want at the moment,' he said.

Knowing he was close to the King, I asked if for this film—unlike *Victoria the Great* where I had no help—I could be granted certain facilities.

Vansittart went to Windsor Castle, talked with the King and came back with the message: 'Ask Wilcox to write and tell me what he needs. I'll do everything possible to help.'

I wrote to the King in longhand and set out what I needed. The King replied in longhand and granted every request except the wearing of the Balmoral tartan, which was private and only for the use of the royal family.

In his letter, the King said: 'If you propose showing Queen Victoria leaving Buckingham Palace for St Paul's on the occasion of her Diamond Jubilee, would you mind using the Windsor Greys. Any other horses would tend to destroy the integrity of the scene.'

Would I mind? It was the one favour I was too timid to ask!

We used the Windsor Greys and, during the scene, I noticed two young ladies darting from one window of Buckingham Palace to another. They were Princess Elizabeth and Princess Margaret!

I read the King's letter to audiences throughout the United States when making personal appearances with the film. It always brought the house down.

Again I had baffled the critics and the trade. They had not realised the vast canvas of Queen Victoria's life. There were several films to be made—all different in theme and period.

All agreed I had gone one better with *Sixty Glorious Years*. Particularly Sir Robert Vansittart—'the angry lion of Munich', as they called him. He was having a most unhappy time and could not make his colleagues at the Foreign Office heed his warnings.

'Wilcox,' he said, 'you've made a film that is a warm tribute to the British empire, and at a time when the first step has been shamefully taken to bring about its disintegration.'

Anna and I tried to comfort him. But he would have none of it. His sweet and lovely wife was equally despondent.

'Mark my words, Wilcox,' he went on. 'Within twenty-five years the British empire will be but a shadow of its might and influence, and our homes like this (Denham) will be peep-shows for hordes of visitors.'

What uncanny foresight! Shades of Woburn Abbey, Beaulieu and Longleat!

Mention of foresight takes my mind back to a meeting with H. G. Wells, who was Korda's guest at the London *première* of *Peg of Old Drury*. He sat next to Anna and it was evident even to her, terribly nervous as she invariably is on such occasions, that Wells was very impressed with our film.

Afterwards, over a drink, he remarked how interesting it was to see famous characters of the past such as Nell Gwyn and Peg Woffington come to life, and paid Anna a handsome compliment on her achievement.

I explained that Anna was a glutton for research, and there were many writings about and paintings of the characters which made the task much easier. After all, I told Wells, it was not so difficult to look back and observe, as against looking forward and predicting—as he had done in *The Shape of Things to Come*, which Korda contemplated filming with Wells supervising the screen play.

I ventured to say to Wells that I hoped the film scenes showing the effect of war in the air would not be quite as fearsome as in the book, since the cinema public might find them too hard to swallow.

In his curiously high-pitched voice, Wells replied: 'When the scientists split the atom, which is not so far off, you will realise how restrained I have been in my book.'

With a strange look in his eyes, which transported him far away from Leicester Square, he went on:

'The earth will be scorched and all life, human and animal, will be snuffed out in seconds—not minutes.'

In less than a decade, Stalin used the very phrase—'scorched earth'—in his directive to his army commanders retreating before the Germans. And only thirteen years after Wells' prediction the end-product of splitting the atom descended on Hiroshima!

If I had difficulty in finding a follow-up to *Victoria the Great*, and had to fall back on another story with the same principal characters, how much more difficult after *Sixty Glorious Years*. I must seek a complete contrast.

Marie Lloyd! Could there be a greater contrast?

Victoria, Queen of England, a paragon of all the virtues, and beloved by her people.

Marie Lloyd, Queen of the Music-Halls, by no means a paragon of all the virtues but, like Nell Gwyn, witty, full of vitality and vulgar. In addition, she was a very great artist and, like Victoria, beloved by her people.

I saw Queen Victoria only once. But, during my spell at Camberwell, I saw quite a bit of Marie Lloyd and her husband, Alec Hurley. When you met Marie, you did not forget her. So I was able to paint a realistic picture of her to Anna.

Who would play Alec Hurley? That was the big question. Cary Grant for some time had told me how much he would like to play in a film with Anna. So off I went to Hollywood with a story outline.

'Why have you thought of me for the part?' he asked.

'Because of your performance in *None But The Lonely Heart* when you played an out-and-out Cockney; because you love Cockney backslang which I'm introducing in a big way; and, last but not least, because of your box office appeal,' I told him.

'I'd love to do it,' said Cary, 'but I can't.'

'Oh, could I know the reason?'

'I'm in love and it's a matter of money,' he told me.

'Name your own fee—that'll help,' I said.

'Not that sort of trouble—we've got too much. It's Barbara Hutton! With her money and mine, the tax collector would have a Roman holiday. So we're trying to sort things out. But for the time being, mine is a one-track mind—Barbara!'

I could see his viewpoint. So I saw our distributors and did some quick thinking. It needed a big star opposite Anna to capture the American market, and none that was suitable was available.

At last I found the answer and cabled Anna: 'Marie Lloyd off. Cary in Love. RKO agree I switch to Nurse Edith Cavell. Catch next boat and bring all reference books and details of clothes.'

II

Dear Anna! To switch her mind from Marie Lloyd to Nurse Cavell! Some actresses would question my sanity, but not Anna. She was on the next boat, reference books and clothes complete. I met her in New York.

From the turbulence of Marie Lloyd to the serene calm of Nurse Cavell.

Calm? How wrong can you be? Although the production was completed in record time and represented the first British-Hollywood co-production—commemorated by the planting of an English oak tree in the grounds of the RKO studios—the film was to prove another Wilcox controversy.

The trouble started from its very first showing at Radio City Music Hall, within three months of the arrival of my British production team in Hollywood. The Second World War had just started and I was accused of intelligent anticipation in making this piece of 'blatant propaganda'. Nothing was farther from my mind.

The *Chicago Tribune*, owned by Colonel McCormick who openly professed his dislike—if not hatred—of the British, devoted big space on its front page to a cartoon and an article telling us to get out of Chicago, if not the United States, and go home.

At the Washington showing, the atmosphere was electric. I fully expected a request to withdraw the film from U.S. distribution. Our ambassador Lord Lothian, however, thought the film a fine one and devoid of propaganda. He advised us to secure the widest exposure possible for it.

Magnificent praise came from some of the critics. Anna was nominated for a Hollywood Oscar as best actress of the year. There was a broadside of criticism alleging breach of the Neutrality Code; but *Nurse Cavell* weathered the storm and was accepted as a film of first-class entertainment.

In Hollywood, a meeting was held to determine the course of action of British artists now that the war was in full swing. Larry Olivier, Cary Grant and I were delegated to fly to Washington, see our ambassador, and ask for a directive.

It was a nightmare flight through continuous thunder and lightning storms. Larry slept. Cary sang. He looked out and shouted to me: 'You can see the rivets!' And in the flashes of lightning you *could*, if you cared to look out—which I did not.

'Don't be so damned cheerful,' I said to Cary.

'Why not?' he answered. 'I'm in love.'

And how—with Barbara Hutton. But Cary was always in love—with life and with someone.

Over lunch Lord Lothian asked Larry and Cary their ages. Cary's reply was a gem. 'For years I've been stepping it down. Now I'd better step it up.'

'The truth will do,' said Lord Lothian, and then: 'Go back and get on with your job. It's important to keep the English idiom and way of life before American audiences. Don't violate the Neutrality Act, but do everything you can to help. And tell those of military age to get back to England and take their part.'

Cary and I were impressed—but not Larry. At our Washington hotel he telephoned his wife, Vivien Leigh. 'We've been advised to stay in Hollywood and get on with the job. Get packed, darling, we're going back to England.'

They did—and Larry joined the Fleet Air Arm, in which he served with spells of leave which enabled him to make his outstanding films.

Cary followed Lord Lothian's advice and also resolved his problems about marrying Barbara Hutton.

I followed Lord Lothian's advice and got on with film production. Remembering his warning about the Neutrality Act, I moved into a field far removed from *Nurse Cavell*. I bought the film rights from Warner Bros. of the musical comedies *Irene*, *Sunny* and *No! No! Nanette*.

In *Irene*, I introduced the technique of switching from black and white to colour to illustrate 'Alice Blue Gown'. It was this film that put Ray Milland in the top box office class. Anna's beauty, with reddish hair for the Irish 'Irene', was such that audiences broke out into applause when she stepped from black and white to colour.

'It took a limey to come to Hollywood to show us how to make a musical,' said the *Hollywood Reporter*.

Irene was the top box office picture for RKO and Anna was on top of the Hollywood world. But she was not happy. Neither was I. The war was on and our families were in it. And here we were making musical films 7,000 miles away. We were following Lord Lothian's advice, but we were miserable. Then I hit on an idea which, if it didn't take us back to England, would at least do something to help the cause by combining inherent propaganda with profits for the British Red Cross.

Since every artist of British nationality or origin working in Hollywood in the early days of the war was anxious to do something useful my idea was the making of a film wherein they all appeared—but without a fee—written by top script-writers, again without fees, and directed by top directors without fees.

The title of the film was *Forever and a Day*, symbolising England and the British empire.

I then sought out Dr Giannini of the Bank of America to finance the basic cost and charge no interest. The doctor, who had a great sense of humour and was alarmingly forthright, said: 'Herbert, first of all I'm an American, and America has no war problems on its hands. Secondly, I'm an Italian and they're fighting the British. Do you expect me to finance your goddam film without interest?'

I told him I did. And he did!

Then George Schaefer, president of RKO, agreed that all studio charges would stand over until the film was released.

I got in touch with my old friend, Cedric Hardwicke, and asked him to join me in the project. One of the most popular Englishmen who formed part of the Hollywood British colony, I knew Cedric's association would facilitate matters enormously.

It did! Subject of course to availability, there was not one refusal from stars and directors—and Oscar Hammerstein agreed to write the theme number 'Forever and a Day' without a fee.

Then dear C. Aubrey Smith, the elder statesman of the colony, Frank Lloyd and Victor Saville, with Cedric Hardwicke and myself, formed a working committee. For very little actual cost, we had a great story and the most impressive array of stars ever assembled in one film. The film turned out to be very good entertainment with no undue emphasis on British propaganda. The net profit, we were told by the distributors, would be two million dollars. It would be a handsome donation for the British Red Cross.

A close American friend, George Washington Baker, suggested that for diplomatic reasons the American profits be applied to an American charity. George was head of President Roosevelt's pet cause, 'The March of Dimes', to help polio victims, and we agreed this was the ideal charity.

A good friend of the President, George arranged a meeting with him so that I could let him know of the project. Before going to

31. Anna in *Peg of Old Drury* with Cedric Hardwicke and Jack Hawkins, 1935.

32. With Anna and Anton Walbrook at Windsor Castle during the production of *Sixty Glorious Years*, 1938. On the left is the cameraman F. A. Young (*Bridge on the River Kwai, Lawrence of Arabia* and *Dr. Zhivago*).

33. At Balmoral, rehearsing a scene from *Sixty Glorious Years*. The pony chaise was the one used by Queen Victoria herself.

34. Anna as the old Queen Victoria.

35. With Anna and Mr Mackenzie King, Prime Minister of Canada, at the Ottawa *première* of *Victoria the Great*.

36. (*left*)　　The critics' reaction to *Victoria the Great*.
37. (*right*)　The *Daily Express* leader on *Victoria the Great*.
38. (*below*)　The American Institute of Cinematography's award.

39. Rehearsing Anna in the first scene of *Nurse Edith Cavell*, 1939. This picture established a new record for long-distance publicity; it was flown from Hollywood to San Francisco and wirephoto'd to the *Daily Mail* for publication next day.

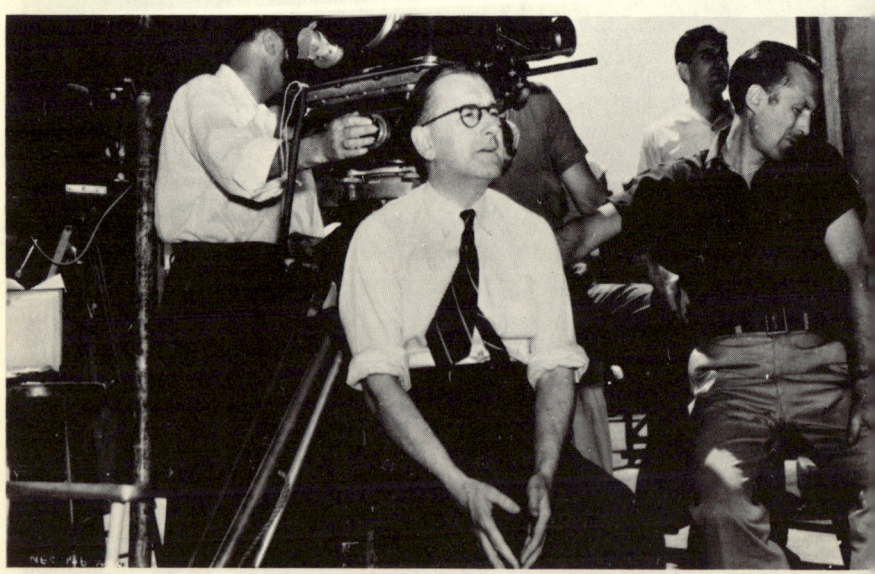

40. Directing a scene from *Nurse Edith Cavell*.

Washington I asked George to put me in the picture about President Roosevelt. Was he pro-British? Remember, America was not involved.

George answered me on this point and told me a story of Roosevelt to illustrate his statement. This was about the time that Winston Churchill made his famous appeal to America: 'Give us the tools and we will finish the job.'

George Washington Baker had an appointment to see the President on another matter. When he was ushered into Roosevelt's room he saw that something was amiss. Without greeting George, or even looking up at him, the President told him of the pessimistic reports from Joseph Kennedy in London, at the time American ambassador at St James's. Kennedy sent reports claiming the British were finished and nothing could save England, and that to send arms or money from the U.S. was throwing it away.

'I thought Kennedy protested too much, George,' the President went on, 'so I sent Bill Donovan (a great American) over to check up.

'Bill told me Kennedy was right—the British were finished—they were up to their knees in serious trouble. "But," said Bill, "they know it but won't admit it—and they never will. They can't be beaten. Send over every dollar and all military aid you can."

'I said nothing,' Roosevelt went on, 'but acted on Bill's advice and almost got those destroyers to England when—dammit—Congress has just heard about it, and the delay of getting it through may be fatal.'

He was referring to the forty-nine American obsolete destroyers which proved a godsend to the British Navy.

When we met the President, he was charming and appreciative to a degree, and his 'March of Dimes' benefited handsomely from the generosity of all these Britishers who had so readily given their time and services.

At the world *première* at the Leicester Square Theatre, Anna read from the stage a telegram from King George VI, who was prevented from attending by much more important matters in North Africa.

'To Anna Neagle: Regret I cannot be present to express my thanks to all those who contributed so generously to the production of *Forever and a Day*. May it enjoy much success. George R.I.'

Following Lord Lothian's directive, whilst I was preparing and setting up *Forever and a Day*, Anna toured forty-seven of the forty-eight States, making personal appearances and appeals for the British Red Cross and other charities.

But although the results were excellent, she was not satisfied. She was restless and unhappy.

One Sunday we were sitting on the Santa Monica Boulevard, watching the hideous and noisy trams taking their human loads down to the beach, and by contrast the humming-birds hovering like fuchsia blossoms against the blue jacaranda trees, when from nowhere Anna said:

'How soon can we go home?'

She had voiced my own thoughts.

Our decision was made. We arranged that I would direct the opening episode of *Forever and a Day* with Anna, Ray Milland, Aubrey Smith and Claude Rains, after which I would hand over to Frank Lloyd. And then to England. I would, of course, have to get the necessary consent of RKO since we both had a long-term contract with them.

Our work on *Forever and a Day* was completed, and we sought out George Schaefer, president of RKO, and found him literally in tears.

'I've just heard from England,' he told us. 'Ralph Hanbury, his son, daughter and grandson were killed in an air raid last night.' (Ralph Hanbury was managing director of RKO, England, and a great friend of Anna's and mine.)

This didn't make my job with Schaefer any easier, but I pressed on and told him of our decision.

'You can't take Anna back,' he said. 'It would be madness.'

But Anna was more determined than ever.

'We're not being heroic,' she said. 'Herbert and I have gone into it so often. We can't stay here any longer. We'd always regret it.'

Schaefer saw our viewpoint and agreed to release us from our contract.

He was at La Guardia airport to bid us God-speed. He had a florist's box enveloped in cellophane, which he presented to Anna.

'Anna,' said George, 'It's orchids we usually give you, but from what I hear these will be more appreciated in England just now.'

Anna opened the box. In it were twelve lemons! How right George Schaefer was—lemons had disappeared from the English scene and when we gave two or three to close friends, their thanks were embarrassing.

Something else happened in the World War II years that emphasised basic values.

The head of the Bank of America, Mr A. P. Giannini, was on his first visit to London. The war was just over but rationing was at its tightest. He particularly wanted to stay at Claridges, which was full and there was no likelihood of accommodation for some months. Mr Van Thyne, the manager, was helpless and disappointed to have to turn away so important a man as Giannini.

Anna and I resolved the problem by moving out.

Claridges was notorious for strict conformity to the rationing and regulations and, when we were invited to have lunch with Giannini in his suite, the simplicity of the meal seemed to surprise him but he did not complain. With half-closed eyes, he entertained us with a survey of the American economic scene and suddenly lapsed into a rather strong anti-British soliloquy.

'You British—you're smart—you ask for more dollars than we've got—and you'll get them—and you'll never pay us back!'

Anna's comment caused 'A.P.' to open his eyes wide as she asked: 'Are we as clever as all that?'

And his humour came out as he smiled at Anna. 'You see what I mean—smart, that's what you are!'

Anna asked him if he was being well looked after—and he turned to her and told her how he missed his customary new-laid egg for breakfast! The multi-millionaire banker spoke quite feelingly about a new-laid egg.

We were allowed six hens at out little country cottage, and we got back to find a miracle—four eggs! Wrapping them carefully, Anna delivered them personally to Claridges, with a note to A. P. Giannini stating that they had just been laid.

The result was a four-page letter of thanks in longhand from someone who could afford to buy the entire output of eggs in the United Kingdom and not miss the money.

Now to bacon, the most missed of all foods.

On our way to Canada to raise funds for Air Marshal Bishop's air cadets (of which more later), a wireless message was received on the *Batory*, the Polish ship in which we were travelling, asking if Anna would do a coast-to-coast broadcast for the Canadian Red Cross. It was to last for fifteen minutes at the outside.

Since Anna had seen at first hand the end-product of the help given by the Canadian Red Cross to blitz victims, her talk was moving and fascinating. It went on and on without interruption for one hour and ten minutes! Gladstone Murray, head of the Canadian Broadcasting Corporation, was so impressed that he telephoned orders to let it overrun without restriction.

In the talk, Anna mentioned rationing conditions and that bacon was 4 ozs. per person per week. Although Anna only made a humble contribution, the result of the Red Cross appeal was eleven million dollars—or one dollar per head of the country's population, man, woman and child. Remarkable and without parallel.

So was the offer she had from a Canadian bacon curer—when she returned to England, would she take back a gift of a whole side of bacon? We decided that our arrival in London with such a gift would not be the best of publicity, so with thanks the offer was refused. We mentioned it to the President of the Board of Trade, Mr Harold Wilson, when we got home.

'Do you know,' said Wilson, 'you refused the ration allowance for the two of you for two years and three months, or for Anna alone, for four and a half years!'

Before returning to my story, I should like to tell one incident of the blitz which is a classic example of the true Cockney spirit—a spirit Hitler had not reckoned with. Anna's old theatre dresser, Louie, a Cockney and worth her weight in gold, lived with her daughter Maudie on the top floor of a block of flats in the Elephant and Castle district. One night all hell was let loose in one of the worst raids ever, so Maudie went in to her mother.

'Get your dressing gown and slippers on, Mum. We're going down to the basement.'

Down five flights they went for safety. Arrived there, Louie rushed out and started up the stairway again.

'Where are you going, Mum?' shouted Maudie.

'Forgot me false teeth,' replied Louie.

'Come back here,' bawled Maudie. 'What do you think they're dropping? Ham sandwiches?'

I had wondered, before leaving Hollywood, whether British films were still being produced. Not only was production active, but great films were in the making. With its nostalgic memories of *Victoria the Great*, I decided on Denham studios.

Nothing in my career has been more inspiring than producing films throughout the war and blitz. Despite timber and other shortages, the black-out which ruled out exteriors at night, and the shortage of technicians and labour brought about by the call-up, some of the really excellent British films were produced at that time—Coward's *In Which We Serve*, Powell and Pressburger's *49th Parallel*, Pascal's

Major Barbara, The First of the Few, The Life and Death of Colonel Blimp and many others.

It was into this atmosphere that Anna and I arrived back in England in 1940 to make the Amy Johnson film, *They Flew Alone*. We were very proud of that film and both Anna and Robert Newton, who played Jim Mollison, gave outstanding performances.

Newton had recently appeared in *Major Barbara* and was a really great actor. But he was also an incurable alcoholic, and his meetings with the real-life Jim Mollison cannot be recorded here. Both were extraordinary and extrovert characters and had no respect for law and order, women or the conventions. After any night they had together, I was lucky to get Newton on the studio floor at all.

I had to secure his temporary release from the Royal Navy, in which he was serving as a matelot on a minesweeper.

One day, with a crowd of two hundred extras, I waited two hours for Newton anxiously and had almost given up hope when, with great relief, I saw the hired car that always picked him up from the Savoy. I looked in as it passed, but to my dismay—no Newton. The car stopped. The driver opened the door and out fell Newton.

'Get him to his dressing room,' I told the assistant director. 'Strip him and douse him with cold water. Then give him some black coffee and dress him.'

'Me and how many?' asked my assistant.

However, we got him on the floor where Anna as Amy and the crowd of extras had been waiting.

Anna was patient. The extras were not. The war was on, rations were tight, and to see a highly-paid star hold up the production and waste time and money did not amuse them.

Bob came on, his face bloated and the colour of a beetroot. His eyes were glazed and he made straight for me, starting to weep as only a drunken man can.

'You're so wonderful, Herbert. The greatest director in the world. I'll never let you down. I'm here—to act!' he declaimed in old-fashioned Lyceum style, with extravagant gestures. I could see the angry mood of the crowd.

'Then act, Bob,' I answered. 'That's what we've all been waiting for, and what you're paid for.'

'Herbert, darling,' he went on, 'I don't want the money. I love you and will act for *you* for nothing.'

Anna on the sidelines must have been at the end of her patience. She also sensed the crowd was becoming more hostile. I took a chance.

'I've never kicked an actor before, Bob, but if you don't shut up and get on with the scene, I'm going to kick you in the backside' (backside was not the word I used!).

'You wouldn't do that to me, dear Herbert,' he whined.

I did. The effect was electric—on Bob, the crowd, and Anna. With an attitude of outraged dignity, Bob did the scene first time and to perfection.

What a waste of outstanding talent—and of life!

Throughout the entire picture, Anna never played one of her close-up scenes with Newton. I had decided to leave them for the sober period. As that never came, she played them all to me with the back of my head in the foreground of the camera.

Bob returned to his minesweeper. The film was shown at the Odeon, Leicester Square, and Bob got the most ecstatic notices! There's no justice! Fortunately Anna scored too, but it was one of the most frustrating periods I had ever been up against.

'Bob is a genius,' said Newton's agent. 'You must make allowances.'

Constance Collier used the same words to excuse Charlie Chaplin's bad manners at the Hollywood *première* of *Victoria the Great*, which I deal with later.

Why being a 'genius' is offered as an excuse for odd behaviour, I have never understood. Neither do I understand why the tag of 'genius' is so loosely applied, when in most cases it should be 'eccentric'.

In looking back over my years in the entertainment world, how many can I with conviction dub a genius? Perhaps half a dozen, and these come readily to mind.

During my short partnership with the H.M.V. gramophone company, I first saw and heard an undoubted genius. At the old Queen's Hall it was, where a boy of twelve had just, unaccompanied, finished playing on his violin the concerto by Elgar. 'Between the two there was enthusiastic admiration of each for the other,' says Elgar's biographer.

This concerto was being recorded under the critical ear of Freddie Guisberg, the guiding hand behind the H.M.V. celebrity stars. Apart from Guisberg and myself, the audience consisted of Yehudi Menuhin's mother and father.

Only by an effort did I restrain myself from applauding—which was just as well. Yehudi's father, with a glance at Guisberg who nodded his head, held up three fingers.

'Three false notes, Yehudi—you must play it again.'

'But I'm tired,' pleaded Yehudi.

'Once more, then you can have some tea and see a film,' said father.

Yehudi's face lit up at the mention of a film, and immediately into action he went again, attacking thousands of notes—of which three had apparently been false in his previous effort. This time there was a kiss from his father and mother, and a beaming smile from Guisberg.

I had an interesting talk with his father after Yehudi had literally dashed out of the hall to his tea and a western. Did he not consider himself a hard taskmaster? I asked.

His reply was simple and sincere. 'Since God has given Yehudi so much, He would expect those nearest to him to see His gift was protected and perfected. My wife and I have accepted that stewardship.'

My next member of the 'club' would be D. W. Griffith, who was a creator rather than a director and to whom the cinema owes a debt that can never be assessed.

Remember Griffith came in at the time of the nickelodeon, and his genius enabled him to see—instead of a few nudes and slapstick comics for a nickel—great themes and a style and technique that has endured and is still in vogue.

Orson Welles! Of course.

Orson's greeting when he sees me is invariably a huge beaming face, like a setting sun, his arms envelop me and a kiss on both my cheeks!

There is a reason. As a matter of fact—two reasons. At the time of producing his first film ever, *Citizen Kane*, Orson had only two supporters at the studio—Anna and me. We saw his 'rushes' with our own every morning at 6.45 a.m., and lavished praise on him when everyone in Hollywood treated him like a leper after word got around that *Citizen Kane* was based on the life of William Randolph Hearst—who, in his newspaper empire, was powerful enough to make or break a star or a movie company overnight.

But Welles ignored the angry silence and pressed on with his task with the mind and eye of a dedicated artist painting his masterpiece.

At the Hollywood *première* at the El Capitan theatre, where the audience was ecstatic, Orson, spotting Anna and me, called out: 'I'll say it first—you told me so,' and burst out laughing as only Orson can laugh, then kissed us both.

Another reason was, when I was directing *Trent's Last Case* with Margaret Lockwood I could not find the right casting for the spectacular role of the heavy! I decided to gamble and started the production with the part not cast. I was sure we could find the right man. By the end of the first week I began to worry, when from nowhere Orson's face came to my mind.

I was lunching in the studio canteen with Margaret. Without explanation I looked at her and asked, 'What about Orson Welles?'

Sharp as a button Margaret was with me and answered: 'What about God?'

But I was already on my way to my office.

'Get hold of Orson Welles,' I told my secretary. 'He's probably in Rome at the Excelsior—or Paris at the Georges Cinq—or he might be in Hollywood. Find him!'

She found him—at Hammersmith! Dubbing *Othello*—but—no one was to know.

Straight from the studios I went. The commissionaire assured me he was not there. 'Tell him Herbert Wilcox is here,' I instructed the man.

I was shown up to the recording stage. The door was locked—the room in darkness. No response to my knock until I called: 'Orson—it's Herbert.'

The door-key turned—the door opened and I saw one of Orson's eyes. He smiled as he opened the door and locked it after me. Without greeting he said: 'Must do this reel—then we'll talk—sit down.'

I saw the reel of *Othello* he was dubbing—it was magnificent and I told him so.

'Why all the mystery, Orson?' I asked.

'I'm already lousy with writs—but they're not satisfied. I'll be all right if I can get this job finished.'

Manna from heaven, I thought, he needs money. What luck! I told him of my mission and explained the part was small, about ten days, but very effective. Orson suddenly turned cagey.

'I might do it—but I'm very busy and very expensive!'

He had apparently forgotten all about the writs conversation.

'What's expensive?' I asked him.

'For ten days—six thousand', he blurted out—not very hopefully.

'No good, Orson, can't pay six thousand,' I countered.

'What's your offer?' he asked as he saw the chance slipping away.
'Twelve thousand!' I replied.
'But I only asked for six,' he cried.
'I heard you—but you're worth twelve—I've got twelve in my budget and that's what you're getting.'

He threw his arms around me and kissed me on both cheeks—he tells everyone about 'Herbert who doubled my salary without asking'—and that's the second reason for the kissing every time we meet.

Poor Orson! As soon as he started work on *Trent's Last Case* the writ servers arrived at the studio—I was personally served with notices of attachment so had to pay it out of his £12,000—Orson finished up with £150.

Having directed Orson in two films, I can vouch for the fact that there was never a dull moment—except for sharing a couple of bottles of champagne with him every morning before breakfast! (I still shudder at the memory.)

Then John Logie Baird, who was the real inventor of television.

Despite financial problems with only his school chum Jack Buchanan to turn to, and not enjoying the best of health, he worked on and made practical his 'pictures out of the ether'—but for which Telstar could still be a good distance off.

Yes—definitely John Logie Baird. Unanimously elected.

The next member got off to a bad start and had a heavy initial handicap to overcome.

'I have found a young writer,' Korda once told me. 'His name is Ustinov. And, Herbert—he's a genius.'

Peter was out with me from that moment. I like to discover my own geniuses.

My conversation started at a stage performance of *Crime and Punishment* in which, as a comparative newcomer, he overshadowed an old stager—my favourite actor, John Gielgud. Peter was from then on eligible for membership of my club.

Even when he was at school at Westminster, Peter Ustinov is said to have picked out characters and reproduced them. He started his writing in those early school-days which was sublimated in his keenly observant political characters in *Romanoff and Juliet*—in my view his best play and performance.

His first film of *Private Angelo* was a gem—at the time way ahead of the critics and beyond the vision of the distributors and cinema owners.

My only experience of directing Peter was in the film of *Odette*. What a joy and inspiration it was! As soon as the camera turned, he would disappear and Arnaud, the resistance radio operator, would come to life with subtle shading of character that completely and always separated the artist from the portrayal. I've had many opportunities of studying the genius of Ustinov, which enables him, with a chuckle, to slip slyly inside the skin and mind of the personality he is describing. And he does not let go until he slips out again and rejoins you as himself, having had as much fun as his audience.

Peter has much to thank me for. I introduced him to an adorable and intelligent young French Canadian actress, Suzanne Cloutier. He married her and they've lived happily ever since.

In 1933 Cedric Hardwicke told me of a young friend of his who was as exciting an actor as he had met. Not only that, but he was a very fast driver of very fast cars.

I was about to produce a film based on the life of Sacha Guitry, called *The King of Paris* with Cedric playing Sacha, and he suggested we give his young fast-driving friend the second lead. My director, Jack Raymond, and I met him—and I must say he was no Jack Buchanan or Ivor Novello to look at, but I had a feeling that he was a mystic. I exerted my influence as producer and persuaded Raymond, saying: 'Cedric would not have suggested him if he did not really believe in him.'

We started the film with a most unenthusiastic director—until the first day's rushes were shown.

'Don't understand it,' said Raymond, 'On the floor, gives nothing—on the screen, he's terrific!'

'That's where the public will see him,' I replied.

And in the most difficult, nondescript part of a Parisian artisan, Ralph Richardson was superb.

Whenever Ralph scored an outstanding hit afterwards, which was often, Cedric's only sly comment was—yes! 'Herbert—I told you so.'

Richardson has the genius of projection and his performance in *The Shape of Things to Come* alone would qualify him for membership of my club, apart from the sensitive *The Fallen Idol*, plus his stage performances in *Flowering Cherry* and *The Heiress* represent the actor at his peak and puts him at the top of his class.

I include Alec Guinness in my short list since, having purchased the film rights of Rattigan's play *Ross*, in which he played Lawrence of Arabia, I saw the play at the Haymarket Theatre eighteen times and never once lost the illusion that I was seeing and hearing Lawrence himself.

To have written plays at the time of his coming-of-age, and to appear on the stage in opposition to these same plays forty-five years later, surely justifies the inclusion of Noel Coward.

Those early plays are not only superb entertainment but, after all these years, stand up as museum pieces which reflect the period of their origin. To challenge and conquer the tricky and elusive cabaret scene when no longer a chicken, and then come back in vintage form as actor and author of his recent plays *A Song at Twilight* and *Double Bill*... Who but a genius could do all that—and also write and direct *Cavalcade* and *In Which We Serve*?

In one day, I have attended matinée and evening performances of Noel's latest play, *Suite in Three Keys*. Writing superb–vintage Coward dialogue, coupled with his brilliant acting. Switching as he does from a hypersensitive terrified victim of blackmail to an adorable hen-pecked American from the Middle West, Noel's characterisations culled the compassionate sympathy of a packed house—which suffered with him in the one, and rooted wildly for him in the other, when it seemed that happiness for the mid-westerner was just round the corner.

Apart from all other considerations, on the strength alone of this day of my Coward bean-feast, Noel becomes a senior member of my club.

Laurence Olivier, of course. And then Charlie Chaplin, who was responsible for this train of thought.

What, not one woman in the club? I must admit, none came readily to mind as full candidates.

Of the artists who have passed through my directorial hands, many women have contributed moments of genius. The look of Sybil Thorndike as Nurse Cavell, with her forgiving smile to her emotional German warder as she was led out to her execution; Pauline Frederick hearing her beloved French son denounced by Herbert Marshall as a German spy; Dorothy Gish as Nell Gwyn locked outside the death bedroom of Charles II; Anna Neagle as Odette, in the scene in her cell at Fresnes prison following her torture, asking the padre who had refused her communion, 'Are they (the Gestapo) so afraid of God?' Undoubtedly all moments of genius.

On reflection I would award full qualification to the young German actress Brigitte Helm, the star of *Metropolis* and other great German films of the late twenties, who refused all Hollywood offers and quietly dropped out of the film scene when still in her twenties.

In turning out photographed stage plays like the Aldwych farces, although immensely profitable, I felt frustrated and dissatisfied when making comparisons with my love of silent films. So, long after talkies had taken full possession of the industry, I decided to make a 'talkie' that did not talk—and without sub-titles. Music, of course, was to be a dominant substitute for words or text.

At that time an extraordinary Hungarian 'Zigeuner' band was performing at the old Kit Cat Club in Haymarket, where the Odeon now stands, and their rendering of The Blue Danube and Liszt's Hungarian Rhapsody had blasé sophisticates (not all sober) standing up at their tables and cheering.

I decided to make a full-length feature film entitled *The Blue Danube*, using only music as an accompaniment and comment. The musical excerpts were of course no problem, but to play scenes, including love scenes, without a word spoken was quite a pill.

As stars I brought from America Joseph Schildkraut, a top stage star of Broadway, and Brigitte Helm from Germany, generally accepted as the finest young actress in Europe. Words with Brigitte were quite unnecessary and to direct her was an unique experience.

The censor had plenty to say about one love scene she played with Schildkraut—so did Schildkraut, who had the reputation of a lady-killer and suggested the scene be repeated at his hotel after supper the same night! Then Brigitte spoke—and her answer was expressive and short! The rafters of the studio rang. They never spoke again either during the production or between scenes.

Brigitte's genius emerged since for the entire production she did not even mouth a word, but conveyed the role of a Hungarian aristocrat in love with a peasant so effectively that one could read the words in her eyes, face and hands.

I'm afraid the reception given *The Blue Danube* did not warrant my self-election to the club. Having been on the receiving end of as much, if not more critical praise and publicity than any of my British film contemporaries, I trust I can take adverse criticism with good grace; but I doubt whether such caustic or bilious reviews have ever been levelled at any film or director. One might have expected a pat or two on the back for assaying to substitute pictorial images against a musical backdrop instead of a spate of talk and photographed stage plays of which I had been a major guilty sponsor.

No pat on the back for *The Blue Danube*—but plenty of kicks in the pants! I had often been hailed by the press as the 'king of film showmen', but now one critic went so far as to say I had abdicated that spot to become the 'king of catgut'. That phrase must have taken some thinking up! The catgut represented the medium to produce what was generally considered the most exciting musical sound from any orchestra of its style.

The reviews resulted in the film's early demise over here, but in Sydney *The Blue Danube* played in one theatre for over a year and to excellent reviews and paying audiences estimated to number approximately one million; so the cost of production was recovered from that one engagement alone.

However, back I went to talkies and photographed stage plays.

12

Meanwhile, how was my plan regarding my children working?

As I said earlier, everything I was denied I promised myself they should have. And I had seen this realised. Since I got so much happiness out of my association with Anna and my work, I wanted my children to be happy.

Apart from stables and a string of horses—including a racehorse bought from Tom Walls (named 'Plunder' after his successful play and our film)—all the children were members of the local hunt. In the grounds of our lovely home, there were hard and grass tennis-courts and a sleeping-out cabin. And I sent two of the girls, Pamela and Patricia, accompanied by a nurse-governess, on a luxury trip round the world, including Australia and Japan.

My plan was a failure—a ghastly failure. The luxuries I provided did not bring happiness to my children, but rather unhappiness and boredom. Their doting mother became a stranger to them and, whilst they were always delighted to see me, we were strangers and had no communion of spirit or heart.

As a parent I had proved myself a flop!

How much more intelligent was the attitude of millionaire Charles Clore when his son reached his majority. He was asked what sort of present he was giving him. Clore replied: 'Something very special when he comes down from Oxford with Honours—not before. Anybody can be twenty-one!'

It is no use falling back on the hackneyed 'broken marriage' excuse, because it was never apparent or revealed to anyone in our home. I realise now that, in providing everything for my children, I really indulged myself.

I confided my thoughts to Anna. She agreed, and told me of something appropriate she had read in Emerson's essays. She recalled that Emerson had stated that to indulge children and provide them with the good things and luxuries of life without effort on their part was merely indulging the whims and vanities of the parents and was wrong, since it deprived the children of the contest and struggle the parents had overcome in acquiring these same luxuries.

'Leave your children to fight for the good things of life,' said Emerson, 'and they will emerge finer citizens and better characters in the process.'

Suddenly from out of a black cloudy sky came an unexpected solution to a situation Anna and I had almost accepted as insoluble. A. P. Herbert, M.P. (now Sir Alan).

How much we have to thank him for! Not only as a wit—'Have you seen a financier bathing? A whale is a little like that!'; or as the author of *Bless the Bride*, *Big Ben* or *The Water Gipsies*; or as our host at Hammersmith on Boat Race day. But as a Member of the House of Commons. It was Sir Alan who introduced and shepherded through a Private Member's Matrimonial Bill, one clause of which made desertion on either side for three years an automatic reason for divorce—and reduced the mud-slinging to a minimum.

At that time I had not lived with my wife for nearly seven years. But I could not contemplate a divorce in which Anna's name undoubtedly would have been bandied about, and I was determined that must not happen.

My wife wished to marry someone else, whose interest in horses and riding-schools was as strong as her own. Her interest in films was nil. My interest in horses even less. There was no problem on finance. The children were launched on their various careers. Realistically, nothing could justify the continuing of a situation where, apart from any emotional consideration, four people would never find companionship and interest.

But now Alan Herbert's bill had been passed and was law.

The registrar at Caxton Hall, Mr J. P. Bond, was most co-operative. No one must know, I stressed, least of all the press. We would announce it in, say, six months. When he heard the circumstances, he told me: 'I understand perfectly. You can rely on me, I am the soul of discretion. I married the Duke of Westminster four times and none of his wives was aware of it.'

Mr Bond suggested, to his own inconvenience, that we marry on a Sunday morning. No one would be about, so Sunday it was—1st August, 1943.

Our wedding morning lingers warmly in my memory. I was still living at Claridges; Anna with her aunt. I was up early. There was no best man, only two witnesses—Anna's aunt (more about 'Auntie' later) and an old girl-friend of Anna's.

I was to meet Anna at the side door of Caxton Hall a few minutes before the ceremony. How the time dragged. I had breakfast at 8.30 a.m.; the ceremony was set for 10.0 a.m. I wandered from Claridges to Berkeley Square. The sunshine was lovely, so I sat down there for a few minutes. It was still only 9.15 by my watch. I decided to walk to Caxton Hall, which took me through the gardens of Farm Street Roman Catholic Church—an oasis of tranquillity.

Passing the church, I heard the intonation of the priest. Mass was being celebrated. As in Gibraltar, I stole in and knelt at the back, and prayed that our marriage would endure.

At the side door of Caxton Hall, I waited for Anna. As usual, she was dead on time. She gave me a smile, and in it I could read her confidence in our future.

That was twenty-four years ago.

The cynics and sophisticates say: 'Oh yes, their gimmick is to keep up the illusion in public, but in private they fight like cat and dog.'

For the benefit of these cynics and sophisticates I (and I'm only speaking for myself) have never for a moment regretted our marriage, and over the years we have never had one row.

'How terribly dull,' I can hear them saying.

However, I mean row in the literal sense. We've had disagreements, and violent ones at that, about our work. And since I am Anna's severest critic, and she is mine, that is understandable and inevitable. But a row in the literal sense of the word. No.

Anna and I are, I hope, too intelligent to waste valuable nervous and mental energy that way. Yes. We have already advised the authorities at Dunmow that we are ready to receive the flitch!

I promised more about 'Auntie'. If I failed to introduce 'Auntie' into my life story, any relative, friend or remote acquaintance who knew Anna and me between 1941 and 1964 would want to know why.

So meet 'Auntie'.

To do full justice to Auntie and her forebears would require another book in itself, so here briefly are the main facts.

Auntie's grandfather, Captain Neagle, came over from Ireland early in the nineteenth century and settled in the London dock area, to which his ship (he was captain of a clipper) invariably returned from its voyages to the East Indies. In those pre-industrial revolution days, that part of east London had an urban charm. It was there that Lister experimented and lived, and also the Gurney family. And the choice for Sunday worship was Old Limehouse Church or Chaucer's church at Bow.

In the Great War, Auntie's brother, Captain Arthur Neagle, conceived the idea of sending ships out in convoys instead of singly.

He was duly thanked by the Lords of the Admiralty, and himself led the first convoy from Genoa.

Auntie was born in the Isle of Dogs. One of her sisters was Anna's mother, who married Captain H. W. Robertson. It was her mother's maiden name of Neagle that Anna adopted professionally—and when her mother died in 1926, Auntie stepped in and devoted her life to Anna. During our married life, she was our constant companion.

A great character who refused to be ignored and was liked by everyone, she could adjust herself to any company and was no respecter of rank, wealth or person. Looking rather like the old Queen Victoria, but perhaps an inch or two more round the waist, she would regale us with stories of Anna's early days down in the East End of London, with a memory and mind as clear as a spring stream.

A stalwart of the Primrose League, she held Sunday School classes and taught the children to outsing 'The Red Flag', which the opposition had just introduced. She was an active worker in getting Sir Ernest Wild, later recorder of London, and Capt. Arthur Margesson returned to Parliament, and was a true blue Tory of the first order.

Up to the time of her death at the age of eighty-seven, she would read three or four newspapers a day and scorned the use of such things as spectacles. Intolerant to a degree, her knowledge of worldly events was always a marvel to me. She travelled with Anna and me all over the world, including a visit to Finland.

It may sound emotional or mawkish, and of course it is, but every year on the anniversary of Auntie's death Anna and I drive down to the family cemetery in the East End of London, where Anna's father and mother are also buried. And every time we go, although early in February, the sun always shines bright and clear.

And, as I mentioned earlier, at Caxton Hall when Anna and I were married, there was Auntie—one of only two who were present.

To have recorded my life and not mentioned Auntie would have been unpardonable, since for many years she was an integral part of my existence.

13

The origin of the 'London Series' could not have been more accidental. I was staying at an hotel at Gerrards Cross, during the production of *The Yellow Canary* at the near-by Denham studios. As always on Sundays, Anna and I went for one of our long walks. Sometimes they would be as long as six or seven miles. On this occasion, we met one of our old friends, Maurice Cowan, editor of *Picturegoer*, the fan magazine.

'I've got a good subject for you,' he told me, and proceeded to outline *I Live in Grosvenor Square*. Before he had talked for two minutes I told him to say no more—it was mine.

Very timely, it not only did outstanding business here, but throughout the world, and Twentieth Century Fox bought it for America. Rex Harrison followed the film there and never looked back. *I Live in Grosvenor Square* had the unique distinction of playing concurrently for a season at the Empire, Leicester Square, and next door at the Warner theatre—and filled both cinemas.

When I decided to make *Piccadilly Incident* as a 'London Series' follow-up to *I Live in Grosvenor Square*, I envisaged Rex Harrison as Anna's co-star. But Rex was in Hollywood.

I wanted John Mills. No luck. Then I tried everyone possible.

Eric Goodhead, the agent, put up Michael Wilding, but neither Anna nor I liked the look of him at all. Goodhead persevered and, since there was absolutely no alternative and the film was due to commence within a few days, in desperation I signed Wilding—but with many misgivings.

In his very first scene with Anna, everything about him—his naturalness, his repose, his figure and, most of all, his smile—shouted out loud that here was a new star.

'Does he hit you as he hits me?' I asked Anna after the first day's work.

'Harder,' replied Anna. 'Sign him up.'

I did, on a long-term contract and within forty-eight hours of starting *Piccadilly Incident*. He made an enormous success in the picture, and I won the British Oscar for the best film of the year. Michael went on to become the number one box office actor in the British and International class. And Anna had seven consecutive years as top British actress and four years as top international woman star.

An extraordinary man was Wilding. Talented in so many ways, he could have made his mark as a painter. He was a really fine judge of pictures, particularly the Impressionists. He got me interested too, and Anna and I finished up with one of the finest private collections of Impressionists in the country.

Michael's charm and sincerity matched perfectly the same qualities in Anna. Small wonder as a team they topped all British box office records. Even today, despite the James Bond series, the Beatles, *Mary Poppins*, *The Sound of Music* and *My Fair Lady*, *Spring in Park Lane* still holds the attendance record for any film in the United Kingdom.

Whilst Michael could grasp this, he could not accept the fact that he personally could make an appreciable impact on cinema audiences. I told him of the mean Lowry-like houses and people in the mining districts of the North, where I served my film apprenticeship. Four walls and a roof, holes for the front door and windows, outside water closets, and not always water. I have never forgotten the grim, unglamorous existence of the people who lived in those districts. That is why I believed in glamour and that is why we were so successful.

Michael was impressed but, as to his own contribution, was still not convinced. There was only one thing to do—show him.

Spring in Park Lane was opening at Worthing so I asked Michael to come to lunch at Brighton, where Anna and I were staying, on the opening day, Sunday. I did not tell him the reason. After lunch, I told him we were going to Worthing. I had engaged an open car. Within two miles of Worthing, the crowds were lining both sides of the road.

'What's happening?' asked Michael. 'What are these crowds for?'

'For you and Anna. Stand up and smile and blow 'em a kiss.'

He did, and Anna did likewise. The crowds grew thicker, and by the time we reached Worthing we could not get to the theatre. I then broke the news to Michael that we were making a personal appearance —his first. The police did their best and, an hour late, we reached the theatre, where a bewildered but happy Michael joined Anna on the stage.

Anna had had crowds like this with *Victoria the Great*, so she was a little more composed. But Michael asked for a brandy.

'Now do you see what I mean?' I asked him.

The success of *Spring in Park Lane* reached its climax when Anna, Michael and I won all three British 'Oscars' as best actress, actor and director of the year.

Walking on pink clouds and sipping pink champagne, we set off for New York in the *Queen Elizabeth*, with my sights aligned on selling the American rights—for dollars.

What a voyage! Red carpet down for us at Southampton, where we were greeted by Captain Grattidge and Chief Purser Lionel Carine. And the trip to New York was one series of celebrations and significant events.

On the evening the captain organised a cocktail party for us in his quarters, the *Queen Elizabeth* broke the record for a day's run with 722 miles and took the 'Blue Riband of the Atlantic'. The photograph inscribed by the officers of the *Queen Elizabeth* commemorating our dual success is reproduced in this book. The *Ocean Times* carried the news of the double triumph, and we were swamped with congratulations and invitations.

Before leaving London, a meeting had taken place between Mr Harold Wilson and Sir Arthur Jarratt, head of British Lion, the distribution company, which had been receiving approximately a million pounds yearly in cinema rentals from my films alone. At that meeting it transpired that I was the top entertainments tax earner and dollar saver, although at this point not much of a dollar earner. Harold Wilson, being President of the Board of Trade, knew the facts and figures. The significance of this meeting was to emerge with startling suddenness on this memorable voyage.

After two days we were forced to call a halt to the hospitality, which had included drinks with the engine-room crew in the bowels of the ship and which Anna—the daughter, sister, niece and aunt of sailors—enjoyed enormously. I planned a quiet day before disembarking, in order to recoup our exhausted strength and to work out my sales campaign.

At lunch in the Verandah Grill, a radio operator informed us 'London' was on the ocean phone for me. It was my solicitor, Stanley Passmore. The Lord Chamberlain's office had contacted him in my absence. My name had been put forward for a C.B.E. (Commander of the British Empire).

'Will you accept it?' Passmore laughingly inquired.

I had never contemplated or sought special recognition since I considered I was amply rewarded for my work in acclaim and money. Now, from out of the blue, it was offered—and I realised I did not wish it and asked Passmore to advise the Lord Chamberlain accordingly.

He was astounded, and inquired if I had heard him correctly. I stood firm, and Stanley was bewildered.

'Knowing you—I'm sure you will withdraw gracefully.'

He put the receiver down rather abruptly, I thought.

I realised as I made my way back to Anna that this was obviously the outcome of the meeting between Harold Wilson and Arthur Jarratt.

'Who was it?' Anna asked when I returned.

'Stanley Passmore,' I told her.

'No trouble?'

'No!'

But Anna was not satisfied and pressed for more information. In confidence, I told her the story. She was stunned and told me: 'The C.B.E. is recognition of a job well done—a workman's recognition—you must accept it.'

Without waiting for my reasons for not accepting, which were nebulous, she called the head waiter and asked him to have a phone call put through to London.

Just in time! Passmore was at that moment contacting the Lord Chamberlain's office. He was delighted at my change of heart, and Anna could not have been happier. By now, I too was glad and excited.

But, of course, I could not tell Michael or anyone—until it was officially announced. So that evening, in our suite on the main deck, we locked the door whilst Anna and I alone split a half-bottle of champagne.

Yes—quite a voyage! And to crown it all, soon after our arrival in New York, Mary Pickford saw *Spring in Park Lane*—and loved it, and a United States distribution deal was made, including a very substantial cash advance.

We had a seven-year deal with Michael Wilding and one day, from out of the blue, Michael said: 'Herbert, can I talk to you about my contract?'

'But you have a first-class agent,' I told him. 'Talk to him. I hate talking business to an artist I work with.'

'But this is something I can discuss only with you,' he replied.

'All right. Get it off your chest, Michael.'

'I've got a seven-year deal. I'd like to make it twenty-one years.'

I was knocked flat, and it was a minute or so before I could tell him how much I appreciated his suggestion and that I knew Anna would feel the same. Anna was not as surprised as I had been. 'That's just like Michael,' was all she said, but her eyes conveyed much more.

The news went the rounds and Fleet Street applauded this unprecedented gesture which—with Anna, Michael and myself literally on top of the box office world—promised enormous possibilities.

But Michael was not as happy as his success warranted. I talked to Anna. We knew his domestic background was rough, but this had been the case for some time.

'It's money,' I told Anna. 'And we must do something about it.'

'If you say so,' she replied.

We decided we would make him a present of £20,000 from our own pocket and therefore tax-free. 'Let's make it in two payments,' suggested Anna.

So round to Michael's flat I went with Goodhead. I told Michael what we proposed doing and pulled out the cheque for £10,000. 'Here's the first instalment—now open a bottle.'

Michael then had another problem. He was in love—with both Marlene Dietrich and Elizabeth Taylor! Did I say 'problem'?

'If you can't make up your own mind, Michael, I'm afraid I can't help,' I told him.

As I was on my way to New York, he told me he had decided on Liz Taylor. On arrival in New York, Marlene and I had lunch together. She was very sad. 'What's Taylor got that I haven't?' she asked. And what had she—except youth?

Marlene is incredible. Sensuous and exciting, she is the most feminine woman I have ever met. She exudes femininity.

I first met her in Berlin when she was making *The Blue Angel* with Emil Jannings. 'Falling in love again—can't help it,' she sang in the film, and overwhelmed every man she met. And now, thirty odd years later, she still has the same effect on a man. She still has a wonderful figure—that of a girl of eighteen—and a great sense of humour. She's a superb cook, too. What more could any man ask? And she's a wonderful 'doctor'. She takes people apart, analyses them and puts them back the right way.

Michael needed Marlene emotionally. But professionally I was disturbed. I certainly don't think age has the importance that every British newspaper attaches to it. But Michael was under a long-term contract to us—as a romantic young lover. I could just see what the age-crazy press would do to him and Marlene.

It was some time after the problem of Dietrich or Liz Taylor had been settled in favour of Liz that Anna and I felt it would be a good time to give him the second £10,000. With the cheque in my pocket, I again went to Michael's flat with Goodhead. Michael was not his usual bubbling self, but I thought our cheque would bring back the sparkle. I put my hand in my pocket for it. Before I could get it out he dropped a bombshell.

'Oh, Herbert. As I'm going to marry Liz, I shall have to go and live in Hollywood. It wouldn't work if we were separated. You and Anna will understand, I'm sure.'

'But our contract,' I gasped, and withdrew my hand from my pocket—without the cheque.

He was sure we would not wish him to stay in England if he would not be happy, and besides, M.G.M. had offered him a very good deal.

'Well, let me negotiate the deal,' I said.

'I've promised Liz I'll do nothing until I see her,' he told me.

And so ended one of the happiest and most successful associations in the British film industry in a way that was sad, unnecessary, tragic.

I went back to Anna and tore up the cheque for £10,000. Anna, as usual, saw his reasoning, so we decided to take care of the wedding arrangements.

What a circus it turned out to be! I went to Heathrow with Michael and smuggled him into the V.I.P. lounge overlooking the tarmac. Anna stayed at home to meet the new registrar from Caxton Hall, Mr Holliday, whom we persuaded to come and have a meal and brief Michael and Liz so as to avoid any hitch.

Thank heavens we did. When Liz's plane touched down, she disembarked escorted by every press relations official at the airport. She started to walk to the main building. Immediately the biggest group of press photographers I have ever seen rushed towards her and, retreating in front of her, clicked their cameras with flashing bulbs going all the time. Liz, as calm as any royal, and looking minute from where we were, waved as only royalty do, smiling here and smiling there. Her composure in one so young was incredible.

As she entered the building, another swarm of photographers gathered and in the rush some were trodden underfoot—cameras and all. Some privileged reporters were waiting in the V.I.P. lounge with Michael and me.

When Liz entered, she took one look at Michael and in a flash she was in his arms and they were embracing madly. The reporters and I were completely forgotten. The embrace lasted so long and was so passionate that we all moved over to the bar and left them to it.

When Michael and Liz arrived at our flat, Mr Holliday suggested a rehearsal of the ceremony and, although they went through the motions, their minds were not on the job. At least, Liz's mind wasn't! She gazed at Michael until it became a little uncomfortable to watch.

Mr Holliday himself was more than a little startled, but he carried on nobly. When he said to Michael, 'Kiss the bride', Liz beat Michael to it, and they fell into a clinch which had to be seen to be believed. Mr Holliday coughed, but Anna saved the situation with a laugh that Nell Gwyn would have envied. Mr Holliday looked at us both and smiled as he coughed again.

'Miss Taylor, excuse me—you've been married before?'
'Sure,' said Liz, coming up for breath, 'but this is it!'
'Did your husband die?' asked Mr Holliday.
'No, I divorced him,' said Liz.
Mr Holliday smiled: 'And you have the papers?'
'Not with me. My lawyer in California has them.'
'But I must see them! I can't marry you without.'
Liz came out of her trance. 'You can't what?'
Mr Holliday told her it was the law, but by now tearful Liz asked him how should she know? He must marry them. The atmosphere was electric.

'Could we phone her lawyer?' I asked Mr Holliday.
'If he could give me his assurance and cable me confirmation to Caxton Hall—I feel it...'
Liz was already on the phone and asking for a California number. Michael asked for a drink. I gave him one, and Mr Holliday too. Within half an hour, all was calm again and the marriage would take place as planned in the morning. When they left, I lay in a hot bath and blessed Mr Holliday.

The wedding was at 11 a.m. next morning. Anna sent our wardrobe supervisor ('Churchie') round to the Berkeley to help Liz dress. But, when Anna (best girl) called for her at 10.30, Churchie was frantic. Elizabeth was still sound asleep.

'And where,' Churchie asked, waving her hand over three cabin trunks and thirty suitcases still unopened, 'do you think her wedding clothes might be?'

I picked up Michael and we sank a whole bottle of champagne before starting out. We all got to Caxton Hall on time, but Anna and our wardrobe supervisor were worn out—their nerves shattered. But not Elizabeth. She was as cool as a cucumber and as lovely a rose as ever came out of an enchanted English garden.

And so they were married. When the excitement had died down, the press boys asked me: 'What about that twenty-one year contract?'

'We released him to make a better deal with Liz Taylor—a lifer!'

Alas it did not turn out that way. And I regret to say that they did not live happily ever after. However, they are the parents of two lovely children whom they both adore—and are still 'just good friends'!

After the reception a huge crowd had gathered in Brook Street to see Liz and Michael leave for their honeymoon. So dense were the fans that to enter or leave Claridges was out of the question.

The management was not amused.

14

Claridges! The quintessence of gracious living and inextricably linked with so many important events in my life; and on many occasions a morale booster.

Whenever the going was rough and I was beset by a problem I would move in—the royal suite, order cocktails and in solitary state get through a good dinner, plus a half-bottle of champagne and a friendly chat with the head floor waiter, Robert, or Stephens thrown in for good measure. Within a day or so the wind would change and the problem invariably disappeared. I then moved out.

Since Anna and I lived there for nearly three years it is understandable that a great deal of my drama and comedy was played against a backcloth of Claridges.

Receptions for a hundred or more after important *premières*.

Our first meetings with Odette and Maurice Buckmaster.

Supper with Lord Mountbatten and his family after Anna had performed Housman's 'Queen Victoria' at Drury Lane.

Jim Mollison over double brandies, recovering from shock after seeing how I had portrayed him in the Amy Johnson film.

The purchase of Universal British Company for Rank.

Memorable meetings with Lord Portal of Laverstoke.

Michael Wilding and Elizabeth Taylor's wedding reception, for a hundred or so.

The day I married Anna—our quiet wedding breakfast for four served in our room by an ever-watchful Stephens.

The blitz, when we went up to the roof and saw London burning all round us. Van Thuyne, the manager, always present in a tin hat.

For some inexplicable reason, the blitz was less disturbing at Claridges than elsewhere, and it is worth recording that despite extensive damage in all directions—sometimes within a few hundred yards—the hotel itself was never hit. It was almost like reaching harbour when the taxi-man, with little more than a crucifix slit of traffic-light at the crossings to indicate his whereabouts, drew up at Claridges. However, that was during what some wags facetiously called 'the good old-fashioned blitz'! The V-bomb period was different: no warning and an uneasy silence after the cut-out as the bomb plunged towards its target.

The night the first V-bomb fell on London was memorable. No alert—just an explosion and a very near thing indeed. After a second bomb fell I slipped on my dressing-gown and decided to investigate.

Outside in the corridor, amongst others, was the young, newly-married Queen of Yugoslavia, pacing up and down—her spaniel at her heels.

It was uncannily frightening and, after several explosions, word was sent to all guests at Claridges to proceed at once to the shelters in the cellars. All responded, including a Mr David Sarnoff. The mysterious bombs continued to fall and the cellars seemed to shake. But all were calm except one lady, who was on the verge of hysterics and who might conceivably have touched off panic among others. Mr Sarnoff, sensing the situation, started to talk to her about extraneous things and soon held her interest and had her exchanging views with him. All without heroics or demonstration . . .

I met the lady a few days later and she expressed her gratitude that 'he stopped me from making a fool of myself'.

It is interesting to know that early in his career, David Sarnoff—now General Sarnoff and, as president of the Radio Corporation of America (R.C.A.), one of the most powerful figures in the world of communications, radio and television—was the central actor in a sea drama during which, as a boy telegraphist in the pioneer days of wireless, he remained on duty for three days when the President of the United States silenced all stations so that news could be flashed out with the names of the survivors of the S.S. *Titanic*.

During World War II Claridges became the H.Q. for American top brass. One day, walking along the corridor to our suite, I saw a tall, elegant, loose-limbed figure coming towards me. He was not unlike Gary Cooper and had five stars on his shoulders. General Patton!

At the time he was in the middle of a raging controversy with his picture in every newspaper.

There was no doubt about it. It *was* Patton.

I then committed an unforgivable sin. I approached him with outstretched hand.

'General Patton, I believe.'

'Dr Livingstone, I presume,' he replied, as he ignored my hand and passed me without even a glance in my direction. I asked for a snub and I got a five-star beauty!

I have so many other memories of Claridges, mostly happy ones and in this year of grace, 1966, I am hoping to emerge from the financial shadows which have shut out a lot of sunshine over the past year or two. When this happens I shall hurry from the bankruptcy court to keep a promised date with Anna. Lunch at Claridges!

When talking about Claridges I always conjure up the image of Luigi in charge of the restaurant: gracious, courteous and, like all the high priests of gracious living, with abundant presence of mind.

Besides Luigi of Claridges, the others who linger in my mind are: Luigi of the Embassy Club of the twenties: Sovrani with his speciality dish of baby bear; Quaglino, 'Quag' to everyone; and Mario, for many years the chief of the Ivy restaurant, who moved to the Caprice on its opening and has been mine host there ever since. All greats in their own sphere with discretion and presence of mind predominant. Sovrani and Quaglino, both Italians, were interned at the outbreak of war and Sovrani went down when the ill-fated *Athenia* was torpedoed.

Presence of mind was certainly needed when 'Bunch' Keys, Tallulah Bankhead, Michael Arlen and I were having supper at the old Embassy Club. The other member of our party was a close friend of the Prince of Wales.

H.R.H., a frequest visitor to the Embassy, came over to our table to have a word with Tallulah. Naturally we stood up, except the Prince's close friend.

Luigi, who was 'hovering', rushed to the table and apologised to our seated guest. 'May I trouble you, sir, one of the legs has gone'— as he took away the chair, leaving our friend standing. Luigi handed the chair with an admonishing finger, to Peter, the head waiter. The substitute chair did not arrive until His Royal Highness had left our table. Michael Arlen's wink to Luigi is a treasured memory.

It was at the Embassy that the Prince of Wales set a fashion that swept the Mayfair scene like a prairie fire.

I was directing Will Rogers, Dorothy Gish and Nelson Keys in George Gershwin's *Tiptoes* at the time and Will Rogers was appearing at the London Pavilion at night. In Bill's famous monologue act, during which he spun a lasso throughout, his incomparable dry humour invariably led to his comments on the horsemanship of the Prince of Wales and his *penchant* for falling off. The house always rocked with laughter, and none more than His Royal Highness.

'Fruity' Metcalfe thought they should meet socially, so he invited Bill, Bunch and myself to join a supper party at the Embassy Club.

Our party was ten or twelve and after a long evening of banter and dancing, at which H.R.H. excelled, Fruity looked at the Prince.

'Your glass is empty, sir; won't you ... ?'

'Thank you, no,' replied the Prince and seeing Luigi, who on such occasions always 'hovered' unobtrusively near at hand, asked, 'Luigi, I would like a kipper, toasted brown bread and coffee.'

Kippers! At seaside boarding-houses, the Isle of Man or the East End—yes. But at the Embassy!

Hoots of laughter gave way to a discreet gasp—which His Royal Highness faultlessly ignored—when it was realised that the Prince was serious. Within minutes the dish was set before the Prince and the sight and smell of the kippers resulted in all at our table ordering the same—and wonderful they were.

From that night every fashionable restaurant and night club in town had a daily consignment of kippers from Douglas, Isle of Man, against the possible patronage of the Prince. The word went out far beyond Mayfair and eventually reached Hollywood. When I arrived there a little later I was offered English kippers at the Cock and Bull on Sunset Strip. They were served with hot English muffins and strawberry jam—on the same plate!

But to get back.

Whereas Anna loves acting—the trouble with Michael was that he did not.

He appreciated the rewards, both material and spiritual, that acting brought, but it was not his life as it was Anna's. Had he felt otherwise, I'm sure—with his looks and charm—he would have reached the heights. His disappearance from the acting scene is a tragedy.

On the opposite side of the medal, Elizabeth Taylor has developed enormously as an actress. I predicted this when one day I congratulated her on her performance in the George Stevens-Theodore Dreiser film *A Place in the Sun*.

She seemed surprised, and with unaffected humility told me: 'I've never considered I could act. I don't like acting enough, so I guess that's why I'm not a good actress ...'

'You may not like acting,' I replied, 'but one day you will make the grade as a top actress.'

Liz seemed very amused; she laughed, and then asked: 'Are you kidding?'

'No, I'm serious.'

'I wish I could think so,' she said.

'To quote Humphrey Bogart,' I told her, "You've got the equipment—good looks and a good brain" and what to me is just as important, humility.'

'I hope you are right,' said Liz, completely unconvinced.

I have now seen her dazzling, incomparable performance in *Who's Afraid of Virginia Woolf?*—a performance from a girl who once said to me: '. . . guess that's why I am not a good actress.'

Such humility in an artist is rare. However, I have personally seen it matched.

Whilst having my hair attended I noticed someone waiting to follow me. His face was familiar but—rarely with me—I could not put a name to it.

Came his turn in the chair.

'How's your wife?' he inquired as he sat down.

'She's fine,' I told him.

'I was a "super" at Edinburgh in her play *The Glorious Days*,' he went on.

'I thought we had met before,' I replied.

'A nice engagement, and Miss Neagle was very kind to all of us. Give her my regards.'

'Thanks. I will,' I assured him.

As I was almost out of the door I turned back and asked: 'Who shall I say?'

'Sean Connery,' he answered.

And I had not recognised him! I could not apologise, so settled for: 'Well—I'm damned!' Connery's generous laugh helped to cover my confusion.

To have referred to his being a 'super' in Anna's play was not exactly the image 'James Bond' had created in my mind.

Confirmation of Connery's acceptance of his unique world popularity came in a quote in a Sunday newspaper from Terence Young, the brilliant director who launched him as 007. Said Young: 'In my long memory only one person has not changed with success—that is Sean Connery. And I cannot even say that about myself!'

With *Spring in Park Lane* breaking all records, I was the white-headed boy of British Lion.

Korda asked me if I would have dinner with him at his penthouse on the roof of Claridges. Knowing that a meeting with Alex was always a tonic plus good food and wine, I went along to find him with Frederick Lonsdale, the playwright, whom I had not seen since a stormy dinner party at Mike Romanoff's in Hollywood.

We had not met or spoken to each other since, and when Alex, knowing nothing of the situation between us, dramatically raised my right arm like a triumphant boxer and announced I had won the championship of the British film industry with *Spring in Park Lane* Lonsdale was not amused and neither was I.

'You asked me to have dinner and a talk, Alex. It was tonight, wasn't it?' I asked.

Lonsdale left. Alex saw him to the lift.

'You were rude to my guest,' he said when he returned.

'Yes. Deliberately so,' I answered.

'Bad manners,' said Korda.

'Yes, but no worse than declaiming—to admiring cronies, mostly American, at Romanoff's in Beverly Hills, six thousand miles away from England—the futility of Winston's handling of the war.'

'I'll order dinner,' was all Alex replied.

Alex Korda was a very superior person. I mean superior in the literal sense. He had erudition, charm, business acumen, artistic sense, and was a gifted linguist. His personal magnetism would have ensured his reaching the heights in many fields.

He had his failings, of course, and the greatest of these was, I believe, an overwhelming desire for power. I saw Alex grow old very fast from this malady. Only a man who realised his superiority over most of his fellow creatures would have expressed a wish that he was to be known as and referred to as 'Alex' by his entire staff from top to bottom. And it was unnecessary for Alex (as was the case with a certain TV executive) to issue a directive that he wished to be addressed as 'sir'.

To some it was not easy to call him 'Alex'—but if he wished it?

He did.

To sit at a conference table and hear Korda debate almost any subject was a revelation. His command of English, his extensive vocabulary and telling delivery must have confounded many a city magnate hearing an artist so faultlessly and effortlessly presenting a case.

That he was effective was demonstrated by the fact that the Prudential Assurance Co. came into London Film Productions for some millions, as did later his friends and comrades in the Secret Service, the Hambros.

It is not generally known that Korda's recognition was not entirely for his work in British films. His important work during the war, of which I knew a great deal that I cannot, alas, disclose here, was much more the basic reason.

I first met Korda in Vienna whilst he was directing his wife, Maria Corda. Young, handsome, with a newspaper background, he impressed one at once as a man who was going places. He did—to Hollywood. After a brief stay that was nothing startling, he came back to Europe and to a very thin time indeed. And this is where he enters my story in an important way.

After the enormous success of what I enjoy calling the renaissance period of British films—Jack Buchanan, Walls and Lynn, Sydney Howard, Elisabeth Bergner—I was persuaded to transfer my distribution from Gaumont British and C. M. Woolf to United Artists of New York, who told me to name my own terms; which I did.

One of them was that, whilst United Artists were distributing my British films, they were forbidden to distribute any other British product. My object was to ensure their entire selling concentration, other than on their own American films starring Charlie Chaplin, Douglas Fairbanks, Ronald Colman and Mary Pickford.

Korda 'phoned. He wanted to see me urgently. Because of my embargo, he told me, he could not get airborne—financially or otherwise. He had an important script completed. He had raised £58,000 and the distributors interested were United Artists. Would I lift my ban for this one film, which he described.

I demurred.

'I'm on my beam ends just now, Herbert,' said Korda, 'but I've always believed that one good film can make a company—a dozen good ones an industry. This is the film to spark everything off for me.'

I was impressed. After all, I thought, one good British film could not hurt me. My objective was keeping out the bad ones. I gave my consent. Korda went ahead and made the film, which turned out an outstanding success. It was *The Private Life of Henry VIII*, which otherwise might never have been made. At a cost of £58,000.

Within a short time other good films flowed from Korda's company and very soon he was on the board of directors of United Artists and a considerable shareholder. Korda was right. One film had made his company, London Films. I found myself on the outside looking in!

Paradoxically, the position between Korda and myself was reversed a few years later.

Out of the profits of *Henry VIII*, Korda and the Prudential built Denham studios. And in 1937, for reasons I have already explained,

41. Our wedding day.

42. 'Auntie' with Anna on Anna's investiture day.

43. Anna and I with our thirteen awards.

44. With Anna and Michael Wilding at the Dorchester, receiving triple awards for *Spring in Park Lane*.

45. A memorable voyage for the *Queen Elizabeth*: our triple awards, and the record day's run of 733 miles.

46. With Peter Ustinov, Anna, Odette and Trevor Howard in Haute-Savoie during the production of *Odette*.

47. Anna in the title role of *Odette*, 1950.

48. Anna and I congratulated by King George VI at the *première* of *Odette*.

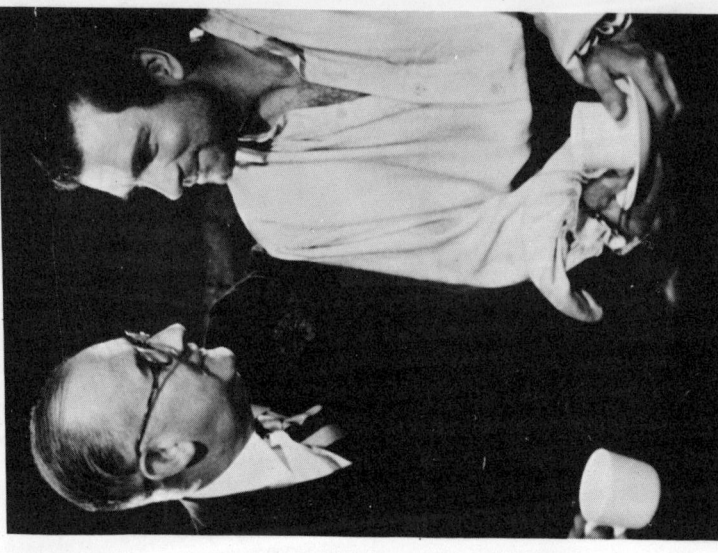

49. Alexander Korda.

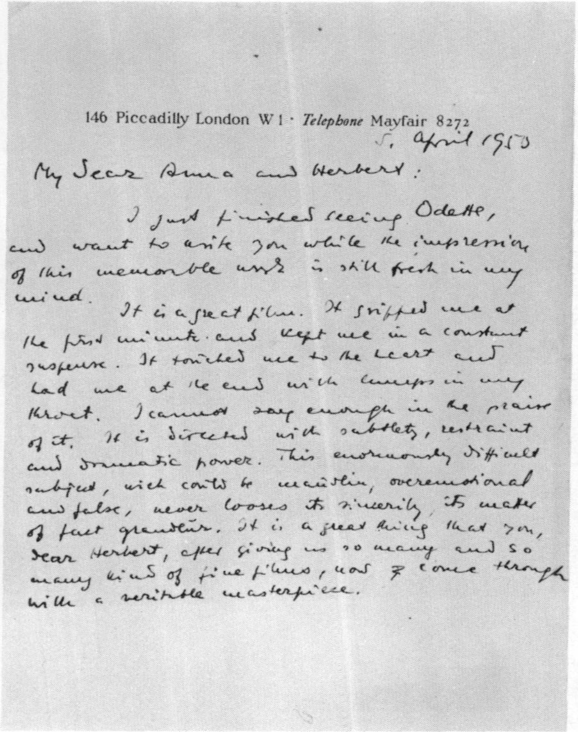

50. A page of Korda's extraordinary letter, received within an hour of his private viewing of *Odette*.

51. With Lawrence Olivier during his playing of Macheath in *The Beggar's Opera*.

I found myself in an independent isolated spot with *Victoria the Great* ready for production. I was £50,000 short of my production budget. Although I had pipped Korda by a short head in securing the right to produce *Victoria the Great*, about which he was wildly enthusiastic, I decided to see him, as one independent producer to another, and explain my problem.

I went to Denham. It must have been a Saturday or a holiday, for no one was about. I wandered on to the big stage. Alone in the centre was Korda, contemplating some structural changes. He greeted me warmly, and—since it was my first visit—proudly showed me round.

'You made this all possible, Herbert, with *Henry*. If at any time...'

'The time is now, Alex,' I broke in, before he could finish. I told him of my problem.

'Herbert, make your Victoria film here and you can have a studio credit for £50,000.'

So here was the reverse of the medal. For without this studio credit, *Victoria the Great* might never have been made!

A man of dignity himself, he boasted that he could adapt himself to any strata of society. He could and did—from his domestic staff to the royals. And never was anybody ill at ease—certainly not Korda—except on one occasion...

Spring in Park Lane carried everything before it—and word came through from Buckingham Palace that Princess Elizabeth and Prince Philip would like to see our film privately. This was understanable because it was very shortly before Prince Charles was born.

They did not wish to see it at Buckingham Palace, so I arranged a viewing at 144 Piccadilly, Korda's offices, which had a small theatre. We were advised it must be a strictly private showing, but they would like to meet Anna, Michael and me afterwards.

Sherry was laid on in Korda's board room. The three of us waiting were delighted with the laughter that was coming from the theatre. The Princess had thoughtfully invited some of her household staff from 'Buck House' and, because of the theme of the film, the laughs were loud and long as the 'lower deck' in the film scored off the 'quarter deck'!

Just before the film finished, in walked Alex! I was surprised but could not very well tell him it was a strictly private occasion, seeing that we were waiting in his board room and drinking his sherry.

Alex was not at all embarrassed. On the contrary, when the royal party arrived, he hurried forward to greet them. Anna, Michael and I waited in the background for the formal presentations. After these were over and they had expressed their pleasure, Prince Philip buttonholed Anna and Michael, and Princess Elizabeth addressed herself to me. Alex joined us.

During the conversation: 'What is your next film?' she asked me. I told her that amongst other things it was a story of the effect of war on women. In a manner it was an exercise in reflection, and I referred to the Prime Minister's comment at a recent Guildhall banquet that many of the ills of today resulted from insufficient time for reflection.

Princess Elizabeth was on the point of expressing her views when Alex unaccountably broke in with: 'The trouble with Herbert, Ma'am, is that he's too reflective. My son has the right idea: act first, then reflect.'

I did not know how to counter this. I certainly could not start an argument in the presence of Her Royal Highness. But I had no need to worry. Turning her lovely blue eyes on Korda and, despite the imminence of her baby's arrival, looking more beautiful than I have ever seen her, she said: 'My husband likes to drive very fast. And last week we were driving from Windsor and, looking out of the window, I could see nothing—just a blurred impression of trees. We were slowed down by the traffic and—I was enchanted by the beauty of the countryside.'

A faint smile never left her face as she said this. What Alex would have answered, I shall never know, since Prince Philip came over and that was an indication to leave.

Having escorted the royal party to their car, I returned to find Alex lighting one of his famous cigars.

'Well, Alex, you asked for it,' I told him.

Taking a long pull at his cigar and blowing it upwards, he looked at me and smiled: 'Herbert, have you ever seen a more beautiful face on any woman?' was all he said.

It was the only time I had known Korda overplay his hand.

I have digressed. So let me take you back to Claridges, where we had just finished a dinner only Korda could think up.

He then came out with the object of the meeting. He had a wonderful story for Anna. Either I could direct it myself for London Films, or he would pay us a handsome fee and a percentage of the profits for Anna's services and he would direct.

He told me the story, and I stared at him to see if he was serious. Apparently he was, so I reminded him that I had established an image for Anna which radiated glamour and, together with Michael, romance. Alex was persistent. I was equally firm. The answer was 'no'.

When I got home, I told Anna of the strange proposition Korda had made. She said she would like to read it. She did and was mystified. She agreed entirely with me that to go from *Spring in Park Lane* to *Mary Poppins* would be fatal!

I still think our decision was right. What Walt Disney and his technical team produced in their lovely film *Mary Poppins* with Julie Andrews was a delightful *soufflé*. In my hands it would have been a Yorkshire pudding!

On the domestic front, my wife married again soon after I did, and our children were left to sort out their own lives. And a remarkably good job they have made of it.

My son, John, as a film production executive was much in demand. He loves detail, schedules and budgets as much as I loathe them. He also has a sense of humour—which he needs in his job—as well as a lovely wife and daughter.

During the war, he served with distinction in the Army—as a film cameraman—and did excellent and exciting work. And, for an extremely sensitive person, some pretty grim jobs such as photographing Himmler, dead after his suicide. Fortunately John's native sense of humour did not desert him, even on this sordid occasion.

'What did he look like?' I asked.

'Well,' replied John, 'for Himmler—remarkably peaceful!'

My daughter Pamela turned out to be quite a writer. During the war, she served with the Office of War Information in Washington and, according to Frank Capra and Carl Foreman, her superior officers, did a first-class job. She had an American coast-to-coast radio series of her own, and won the Stephen Vincent Benet Award for the best radio script of the year. Then she spent four years with the BBC as writer, producer and director of documentaries and directed firsthand programmes with Robert Graves, Compton Mackenzie, J. B. Priestley and C. P. Snow.

Pamela also produced and directed *Square Story*, an exquisite and moving short documentary film of the London squares, written by Christopher Hassall—a great success on release. Also a brilliant short colour film on Brighton.

My second daughter, Patricia, was too young for war service and is now a full-time and wonderful mother with a young son and daughter.

My youngest daughter, Sheila, also too young for any war work, decided to discover Australia; she discovered it and settled for England, and is now serving at the Foreign Office.

All without any help from me. Emerson was right.

15

A production crew of 105 had assembled in a room at Shepperton studios—the cream of the technical cinema world. Addressing them was the star of the picture and my co-producer, Sir Laurence Olivier.

It was a pep talk, which we both thought would bring results. The point of emphasis was that we were embarking on what must emerge as the outstanding British musical film of all time. The talents were there: Christopher Fry, screenwriter; Sir Arthur Bliss, composer of the musical score; Peter Brook, the brilliant young stage director—his first essay as film director; and a story that had been successful over and over again since its *première* more than two hundred years before.

It was *The Beggar's Opera* by John Gay, with Sir Laurence Olivier playing Macheath, Dorothy Tutin as Polly Peacham, Stanley Holloway, George Devine, Hugh Griffiths, Daphne Anderson—and a £500,000 budget in Technicolor! Nothing could have the sweeter smell of success!

With rather more than his usual assurance, Larry addressed the assembled cast and technicians.

'A long time ago in the early twenties, I was playing at the Fortune theatre in a play which Herbert Wilcox came to see. He came round to my dressing room afterwards to offer me a contract—at £100 a week! I rushed home to my wife and said: "Darling! No more worry, no more problems, Herbert Wilcox has offered me a film contract and—you'll never believe it—£100 a week!" Agent trouble caused the deal to fall through but—'

'Don't worry, Sir Laurence,' piped up my production manager (who was my son, John), 'the offer's still open—same salary!'

That was the end of the pep talk and we all adjourned to the bar! £100 a week! And I had to bargain very hard to get Larry for *The Beggar's Opera* for his current fee of £50,000 and a share of the profits; and then he only made a deal because he was so interested in working with Peter Brook on his first film assignment, so much so, that he agreed to defer £30,000 of the £50,000. 'I am expecting to learn a hell of a lot from Peter,' Larry told me. But the production of *The Beggar's Opera* was a chronic headache. At the same time I was producing and directing *Laughing Ann*, a Conrad story in colour with Margaret Lockwood, on the next stage.

If I had not had Larry to watch over *The Beggar's Opera* and to take full responsibility for both of us, I cannot imagine what would have happened to my production. From the outset, the complete harmony which I knew all of us hoped for and had been looking forward to with justifiable expectation was, for some extraordinary reason, unaccountably lacking. Larry and I were in complete harmony, but we could not get to first base with Peter.

Larry, with his wide experience of the stage and screen, and I, with nearly thirty-five years of continuous production behind me, endeavoured to combine Peter's experimental approach with our experience—and give him the best of both worlds. But Peter would have none of it. Stage genius though he had undoubtedly proved himself, and as Larry and I freely conceded, we could not get him to accept our practical suggestions—all of which he seemed to regard as criticisms. The insoluble problem was that Peter enjoyed a superiority complex that shone from his young blue eyes like highly polished brass buttons, insolently surveying and cocking a snook at the conventional; whereas long experience embracing success and failure had mellowed any suggestion of superiority Larry or I may have nursed in our early professional days.

Larry bent over backwards to co-operate, and how he worked. Not even the usual lunch-hour, of which he spent forty-five minutes with his Italian singing-master. Unlike most stars, Larry refuses to be doubled in any aspect—singing (a tremendous role), riding, swordsmanship, the lot. His riding alone—with cameras mounted on cars doing forty miles an hour—would have made most of the Hollywood western stars have a heart attack. On one occasion, he rode up 'Dead Man's Hill', an incline of one in six, so many times that the horse had a heart attack!

The sad thing was that Peter was fanatically keen to turn in the action film of all time, but he lacked the know-how.

The climax came when, in the film, Macheath had to chase his enemy through a gaming saloon, both armed with rapiers. Macheath (Olivier), in an effort to cut off his opponent, vaulted and mounted a gaming table, his rapier at the ready. A dangerous job and one for which any Hollywood artist would, with justification, have demanded a double. Not Larry. He must do it himself.

The cameras turned, he leapt like a ballet dancer, and let out a yell as he landed on the gaming table. Then he turned on his opponent and said: 'You bloody fool! You struck me as I jumped!'

The 'bloody fool' had not struck him, but, as he landed, he tore a calf muscle—and was out. I telephoned our friend, the late Hugh Dempster, the osteopath, to jump in his car and get to us as soon as possible. Larry, the most courteous man I have ever met, couldn't move and the pain was intense. But he sent for his opponent and apologised.

I had visions of an unfinished film on which I had already spent £250,000. Dempster could not promise to have him back on the set in less than three weeks.

Despite my own film which I was producing and directing, I had to attend meetings with solicitors, agents, accountants, assessors, who—knowing of the strife existing between Peter and Larry, which had thrown the schedule badly—recommended I made a change of star or director. This I could not do, since I had entered into financial commitments and distribution contracts for £500,000, in which Peter Brook was nominated as director and Olivier as star.

Film Finances, a company which guaranteed completion, demanded I change directors. But I refused and I took over their potential liability of excess cost and relieved them of all liability. This eventually cost me personally £31,000.

In three weeks Larry was back, and I had a talk with him.

'Larry,' I told him, 'we've both decided that Peter might turn out something really great. Let's give him his head.'

Larry agreed, and the film was completed without further argument. Goodness knows what we had—the greatest film ever or the biggest egg ever laid. However, it was completed.

Both Larry and I were substantially interested from a financial point of view. The £31,000 it had cost me to step into Film Finances' shoes had to be recovered, and £30,000 of my fee of £50,000 was second money. Larry's fee of £50,000 was also largely deferred. So we set to work on editing.

We had 600,000 feet of film to edit, anything was possible. By good fortune, we also had the best editor in the business—Reggie Beck, a quiet genius of long experience on *Hamlet*, *Richard III* and all Larry's films.

A miracle! Despite everything, we had a great picture—or so it seemed to us. All the heartaches and headaches would soon be forgotten.

Alex Korda, who had advanced finance against the foreign rights, made a deal with Jack Warner for the western hemisphere. 700,000 dollars was the figure! Alex rang me up from Cannes to seek my confirmation.

'Herbert, I have an offer for *The Beggar's Opera* from Jack Warner—700,000 dollars. Do I accept?'

'Yes, Alex, on one condition. Sight unseen.' (I remembered the lesson of my deal with Al Woods for *Southern Love*—250,000 dollars 'subject to viewing'.)

'Herbert. I told you it was Jack Warner! Do you expect Jack to pay 700,000 dollars "sight unseen"?'

'Yes, Alex, and tell him he's lucky to get it.'

Alex was not amused. But he made the deal on my terms. I gave instructions at once that no one, anywhere in the world, was to see the film until it was delivered to Warner Bros. in New York.

Then came a problem. Showmanship was badly needed to put the film over. I therefore planned the London *première* as the first film to be shown at the Royal Festival Hall, and arranged for a constant service of ferry boats from Westminster Pier to take over the V.I.P.s, press and guests. I had to install equipment but, after the Albert Hall experience thirty years previously, this held no terrors.

About that time, the Queen's guests were over for the Coronation and were staying at Windsor Castle. It was not easy to entertain the crowned heads of Europe and their families, amounting in all to one hundred. Could I help? Could I arrange a special pre-*première* for the Queen's guests in London at once, I was asked.

Oh, if only I was ready at the Festival Hall. But that would take some time. However, yes, I could, I sent word back.

And I did—at the Rialto. Every crowned head in Europe and their families. But no press, I insisted; and the Lord Chamberlain's office also insisted—no gate-crashers.

The royal visitors loved it, and I flew to New York to complete the delivery to Warner Bros. and pick up the 700,000 dollars. I had a most enjoyable dinner in New York with affable Jack Warner at '21'. The film was to be delivered the following morning.

At 10.0 a.m., a message came from our representative: 'The film's arrived. They want to know when they can see it.'

'Take the film to their office,' I told him, 'and hold out your right hand. When you receive the cheque for 700,000 dollars, hand over the film. That's when they can see it—not before.'

'But Jack Warner has asked to see it personally.'

'He might not like it,' I repeated. 'Don't forget I have partners in this, including Alex Korda and the Bank of England.'

Our New York representative—wonderful salesman and diplomat—carried out instructions to the letter. He phoned me: 'I've delivered and got the cheque. What now?'

'Take it to the bank and have it certified.'

He did. Within a few hours, I had a call from the head of Warner Bros. distributors.

'Herbert,' he said, 'you've made a hell of a film.'

I was effusive with thanks.

'Now tell me how to sell it!'

I regret to say I couldn't, and they didn't.

But the sequel is important. The governor of the Bank of England was in his office, as usual, discussing international exchange, when someone came in and said: 'The Wilcox film *The Beggar's Opera* has been sold to the U.S.A. for 700,000 dollars.'

The governor looked up. 'Did you say 700,000 dollars?'

'Yes, sir. Here's the cheque.'

'Let me see it,' said the governor.

I wonder what Montagu Norman would have said to Wyndham Portal?

What was the final result? Well, rather sad, I'm afraid. It was taken off after the first night on a circuit booking over here in England, and compensation was paid by the circuit not to show it. As one manager said: 'They didn't even come in on Monday to tell their friends not to come in on Tuesday.'

An inexplicable disaster... and I assure you it was an extremely good film. What's the answer? Please don't say, 'That's show business.' I've heard that one.

The final result? Balance of payments helped by 700,000 dollars. Larry lost his £20,000 deferment. Korda's company made a handsome profit. I lost my £30,000 deferment.

And my friend Jack Warner? I haven't heard from him or seen him since.

As a box office star-maker, my masterpiece was, of course, Anna Neagle—for seven years top woman box office in the international class. And then Michael Wilding, number one international star against all comers.

However, during my career as entrepreneur, as Her Majesty's Inland Revenue dubbed me, I have, through my Irish impetuosity and independence, missed one great world star and failed to see others.

The biggest star I missed was Audrey Hepburn.

Introduced to me by Michael Wilding, I found her enchanting with the overworked word 'star' reflected in every facet—her movements, speech, repose, her clothes sense and bewitching smile which broke through eyes that appeared to have seen hardship and horror. (It was not until after our meeting I learned of her experiences in occupied Holland.)

Terms were agreed between Audrey and myself in Michael's London flat—and we cracked a bottle! The terms were fair and, if she emerged, the sky was the limit for Audrey. But her agent had other ideas, and said so in no uncertain manner. I have no doubt we could have come to terms, but I was riding high, with *Spring in Park Lane* breaking records, so I decided to forget the whole matter—which I must confess was as fortunate for Audrey as it was unfortunate for me.

I feel I could not have equalled the performance of her stage and film sponsors—dating from her stage appearance in *Gigi* for Gilbert Miller on Broadway. I was present at the first night when this unknown elfin charmer exploded on New York. I will never forget Audrey taking her call before a wildly enthusiastic audience, and in her joy turning a complete somersault and winding up with the 'splits'.

Unknown at the time—since Gilbert Miller in his wisdom refrained from over-selling her in advance and astutely denied her prominent billing—next day Audrey was the toast of the critics and the New York public. Gilbert promptly promoted her to top star billing.

Apart from Audrey Hepburn, who has now reached the heights, I tested and rejected Claire Bloom, and a rare and sensitive actress she has turned out to be; also Dana Wynter, and predicted she had not got 'what it takes', whereas she also became an international box office star and, but for deciding on domesticity against a professional career, might well have become one of the 'greats'.

With Margaret Lockwood, a director's joy who can shade a performance or a character with computer accuracy, I went to exceptional lengths in the two films we made together, to find the deep sympathetic understanding I had with Anna.

Not Margaret's fault, I'm sure—but it did not come off. Perhaps Anna, with her fair loveliness, blue eyes and beautiful skin, plus her innate integrity as an actress, sublimated, both as woman and artist, my spiritual and physical needs and ideals, and I had subconsciously developed a blind spot for brunettes! It could well be.

I have often been asked the rarest quality to find in a star and I say without hesitation—a sense of humour. Whether it is the toughness of being at the top or the fear that the higher you go the harder you fall has any significance I cannot say, but seldom have I met a star, particularly a woman star, who has enjoyed her success to the full and maintained a reasonable perspective.

Anna has the sense of humour that enjoys a sense of humour in others. She is a wonderful audience and her uninhibited Nell Gwyn laugh when anything funny is said is a great tonic. I have been on the receiving end quite a lot. But Anna herself does not profess to being a humorist.

The wittiest woman I have met is undoubtedly Dorothy Gish. Usually without malice, but sometimes—for instance, whilst in New York I took her to the Pavillon, the smartest and darkest restaurant in the city. About that time a columnist who called herself 'Hortense' was dishing out her daily column of poison. 'Hortense' was universally loathed, particularly by her pet target—film stars.

Whilst eating I thought I saw her at a far table, but in the low-key lighting was not certain.

'Isn't that Hor*tense* over there?' I asked Dorothy.

Dorothy looked and without a flicker of a smile answered: 'She looks perfectly relaxed to me.'

Until the film of *Nell Gwyn* Dorothy's beautiful legs and breasts had been obscured by D. W. Griffith in period costume and the rags of *Orphans of the Storm;* so when as Nell her charms were revealed, Dorothy suddenly found herself very much in demand and propositioned by men of all ages, particularly by a certain famous young poet (let's call him 'Johnny'), a close friend and drinking companion of Scott Fitzgerald.

It was literally a fixation. He chain-smoked chain-drank and chanted his poems as he pursued Dorothy madly on any location.

'I was only safe or private in one place,' she confided to me. 'And then I double-locked the door.'

Dorothy, who could handle any man, was disturbed.

'What have you done to me?' she asked.

'Apparently exposed you,' I told her.

She was enormously relieved when the amorous poet went West—to Hollywood on a script assignment.

Dorothy Parker came in from the coast and met Dorothy Gish.

'How's Johnny?' asked Dorothy 'G.'

'Didn't you hear?' said Dorothy 'P.' 'He's had a nervous breakdown.'

'How could they tell?' replied Dorothy 'G.'

One of the legends of the book world in the twenties was Elinor

Glyn, whose novel *Three Weeks*, daring to a degree at the time, was being made as a silent film. Elinor was technical adviser to the Hollywood production company. Dorothy Gish was working on a neighbouring set.

'Was Elinor on the set at all?' I asked Dorothy.

'Never off it,' she replied, 'and ready to walk on herself at any minute.' (Elinor Glyn was famous for her heavy make-up which almost amounted to a mask!)

During production Elinor created a sensation when she refused to allow thousands of artificial roses to be used for the nuptial bed of her hero and heroine. 'Real white roses or nothing,' Elinor decreed. California was combed—real roses replaced the fakes—and the scene and film was completed.

Incidentally, it was Elinor Glyn who, seeing Clara Bow at work declared, 'That girl has IT...' and 'IT' passed into posterity as the password for sex.

When the film of *Three Weeks* was ready for release in England I was asked to advise on its special presentation. I met Elinor Glyn—and when you met her you really met her! She not only flattered but overwhelmed me.

To my horror a special Sunday *première* at the Oxford Music-Hall (where I had shown *Flames of Passion*) had been arranged by her society friends. I endeavoured to have it cancelled since I felt confident that the reaction of a sophisticated society audience would be a 'send-up'.

I was not heeded, and personally escorted Elinor Glyn into the theatre. She was hanging on to my arm as we entered—not unlike royalty! She sat next to me.

The film unfolded without incident until the famous rose-bed seduction scene. Some bright publicist had arranged for white rose scent to be pumped into the theatre at that moment which, mixed with cigar smoke, lost much of its fragrance. When the lovers really got to work on the bed of roses a very county Jimmy Edwards type commented in a voice that echoed through the theatre like thunder: 'Ha, ha, prickly—and damned uncomfortable!'

From then on the *première* was a total loss, but nevertheless the film went out and made big money with real cinema-goers.

The wit of Dorothy Gish again: about the same time as *Three Weeks* was published another book that shocked made its appearance—*The*

Well of Loneliness, by Radclyffe Hall, which dealt with the problem of lesbianism. Michael Arlen sought Dorothy Gish's advice about casting for his play *The Green Hat*.

Dorothy suggested a name.

'Thanks,' said Michael, 'but isn't she a lesbian?'

'A lesbian?' replied Dorothy. 'My dear—she's the wooden bucket itself from the Well of Loneliness!'

16

In summing up the happenings of a professional lifetime, it is natural to assess the things that one feels were worth while, and those that were not. The 'were nots' greatly outnumber the 'weres', so let me tell you about the reflections that please me most.

In the first place: watching some of those technical artists to whom I gave their first or early chance reaching the heights and taking their place among the 'greats'.

F. A. (Freddie) Young. My cameraman for many years on many of Anna's films. Now generally regarded as the top cameraman in the world. His credits include *Bridge on the River Kwai*, *Lawrence of Arabia* and *Doctor Zhivago*.

David Lean, my editor on *Escape Me Never*, now supreme as a director on whose record comment is superfluous.

John Woolf, my personal assistant at Elstree on his first studio job. With his brother 'Jimmy' Woolf, headed Romulus Films with its long list of successes from *African Queen* to *Room at the Top*. John Woolf has also, since its inception, been the inspiration and chief of Anglia T.V.—with its prestige and profit record.

Emile Littler! It was his first job after leaving school. Emile enjoys telling this himself but now I am going to tell it.

His father operated the Royal Artillery Theatre, Woolwich. He was a top showman and advised me never to over-light a scene. 'If they can see everything, Herbert,' he said, 'someone's sure to criticise—but keep the scene in shadow and mysterious and they'll be afraid to say anything in case they're wrong.' I have not forgotten this advice.

One day he inquired: 'I've a son straight from school—set his heart on show business—could you use him?'

'How strong is he?' I asked.

'Does that matter?'

'So long as he can lift and carry a camera weighing 120 pounds—it doesn't!'

'What's the pay?' he asked.

'£4 a week,' I told him.

'When does he start?' asked Littler senior.

And that's how Emile Littler, now one of our top impresarios, started. He owns and operates the Palace and Cambridge Theatres,

London, and has presented many outstanding stage successes, the greatest of which is *Annie Get Your Gun*.

George Black junr (son of my old friend, George Black) was my second assistant director in his first studio experience. For many years now, in partnership with his brother Alf, he has been responsible for countless stage successes. With his brother he controls the Tyne and Tees T.V. station.

Elmo Williams, my assistant cutter on *Victoria the Great* and on my Hollywood pictures, was appointed managing director of Twentieth Century Fox production activities by Darryl Zannuck after the success of *The Longest Day*, on which Elmo made a major contribution. He was also executive producer of *Those Magnificent Men in their Flying Machines*.

Lord Brabourne, my assistant director (his first job in production), has gone on to produce first-class films such as *Harry Black*, *The Battle of the River Plate* and others. He is now head of the recently launched TV operation named 'Home Viewing'.

Jack Cardiff came to me for his first job as clapper boy. He moved on to become one of the 'greats' in the camera world, and on again to become an outstanding director.

Ivan Foxwell joined me for his first work in films as an assistant cameraman, and has moved on to produce top international films including *The Quiller Memorandum*.

Kevin McClory was my sound boom operator. He has progressed to producing *Thunderball*—Ian Fleming's story (and Kevin's) starring Sean Connery, which is reported to have already taken over fifty million dollars at the box office. Kevin also fell in love and married the beautiful American heiress, Bobo Sigrist!

All those I've mentioned have made their mark in a big way. That they have done so is entirely due to their native talent and artistry—and not me. However, it is pleasant to reflect that I gave them all a push forward that sent them in the direction of the 'greats'. Most certainly, they represent a 'worth-while'.

Another 'worth-while' stands out in my memory. A wartime episode.

Before returning to England in 1940, my old friend of the Royal Flying Corps, Air Marshal W. A. (Billy) Bishop, V.C., D.S.O. (two bars), D.F.C., paid a visit to Hollywood in connection with the film of his life story which Warner Brothers were making.

Billy told me discreetly that the war situation was very difficult and the tide was running against us, Air Force-wise. Recruits for the Royal Canadian Air Force were badly needed, but he could not get a grant from Parliament for cadets' uniforms.

'Could you bring Anna to Canada so she could make some personal appearances and appeals?'

'I can do better than that,' I told Billy. 'I'll stage a live show which Canadian audiences have never seen, and take it from coast to coast. But first of all I must go to England to make a film of Amy Johnson's life. As soon as that is completed, I promise you I'll be on the first ship back.'

In carrying out my promise to Billy Bishop, nothing I have ever done has been fraught with so many difficulties or frustrations.

The first hazard was a flight from Toronto in a three-seater open plane, flown by a 'bush pilot'. Our destination was Muskoka Lake, where Bishop lived. My visit was necessary to agree upon the technical requirements of the tour, and the *Toronto Star* newspaper laid on the plane squeezing in a woman reporter to interview Anna—she almost had to sit on Anna's lap.

The bush pilot used no map and frequently crossed the main commercial route of Trans-Canada Airways, on two or three occasions missing the giant aircraft by feet only. The petrol from our tank seemed to be leaking and the smell overwhelming, but all the time the pilot had a lighted cigarette hanging from his lips!

Anna was too busy giving the interview to notice the hazards, but I saw them all and as through a magnifying glass. However, the pilot coolly put us down on the lake within a yard or so of Billy's back door where he was waiting to greet us.

Our discussion over, we faced the return ordeal—as on the following day we were booked to fly to England by clipper to make our film, and then return to Canada to cast and rehearse the tour.

Our flight from New York by clipper was memorable, in as much as Anna was the first woman to fly West to East since the war had started. All well as far as the Azores where the Atlantic clippers refuelled. The sea was running high and we hit a wave on touching down. The impact burst a petrol tank. We still had some hours to go before landing at Lisbon, and it was decided to make it. But all passengers were instructed—no smoking, and lifebelts must be worn until landing.

Not pleasant! Having flown in the R.F.C. and R.A.F., even with expert mechanics to maintain the aircraft, I was invariably in a state of 'wind-up'. But this flight proved a positive nightmare.

But we made it. Our flying time from New York to Lisbon was twenty-nine hours, or ten hours longer than I had been in the air for instruction to gain my wings in 1916.

The film of Amy Johnson completed, I cabled Billy Bishop that we were on our way back as soon as a passage could be arranged. Easier said than done. We were refused exit permits from England. 'There's a war on,' we were told. We hadn't noticed!

Our tour, so vital for his Commonwealth Training Plan, according to Bishop, was regarded as a bit of a lark by the Foreign Office.

I contacted Bishop and, within the hour, he was on the 'phone to Vincent Massey, Canadian High Commissioner in London. Massey sent for me, heard what the tour meant to the R.C.A.F. and was not amused! He 'phoned the Foreign Secretary, Ernest Bevin, and there was some very forthright talking on the part of Vincent Massey. The green light was given.

Passages were arranged for Anna and me, and we were due to sail the night she appeared on the BBC in 'Hi Gang'. (What a splendid war contribution Ben Lyon and Bebe Daniels made! As Americans they stayed on here with all the attendant dangers and shortages when they would have been fully justified and not criticised had they returned to Hollywood and plenty, with lucrative engagements galore awaiting them.)

Anna's appearance on 'Hi Gang' was almost fatal to our return to Canada. Our time-table was so tight that cancellation of her appearance on the programme was contemplated, but in confidence we divulged to Ben our problem and that Anna, after her item with him, would need to rush straight to the station to catch the train.

The programme was transmitted from the Paris Cinema, Lower Regent Street, and Ben told us he would advance Anna's spot to precede instead of follow Vic Oliver and promised he would get us away in good time—providing all went according to schedule.

But it didn't! Anna started rehearsing with Ben as soon as the band arrived and half-way through her duet with him the alert went—and in all directions. Anna and Ben carried on, but eventually the din, in one of the worst raids of the blitz, smothered all studio sounds and Ben called a halt and told everyone to get out and go to the stairs or down to the shelters. The band and most of the artists made a bee-line for the shelters in double-quick time, but with Bebe, Ben, Anna and Vic Oliver I sat on the stairs waiting for the din to subside.

It did not subside but got louder. Suddenly Bebe said, 'Ben, have you looked up?' Ben looked up. 'Holy smoke,' he cried—'no goddam roof.' We all looked up. It was true! Our 'refuge' had a sliding roof which someone had slid and failed to slide back and we could see the searchlights dancing in all directions on a dark sky illuminated by the crimson glow of countless fires. Our dash back to the recording studio was orderly but rather hurried!

However, came the 'all clear'. The programme started on time and Ben kept his word. When she finished her 'spot' the compère thanked Anna and told the studio audience and millions of listeners on the air how much they appreciated her coming and wished her 'Godspeed' on her voyage!

With security as tight as a drum and for Anna to be on her way to a ship outward-bound! All hell was let loose!

We boarded the train for Glasgow and on arrival were met by plain-clothes police, who smuggled us through the rear entrance of the hotel with strict instructions to lock our door and not to leave until called for. Meanwhile we were ravenous—but no food or drink was permitted. With Anna's face and personality so well known, no chance could be taken.

We were taken by taxi deliberately to the wrong station, changed into another taxi and found ourselves at Greenock, breathless and hungry. A special naval launch took us to the *Batory*, the notorious Polish ship, with the spies (if they existed) on the decoy train to another port.

It all sounds melodramatic and unnecessary, even in these days of James Bond, but at the time it was a very serious slip-up by the compère which no doubt had severe consequences for him.

The *Batory* and one other ship, the *Letitia*, comprised the convoy. And our Royal Navy escort was one of the forty-nine obsolete U.S. destroyers President Roosevelt mentioned to our friend, George Washington Baker. There were 3,500 R.A.F. personnel aboard the *Batory*, which usually carried about fifty passengers. Small wonder the security authorities were concerned about the indiscretion. I've often wondered why our crossing was not cancelled or postponed—it would have saved an awful lot of cloaks and daggers.

About half-way over, Anna was singing 'Alice Blue Gown' at the ship's concert with the entire 3,500 present, or so it seemed. Suddenly there was an explosion that seemed to split the ship. We'd had it, I thought.

An R.A.F. non-commissioned officer stood up and, in a voice almost as loud as the blast, shouted: 'Quiet, please!' The laugh that went up prompted the orchestra and Anna to continue.

The *Batory* had dropped a depth charge. But, in my imagination, we had been torpedoed and I then knew what it was like. Not pleasant. Could there be any more hazards?

There were! With R.A.F. personnel including some top brass aboard, we were an attractive and legitimate target for a U-boat attack. And twenty-four hours out from our port, Captain Daghakowski—an extremely fine and able sea captain who got his ship out of Gdynia after the fall of Poland—warned us that U-boats had been reported in the mouth of the St Lawrence.

Another period of intense fear followed, and we lived in our life-belts and no one went to bed. However, nothing happened and we made port in time.

For the Canadian tour, in support of Anna, I got together some top British artists in Hollywood; staged a short play by Noel Coward—*Brief Encounter;* and a TV play by Monckton Hoffe—*The Lady who wished to be known as Madame*. There were no fees for actors or authors, who willingly gave their services and material.

'I want a band,' I told Billy.

'Would the R.C.A.F. band do?' he answered.

'How many?'

'Eighty.'

'That will do,' I replied.

I called the evening 'Celebrity Parade', a coast-to-coast theatre tour of one-night stands.

With the band and a company of a hundred, the travel costs were prohibitive. So I approached the Canadian Pacific Railway. They would lay on a special train complete with restaurant cars and food—no charge!

I asked Billy Bishop to travel with us and appear at the end of the performance. He did, and 'Celebrity Parade' opened for one night in Toronto—97,500 dollars. One night Montreal—80,000 dollars. And in seven nights, Ottawa, etc., we raised 250,000 dollars, five times our target. Those who saw it considered it the best stage presentation I had ever produced, and Billy thanked us all at the final performance at Victoria in a speech which meant more than any money could buy.

With uniforms galore available, cadet recruiting shot up—and all those who participated in 'Celebrity Parade' shared a feeling with me that we had made some contribution to the war effort.

It can now be told that Billy Bishop, through his great friend Homer Smith, was recruiting for the R.C.A.F. from the Waldorf Astoria, in the heart of New York, long before Pearl Harbor! He was also responsible for the sending of instructions to all sentries patrolling the 49th Parallel that if a young, able-bodied American, who looked as if he might be interested in flying, approached, to ask no questions but to turn their backs until he was safely on Canadian soil.

Apart from being a rewarding experience, the tour gave me the opportunity of meeting and introducing to Anna two outstanding characters of World War I.

In Winnipeg, we met Group Captain Roy Brown, D.S.O., the Royal Naval Air Service pilot who was officially credited with the shooting down of the German ace, Von Richthofen.

At Patricia (Pat) Bay in Victoria, we met Group Captain 'Poppie' Pope, an extraordinary character if ever there was one. A wonderful pilot and fearless leader, his most startling 'show' was when—while suffering from acute dysentery and its attendant inconvenience, calling for a spell in the sick bay—he insisted on leading his squadron in a dog-fight with his pilot seat removed and replaced by an intimate domestic utensil.

That 'Poppie' Pope suffered stomach disorders is not to be marvelled at, since his parlour trick on guest nights was to drink the contents of every inkwell in the mess! He had given that up when we met at Pat Bay—and was then on Martinis!

Our return home was almost as adventurous as our coming out. I had to go to New York to settle the *première* of the Amy Johnson film and check the editing of *Forever and a Day* prior to its London opening. We decided to fly from our last stop of the tour at Vancouver to New York.

We put down at Seattle, where we were promptly arrested (they called it detained) for illegal entry into the United States! It was not until Billy Bishop and John Grierson, in charge of Information at Ottawa, personally phoned that we were allowed to proceed on our way.

My business in New York completed, we set off for Halifax and home. Again we were held up—we had no exit permit from the States or re-entry permit into Canada. Over the phone Billy's friend, Jack Bickell, a top Canadian industrialist, vouched for us, so we were let out and let in.

But that was not the end of our adventures. We were told to stay in our hotel at Halifax. At midnight we were picked up and taken to the docks, where we boarded a banana boat, *Cavina*, of 5,500 tons, which was carrying the bacon ration for England for a month—stored everywhere. The smell of uncooked bacon for an hour or so is bearable. But, when I asked, I was told our convoy was a seven-knot one—and the voyage would take seventeen days.

The *Cavina* usually carried ten passengers—we carried 150. We joined the convoy of forty-two ships, a wonderful sight, off New York and made for home.

A complete black-out—no one allowed out after dark, and on the second night we met mountainous seas and our ship almost stood on her beam. What with that, the smell of the bacon and my being a very poor sailor! Anna faced up to it better than I did. But as soon as it was daylight, I made a dash for the deck and fresh air.

I looked around—no convoy or escort. We were alone in the North Atlantic in a tiny ship built for the Caribbean banana trade, and a sitting duck for any U-boat. I sought out the skipper, Captain Sam Brown, a great character who had already been torpedoed three times.

'What's happened to the convoy?' I asked Sam.

'Couldn't hang about and wait for them—too bloody dangerous, so I decided to get on and leave 'em behind!'

It was some days before we caught up with them! That same night, an explosion rocked the ship. I jumped out of bed, grabbed my lifebelt and made for Anna's cabin. She was already up.

'Grab your lifebelt,' I told her. 'This is it.'

We went to our boat station where the rest of the passengers were lining up. I was not loving Billy Bishop or his Commonwealth Training Plan at this point!

Suddenly Captain Sam Brown came in and stared at us. 'What the hell are you all doing?' he bellowed.

Someone told him.

'Get back to your cabins,' he said. 'When there's trouble I'll sound the siren—and when I sound it, you'll hear it.'

I went on deck the next morning to discover the rail and part of the deck had been stove in by a giant wave. Another scare, but happily the last, and we crawled home in seventeen days as scheduled.

On looking back, a very much 'worth while', but at the time...

Anna has a most treasured souvenir of this tour and other war efforts in Canada. The inscription is simple but sincere:

ANNA NEAGLE
Canada thanks you for your generous help

Canada!
Whenever I see it in print or hear the word spoken, a face as full of

character as the Rockies themselves crowds in on the image it creates: Lord Beaverbrook.

Due no doubt to the fact that in the twenties, when I decided to produce an historical trilogy of Canada, Australia and South Africa, I visited Beaverbrook at Cherkley and I asked him if he would consider writing the screenplay of 'Canada'. A newspaper charity named by him to receive any fee he cared to mention. The amount of which I would not question.

Without giving an answer Beaverbrook started to outline the points of the story to bring out Canada's military history, starting with the storming of the Heights of Abraham, her mineral wealth, the lumber and pulp industries and her contribution to World War I, when she was the first member of the British empire to throw her hat in the ring. He seemed transported and went on at length without, of course, any interruption from me.

In the process he had virtually written the first draft of the screenplay, and I was hopeful—but although his heart was obviously with it, his numerous activities ruled out his giving the necessary time.

The picture he painted of Canada in those twenty minutes or so has remained in my mental album of events ever since.

Beaverbrook was a strange contradiction of tremendous, ruthless driving-force and a mischievous imp. I've seen both sides.

On the promenade deck of the *Queen Elizabeth*, *en route* to New York in December 1951, I spotted a lone traveller taking his constitutional. Conscious of the fact that his top editor, Tom Innes, had left the *Sunday Express* to join my production staff, I hesitated before greeting him. However, I did so with: 'Am I forgiven?', instead of the usual 'Hello'.

Beaverbrook looked at me and replied: 'Is Anna with you?'

I told him she was.

'Does she like fish?' he asked.

'Very much,' I answered.

'Dine with me tonight, Verandah Grill, eight o'clock.'

It was as well that Anna liked fish, since a whole one between two and three feet long was carried to our table by two stewards, under the watchful eye of the chief steward. It was delicious, even after the third helping. Champagne from a dark green, almost black bottle, helped it down (Dom Perignon). Anna drinks very little, two glasses at the most, but two bottles were consumed that meal.

Next day a call on our room telephone: 'Does Anna like pheasant?'

'She prefers chicken,' I replied.

'I've ordered pheasant—same time,' came the reply.

Again that champagne and again the two bottles between us, less two small glasses for Anna.

'You must have dinner with us tomorrow,' I ventured.

'It's ordered,' replied Beaverbrook, 'same time.'

'And same champagne, please,' I added.

And so for the voyage. The last night he learned we were bound for Montego Bay for two weeks' holiday.

'Good,' he said, 'I'll be there about the same time. Come up to the house and have dinner with me.'

'Thanks,' we murmured, and I added, 'Same champagne, please.'

'You really liked that?' he inquired.

I assured him I did and could he let me know . . .

'No,' he cut in, 'that's my secret, a private cuvée.'

When we landed in New York I noticed amongst our luggage a parcel which did not belong to us. Six bottles of that champagne and addressed to me!

'What can we do to return his hospitality?' I asked Anna after we arrived at Montego Bay.

The answer came soon in a telephone message from the airport. 'Just arrived. Car calling for you at seven for dinner—informal.' It was not an invitation but a command.

For the next three nights it was repeated and we had the rare experience of being alone with Beaverbrook except for his granddaughter Lady Jean Campbell, whom he adored. It was an illuminating experience because he seemed to prefer listening to Anna and me to talking himself. We found him on these occasions utterly charming and simple, and loved every minute of our time with him; and again that champagne.

Then another message. 'Mike Wardell picking you up at noon for lunch.'

Ten sat down, with Beaverbrook at the head of the table. He took stock of his guests and the mischievous imp took over as he decided to cut them all down to size. He picked on his victims at random; he dodged Anna, but had a go at me. Anna and I had been discussing Odette with one of our fellow guests and he had listened in.

'Herbert Wilcox set out to make Odette famous and he's done a good job.'

Before I realised it I snapped back: 'On the contrary Odette has made Anna and me famous.'

A moment's silence with everyone looking at Beaverbrook for his reaction. He had his eyes fixed on me and I got ready for the axe.

'Well said, Herbert,' was the unexpected reply and he then turned to his next victim, a young man at least six feet four who had eyes for no one but Jean Campbell. When Beaverbrook finished with him he looked as tall as Charlie Drake.

A most uncomfortable occasion, the more so because he had been so simple and friendly when we were alone with him. But in company the imp predominated.

One amusing moment at Montego Bay was when Beaverbrook invited Anna down to Doctor's Bay to swim. He turned up with a valet who paid great attention to his lordship's feet with powder and pomade, which were eventually covered by canvas shoes. All this because a beach fungus had been reported.

Anna, watching the proceedings, said, 'You should not wear shoes—I never do.'

Next day we arrived at his house for lunch. Beaverbrook was barefooted—so were the entire household! We conformed and removed our shoes in the hall.

The last time I saw Lord Beaverbrook he was entering the ball-room at the Dorchester on the arm of his son, Max Aitken. It was a big occasion. A dinner given by Roy Thomson celebrating Beaverbrook's eighty-sixth birthday.

He made a magnificent speech, summing up his life, without pulling any punches—having a sly dig at his host and reducing all his own great personal achievements to the apprenticeship stage. Many considered it his finest speech.

Two weeks later Beaverbrook was dead.

He was a good friend and wise counsellor.

The most fitting and gracious compliment to Lord Beaverbrook was that paid by his son Max Aitken who, following his father's death, said:

'I take this early opportunity of declaring I have renounced the title of Lord Beaverbrook. The title was earned and won by my father. He brought on it a unique distinction which belongs to him alone. Certainly in my lifetime, there will only be one Lord Beaverbrook'.

17

I am often asked the question—which film would I like to be remembered by, *Victoria the Great* or *Spring in Park Lane*? Since nine out of ten people who meet me quote one or the other, I suppose the question is a valid one.

The answer is neither. Although both gave me immense satisfaction and profit, I would like to be remembered as the man who made *Odette*. Apart from the film itself, on which I do not propose to dwell, it brought me into contact with Odette herself, a remarkable woman in every sense of the word. It also provided Anna with a story that resulted in her greatest dramatic performance, for which she won the British Film Academy's award for the best actress of the year—an award often known as an 'Oscar', after its American equivalent.

Anna and I are not given to lavishing personal praise on each other's work—on the contrary, plenty of legitimate criticism, if justified. So what I am about to put down here will surprise Anna more than anyone else reading this chapter.

Being as objective as my situation with Anna permits, I am convinced that her performance in *Odette* not only surpasses any given by an actress who has over the past forty-seven years passed through my hands, but also in my opinion compares favourably with performances given to the cinema by the great historic actresses . . . Garbo in *Queen Christina*, Katharine Hepburn in *Morning Glory*, Greer Garson in *Mrs Miniver*, Bette Davis in *Of Human Bondage*, Lillian Gish in *The White Sister*, and many others that do not come readily to mind.

As a performance, I place *Odette* above *Victoria the Great*, since there the externals of clothes and make-up eased the task, whereas Odette—with her ordinary woman's clothes, the slightest of French accents, and the burning inner spirit—was much more difficult but overwhelmingly effective.

However, even if the result would be just as gratifying, I would never ask Anna to repeat the part. Strong and healthy as she is, she came near to a complete breakdown. The emotional strain of undertaking the portrayal of such a tragic character was great enough. But to re-live, as we did, the various phases of Odette's life in the hands of the Gestapo was nerve-shattering.

The strain started on the snow-covered Semnos mountain near Annecy, where we re-enacted the scene of Peter Churchill's parachute-landing on the night of their capture.

In real life Odette, making her way up the mountain to meet Peter Churchill's plane, slipped on some rocks and broke some bones in her vertebrae. Picked up by the Gestapo the same night, and taken to Annecy gaol, she received no medical attention, but by a miracle the vertebrae eventually healed themselves.

In the film, at the very same spot where Odette injured her back, Anna had to rush towards the camera to meet Peter (Trevor Howard) as he descended in his parachute. The scene had to be acceptable first time as it was virgin snow and any retake would have shown the footsteps.

It was a night scene and, as Anna rushed forward, I suddenly saw a collection of camera boxes hidden from her sight. She was racing towards them. I shouted to her to stop but, so apparently lost was she in the scene, that she rushed on and fell on the steel boxes with a deadly thud, and lay still. At the very same spot Odette had injured her spine.

Although Anna was obviously hurt, I was furious she had not stopped when I shouted to her.

'Didn't you hear me shout?' I bawled at her.

'Yes,' she said.

'Why didn't you stop?' I asked her.

'Did you get the scene?' she replied.

I told her we did.

'No more takes?'

'No.'

'Help me up. I'm only bruised a bit.'

Back in England I noticed her walk was erratic and one-sided. Anna was on the verge of a nervous breakdown.

We consulted our friend, the osteopath Hugh Dempster, who discovered some vertebrae were injured and her nervous system badly disorganised. It took weeks of solid rest and doing nothing before Anna fully recovered. Not for a dozen 'Oscars'—Hollywood or British —would I ever expose her to such hazards and strain again.

The tension started the moment I had bought the film rights of the book. Anna felt it needed a French actress, preferably one who had experienced living in occupied France. I tried Michèle Morgan but she was not interested. Then, as an alternative to a French woman, I approached Ingrid Bergman, who read the book and declined it with the observation that she did not think cinema audiences would be interested in so harrowing a story.

I then asked Odette herself for suggestions. She told me she had agreed to the sale of the rights (incidentally she did not benefit financially herself) since she understood Anna would be playing her part. I explained Anna's point of view but Odette was firm.

Could she meet Anna? She did—and Anna agreed to play Odette! Thank heavens Odette persuaded her, for I cannot visualise any actress giving a more gripping and sincere performance.

Odette herself is a remarkable women, very beautiful despite everything, a great character with a realistic French outlook but full of compassion. Like Nurse Cavell, she has 'no hatred or bitterness towards anyone'—not even the Germans.

'I failed when I was taken by the Gestapo,' she would say. 'What they did, horrible though it was, formed part of their work to get information, whatever the price.'

Although she didn't hate the Germans, she despised them. When they pulled out her toe-nails, ran a hot poker down her spine, starved her in a dark cell for ten days, she prayed for the strength to bear it, but always held on to the thought that, when the pain was unbearable, she would lose consciousness. It was courage without parallel, but that was her viewpoint. To have given away her friends would have been something she could not have lived with all her life. To have developed T.B., and to have defied all the theories by seeing it cured in a dungeon at Ravensbruck without fresh air, light or good food, is proof that her spirit and faith in God could match any man-made medical help.

'I would even have given telephone numbers—if it had been me,' I told Odette. 'I could not have stood what you did.'

'You never know what you can stand until you're tested,' she replied, 'and you'd be all right, I'm sure.'

I was not so sure.

When the King invested her with the George Cross at Buckingham Palace, Odette thanked him and said: 'May I accept this also on behalf of my comrades who have not returned' –her twelve FANY friends who lost their lives.

It was a strange turn of fate that thirteen women in the FANY Corps, who were engaged on Special Operations Executive work, were taken prisoner by the Germans, but only Odette was sentenced to death. Yet she was the only one to return alive! The others either died or were executed.

At St Paul's, Knightsbridge, the FANY monument to Odette's friends, including Violette Szabo and Noor Inayat Khan—both posthumously awarded the George Cross, is seldom without fresh flowers from those who still remember.

Before writing the screenplay, I decided to take Odette, Anna, Peter Churchill and the script-writer Warren Chetham Strode on a complete reconnaissance, covering the ground of Odette's activities.

What happened during out journey was sometimes more dramatic than the film itself. We stayed at the Hôtel de la Poste near Annecy, in Haute-Savoie, where Odette and Peter were arrested. Through the proprietor, we learned much of the S.O.E. activities during the occupation. We also met some of their French Resistance comrades, many of whom almost passed out when they saw Odette and Peter alive and well—having imagined both were dead. The reunions were a joy indeed, and the courage of the French partisans, particularly those of the Maquis, must have been of the highest order.

To Marseilles, Arles, Cassis, we went . . . and finally Paris.

One night, we visited the house in the Avenue Foch where Odette was tortured. In those days it was Gestapo Headquarters. Now it was the residence of a financial tycoon. We went up to the torture room and Odette calmly took us back again to the grim happenings. Even the stove was there where the poker was made red hot.

In adjoining rooms on the top floor and unoccupied by the present tenants, prisoners were brought several times before being questioned, and the thin walls permitted everything that took place in the torture room to be overheard, including the screams of the victims. The softening-up process, they called it. Many prisoners escaped torture by giving information after a number of visits to these rooms.

In the one where Odette waited on several occasions, a wardrobe stood against the wall and Odette suggested we move it. Her instinct was right. On the wall behind were messages scribbled in pencil or by finger-nails. Some messages were to relations at home. Some were messages of defiance to the Gestapo; some pathetic patriotic messages.

We started to walk down the main staircase. I felt sick, and needed to reach the fresh air and a stiff cognac.

Throughout the entire journey, and even in the torture room, Odette had been calmly objective. But, as she started to walk down the main stairs, her feet hurt and she walked on her heels—as she had done when she came out of the torture room without toe-nails. She apologised—and for the first time she was near tears as she re-lived that terrible occasion.

Out in the Avenue Foch, I could hardly think straight. I was overwhelmed with emotion. 'I can't go on with it,' I told Anna. I meant it, and could appreciate Ingrid Bergman's viewpoint. 'If Odette can see it through, I'm sure we can,' replied Anna, although I've no doubt she was feeling much the same as I was.

On the Sunday morning, it had been arranged by the British embassy for us to visit Fresnes Prison, where Odette and Peter were taken from Annecy gaol. A grim prison, Fresnes was reserved for the worst criminals. But the sun shining brilliantly and shafts of sunshine through the long windows gave the main hall a cathedral-like atmosphere. The governor received us, embraced Odette and Peter, and then proceeded to give us V.I.P. treatment and a tour of the prison.

Outside one cell, Peter stopped: 'This was mine.' He turned to the governor. 'Can I go inside for a moment?'

The governor explained that two desperate prisoners were inside but if Peter wanted to, he could. Peter did, so a warder opened the door and he went in, closing it after him. The governor looked through the spy-hole.

'He's shaking hands with them, and giving them cigarettes.'

After a few minutes, during which the governor kept his eye glued to the spy-hole, Peter came out and moved off without saying a word.

The governor asked Odette if she would visit the kitchens and taste the food served to the prisoners. We all went down to the kitchens. A strange sight it was to see Odette, here before when under sentence of death, now doing a V.I.P. tour and tasting the quality of the prisoners' food, which she pronounced excellent.

On the way out, Odette turned to the governor.

'Did they ever catch Roger?' (the stool-pigeon who betrayed Odette and many other resistance workers).

We were in the main hall with galleries on all four sides up to the roof.

'If you look up and to your left, you will find Roger looking down at you,' said the governor. Odette looked up, but said nothing. Peter did not look. Nor did we. The governor did.

'He thought you were dead, and that no one else could testify against him. He's been having an easy time running the library. It won't be so easy for him now.'

We left Fresnes. Shortly afterwards Roger left the prison for the last time.

Throughout the film, Odette acted as our technical adviser. And, of course, Colonel Maurice Buckmaster, head of the French section of S.O.E., playing his real-life part in the film, was at hand to see that every detail was correct.

Odette was never emotional, but realistically practical—until the shooting of the torture scene. Anna was magnificent in this scene, where she was being examined by the Gestapo. And when the torture started, I saw Odette was crying. I stopped the cameras.

'Odette, dear,' I said, 'you've been so wonderfully helpful and we've rehearsed the scene. So would you like to go to your dressing-room as this might be too much for you.'

'I'm not thinking about myself,' she told me. 'I'm so sorry for Anna having to go through all this.'

The film completed, it set Fleet Street and Wardour Street on fire.

Through a friend, I approached Buckingham Palace. The King sent word that he would break precedent and attend the *première* with the Queen.

An incredible *première*. The customary presentations preceded the performance. It was for charity, and 100 guineas was paid for every seat in the royal circle at the Plaza. Anna and I sat immediately behind the King and Queen.

At the end of the film there was not a sound. No applause. Just silence. I was stunned and just couldn't believe it. After a second or two, the applause started and went on and on. No crescendos, just steady applause. The lights went up, and the Queen turned to the King and held out her hand to him. He gave her his handkerchief.

Contrary to custom, Lord Cromer whispered to me to bring Anna, Odette and Peter out as the King wanted to have a word with us. The Queen made for Anna and took her hand. 'Thank you so much—your performance was wonderful.' Then, turning to Odette: 'And thank you for having made it possible.'

'Thank you, Ma'am,' said Odette. 'And on behalf of my friends who are not here.'

The King, talking to Peter Churchill, looked at Odette and asked: 'How much can the body take before the spirit cracks?'

'In what way, sir?' asked Peter.

'Just look at her! She's so lovely after all she has been through.'

He must have been considering his own case, for not long afterwards the news of his fatal illness was made known.

A few weeks later we were invited to the royal garden party at Buckingham Palace. The Lord Chamberlain singled out Anna and me.

'The King would like a word with you,' he told us.

With over 6,000 guests present, we felt very flattered indeed to be two of the favoured ones.

That meeting with the King was memorable. At the *première* of *Odette* I had told him of Anna's mishap on the Semnos mountain. He made a bee-line for Anna and held out his hand.

'Are you feeling better?' he asked.

Anna told him she was.

'Fully recovered?'

'Well, not quite, sir.'

'I've been thinking about the film,' said the King to Anna. 'I can understand how in a play you can progress and build up to a climax. But in a film, doing short snippets and out of sequence—it sounds like a jigsaw puzzle—very difficult.'

'I'm glad to hear you say that, sir,' replied Anna. 'Film acting is much more difficult than the theatre since one misses immediate audience reaction.'

'Playing an emotional scene and starting so early in the morning,' the King went on, 'Supposing you don't feel like acting?'

'It's a matter of discipline, sir,' I ventured.

The King turned to Anna. 'A hard taskmaster, eh?'

And Anna, in front of the hundreds of people who were looking on, put her hand on my arm and said: 'Oh no, sir! He's wonderful!'

The King's laugh was hearty, and Anna and I joined in. Turning to me he asked: 'How's it doing?'

'Thanks to your presence, sir, it was a record *première*,' I replied.

The King waved that away and said: 'No—not that. How's it doing with the *real* people—at the box office?'

That the King, with so many other more important problems, should be so interested and have such an insight into film production, astonished me.

The *première* of *Odette* triggers off a thought of all my *premières*—which one remains most vividly and warmly in my mind?

Certainly the *première* of *Victoria the Great* at the Venice Festival was unforgettable in every respect. I shall never forget arriving at the station with Anna, and being told by Neville Kearney of the Federation of British Industries that we had been awarded the Gold Cup of all Nations, the first ever for a British film.

I shall never forget the cocktail parties aboard H.M.S. *London* and her Italian counterpart, as officers fraternised and exchanged ships as hosts. Dr Giannini, the American banker, was lachrymose as he said to Anna and me: 'Your film has done what the statesmen and politicians could not do. Brought both sides together. That's the road to peace.' (Within a short time, the same two crews were knocking hell out of each other!)

I shall never forget the showing of the film on the huge screen in the open-air Lido theatre, the gentle lapping of the Adriatic waves merging into the Elgar background music.

I shall never forget the open-air banquet and dance for five hundred guests that rounded off the evening, every table garlanded with tuber roses, the heavy scent of which was almost overpowering.

I shall never forget Anna dancing with Alfieri, Count Volpe and other top Fascist leaders, and with Grandi, the Italian ambassador in London...

I shall never forget asking the head of our distribution company whom we should thank for the hospitality before leaving.

I shall never forget his answer: 'Didn't Kearney tell you? Anna and you are the hosts!'

I shall never forget looking at the bill. It was £1,800!

Definitely an unforgettable *première*.

The Hollywood opening of *Victoria the Great* was, to a lesser degree, also unforgettable. It was at the Four Star Theatre, which was honoured by the British consul and his wife, Francis and Mary (now Sir Francis and Lady) Evans. He was later British consul general in New York, British ambassador to the Argentine and the first British ambassador to Israel.

Although not invited, Charlie Chaplin sat immediately in front of me with Constance Collier. The royalist theme did not please Charlie and he kept up a running barrage of comment which, in my nervous state—this being my first big *première* in Hollywood—almost drove me from the theatre.

During one ceremonial scene, Chaplin turned to Constance and said (in a voice which sounded to me like thunder): 'Whilst that was happening, I was in the workhouse.'

Mary Evans, the most tranquil and elegant lady imaginable, said afterwards: 'I wanted to hit him.' I nearly *did*. Since he was not invited, but was the escort of a guest, it was not too much to expect a silent protest against what the film stood for. The sequel came soon and was rather amusing.

The following evening Louella Parsons gave a 'Welcome to Hollywood' dinner to Anna and me. On my right sat Constance Collier

52. A good friend and wise counsellor: Lord Beaverbrook, by Walter Sickert, R.A.

53. At the *première*: Anna and Michael Wilding talking to Princess Elizabeth and Edwina Mountbatten. It was the night before the King's operation.

54. The royal *première* of *The Lady with a Lamp*, 1951.

55. Elizabeth Taylor and Michael Wilding.

56. A presentation cigarette-box marking the raising of £50,000 for the Royal College of Nursing.

57. Anna presenting the crest of H.M.S. *Amethyst* to Commander J. S. Kerens, R.N., D.S.O., after the making of *Yangtse Incident*—later to prove disastrous. On Commander Kerens' left is Richard Todd.

58. T. E. Lawrence with Captain Liddell Hart, military adviser on *Ross*.

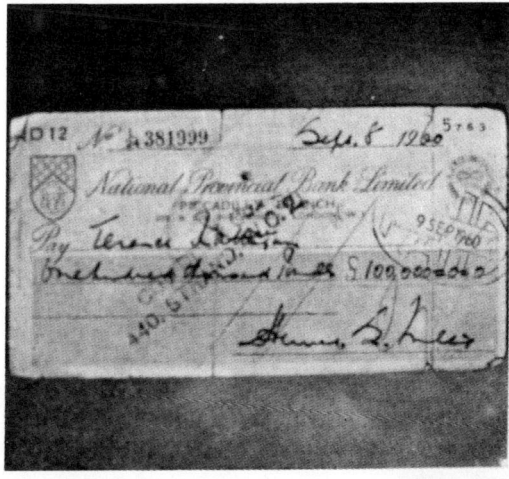

59. My unhappy £100,000 cheque to Terence Rattigan for the film rights of *Ross*, which I never made.

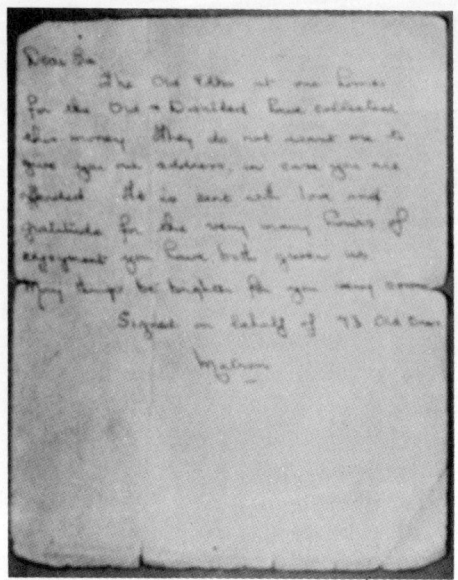

60 The letter enclosing £5 which I received following the news of my bankruptcy.

61. The first day out of bankruptcy.

62. Anna in our living-room in Park Lane.

whom I had never met. During dinner I told her how my evening was marred, if not ruined, by Chaplin. She asked if I had anything to do with the film, and I told her I directed and produced it.

'I'm sorry, he was very naughty,' she said. 'But Charlie is a law unto himself. He is a genius. He has no time or respect for the conventions. But never mind, you must forget it. Meeting you has been worth it all. I've always wanted to meet you. I so adored your *Thirty-Nine Steps*' she gushed—and went on to mention all the films that Hitchcock ever made!

I nearly told her my name was Wilcox and not Hitchcock. But I didn't. I wonder if she ever found out...

For high drama—the *première* of *The Lady with a Lamp* was an easy first.

Lady Mountbatten, as dedicated to nursing as Florence Nightingale herself, was launching an appeal for the Royal College of Nursing—objective £500,000. I suggested that instead of a London *première* I would arrange simultaneous *premières* throughout the British empire—ten in all.

The idea was warmly received, and T.R.H. Princess Elizabeth and Prince Philip consented to attend the London *première* at the Warner Theatre.

In advance we heard the result was overwhelmingly successful and beyond our wildest expectations. It was a great occasion, in which London led the field a few minutes ahead of any other capital.

The film was due to be shown at 8.15 p.m. By 6 o'clock, Leicester Square was packed with a gathering estimated by the police at 25,000.

At 7 o'clock precisely, Anna, Michael and I arrived at the theatre, and a roar went up that must have been heard at Buckingham Palace—where our royal visitors were due to leave at 7.45 p.m. With other principals and executives, we lined up in the upstairs lounge for the customary presentations, over which Lady Mountbatten presided.

At 7.15 p.m. a royal car arrived and two officials stepped out. They hurried into the theatre. The crowd had started to cheer as the car approached but suddenly became silent, as though sensing something was amiss.

Edwina Mountbatten was called aside by the officials. The King was very ill—our royal visitors might not be attending.

How it got to them no one knows, but the news had reached the waiting crowd. A long sustained murmur, and then silence. Meanwhile, we remained lined up and waited, having been told the news by Lady Mountbatten. It was decided to inform the crowd at 8 o'clock, and start the film on time.

At 7.45, Lady Mountbatten was called to the telephone. Her husband was at the other end. Princess Elizabeth and Prince Philip were coming and would be on time. Edwina hurried downstairs to receive them, and it became evident to the waiting people what was happening. When she took up her position at the theatre entrance, a murmur of relief went up.

A few minutes before 8 o'clock, Her Royal Highness and Prince Philip arrived, and he helped her out of the car. An incredible thing then—not a sound nor a cheer. There must have been an instinctive telepathic feeling that this was no time for cheers.

Princess Elizabeth, as she ascended the stairs in a glorious white dress and carrying yellow roses, looked lovely beyond description and serenely happy. Not a care in the world, one would have thought, as she exchanged an apt word with the twenty or so who were presented.

The film over, Their Royal Highnesses had a few minutes with Anna and me. 'What a fighter she (Florence Nightingale) was,' she said to Anna.

As they bade us goodnight, Anna ventured: 'I do hope the news will be better, Ma'am.'

'Thank you,' she replied.

Then that crowd again. Not a sound as they entered their car, but as it started a roar went up that would have done justice to Hampden Park. A token of appreciation of dedicated and gracious people—my hat went off to that sensitive, understanding crowd.

The *première* was on a Saturday, and the Sunday newspapers carried a big front page picture of Anna being received by Princess Elizabeth. Over it, a banner line extending across the whole page: THE KING: AN OPERATION.

Before they left Buckingham Palace, the royal couple knew that the operation would take place within an hour or so. From the picture reproduced, one can appreciate the magnificent character and courage of Her Royal Highness.

Before leaving the *première*, Edwina Mountbatten invited Anna and me to have lunch at Wilton Crescent. The *premières* had realised £50,000 or 10% of the total target from all sources.

After a delightful lunch with the Mountbattens, she presented us with an antique cigarette-box with a simple inscription, a photograph of which is reproduced.

I took advantage of the occasion by asking Mountbatten some

questions about India, since I had been approached to consider film production and the sale of my films there. As on every subject, he was intensely interested and, when we left at 5 o'clock, I had a vivid picture of the Indian scene from its last viceroy. That he gave me three hours of his time when other calls must have needed his personal attention is a gesture I shall not readily forget.

Odette, with the 'real people', was our record film for profit, and represented the peak of the years of plenty. Rather dangerously so, for it seemed to me that the pattern was permanent. And I behaved accordingly. None of my production team was ever 'laid off'. Fifty-two weeks a year, whether working or not, their pay packets were there—and not without serious thought. But measured by the methods of other companies—even the giants—it was quixotic on my part.

But I regarded my production team from top to bottom as the finest in the industry all of whom played an integral part in our overall success. And the profits were rolling in anyway.

This period of too much success was probably one of the reasons for the setbacks of a year or two later. I also think I became a little too cock-sure of being able to turn out hit after hit without an intervening failure. I was also too optimistic.

For instance, at the height of the most prosperous period, I had a 'phone call from Isaac Wolfson, the genius heading Great Universal Stores.

'Herbert,' he said, in his strong Scottish voice, 'I'm in trouble. Will you and Anna come and have dinner with us?'

Isaac Wolfson in trouble! With his millions and his outstanding business genius!

After dinner, Isaac told me about his 'trouble'. He and Lord Kemsley owned a television station covering Manchester and the Midlands. They were concerned over top management. Would I come in and take over?

'I'm not your man, Isaac,' I told him.

'Why not?' he asked.

'I know nothing about television,' I answered.

'But with your film experience you can learn.'

'Not at your expense. I beg of you not to press it.'

'But you can write your own ticket for salary and we'll allot you a big block of shares,' he went on.

I was firm in my refusal. After all, I did not want the money and

I was on top of the film world. And remember that this offer was made before we knew how the British viewers would react to commercial TV. I had serious doubts about its acceptability! And told Isaac so. I also asked why he wanted to become involved in a new, untried medium, when he had such a magnificent and ever-expanding enterprise which demanded his whole time and thought.

'I believe commercial TV is going to be very big and very profitable,' he replied.

'Well, I don't,' were my fatal words.

I told Isaac of my meeting only the previous day with Harley Drayton, and his considerable problem with Associated Rediffusion—the estimate for which to launch and turn the corner was one million pounds. Up to the time of our meeting they had spent nearly three million pounds, and Rothermere had decided to pull out and sell his holdings to Drayton.

Furthermore Drayton told me of the teething troubles of Granada and ATV, despite both stations being operated by two outstanding and widely experienced leaders of the entertainment world, Sidney Bernstein and Lew Grade.

Isaac listened and was impressed.

'What would you advise me to do, Herbert?' he asked.

'Cut your losses and get out,' I answered.

Whether or not it was because of my advice I don't know, but Isaac Wolfson and Lord Kemsley pulled out. A.B.C. stepped in and took over the station, and after the first year the profits have averaged several millions per year.

My lack of vision, and unwise pitting of my opinion against that of Isaac Wolfson, has cost me personally well over a million pounds.

Some time later, with success for commercial TV assured, I was with Roy Thomson (now Lord Thomson), whose mercurial progress in the newspaper world now owes much to his initial success in Scottish TV. Roy told me he was curious as to why I had not jumped into TV at the outset, and I told him the sad story of Isaac Wolfson. He looked at me and said: 'I suppose you feel pretty badly about it, Herbert?'

I told him I did.

His eyes twinkled as he went on: 'Don't feel too badly—you only made two mistakes. Not going in yourself and advising Isaac to get out!'

But Isaac himself, although having missed several millions, has never reproached me.

This was undoubtedly my greatest business error. I should also have remembered the advice of C. M. Woolf: 'Stay where the money is, Herbert.'

Before leaving this sad episode, a word about Isaac Wolfson. Apart from his fantastic business mind which, of course, is common knowledge, he has a glorious sense of humour and can tell stories, mostly against himself, as wittily as Monty Woolley or Robert Benchley. Had the call of the City been less strong, the stage might have been enriched by an outstanding comedian.

Here endeth spring and the years of plenty.

18

And then came autumn and the lean years.

It started with the failure and reconstruction of British Lion Film Corporation.

Since we were grossing, with our films distributed by British Lion, approximately a million pounds per annum—on which they received 50% of the profits plus distribution fees—Anna and I bought up as many shares as our cash reserves permitted. Over 400,000 shares in all.

Unfortunately for our investment, other producers were losing as much and more for British Lion as we were making. The net result? Insolvency.

The Government stepped in and advanced £600,000 but also wiped out, without a penny of compensation, the shareholdings existing at that time. Of these, over £100,000 represented the investment of Anna and myself. Not a bad start to any disaster.

The second stage was the attitude of the banks.

Ours was an American bank from which, in the days of the late Giannini brothers, I had borrowed and repaid with interest over seven million pounds. They, as nominees, had purchased most of the British Lion shares for us and had granted an overdraft against the security of the shares. Now that these shares had been rendered valueless, the bank—not unnaturally—called in our overdraft of approximately £50,000.

Then came another dramatic setback.

I decided to produce *Yangtse Incident*—the story of the escape down the Yangtse of the frigate, H.M.S. *Amethyst*, after she had been shelled by the Communists and driven on to a mud-bank, an episode of British naval history that thrilled the world at the time.

I had American financial partners, R.K.O. for England and an American group for the U.S.A., and a great script by Eric Ambler. I needed, of course, naval co-operation and this was readily forthcoming. My reputation as producer-director of *Victoria the Great*, *Odette* and *The Lady with a Lamp* stood me in good stead. I got as high as seeing the First Sea Lord, Earl Mountbatten.

'You can count on the full co-operation of the Navy,' he informed me.

'Thank you. First of all, I want to borrow *Amethyst*.'

'Afraid that's impossible,' he told me. 'She's on her way to the ship-breakers.'

'She hasn't left Devonport yet,' I answered, 'but is cocooned.' He looked a little surprised.

I explained that I had engaged Commander Kerans, D.S.O., who had actually taken *Amethyst* down the Yangtse, and had sent him on a recce to Plymouth. He was my informant.

Mountbatten picked up his receiver, and in a few minutes told me I was right. The actual ship would be placed at my disposition and would be de-cocooned at once. The smile on that charming face of his indicated his appreciation and not irritation at my contradicting the First Sea Lord on the whereabouts of one of his vessels.

Commander Kerans was an extraordinary character. He was in constant consultation with Eric Ambler and myself on the events and, of course, the vernacular of the Royal Navy.

'We all know what happened,' said Ambler one day. 'But what I'd like to know is what were your thoughts when you were deputed to do the job?'

Kerans' answer was the quintessence of naval understatement. 'Well, I was at Chunking—the captain of *Amethyst* had been killed—and I was sent up to take command. "She's stuck in the mud," I said to myself. "Better get up to her, get her off the mud and get her down to the open sea!"'

Not very helpful to a scriptwriter, but very much to the point.

Of the many exciting incidents attending the production of *Yangtse Incident*, I shall always remember Kerans on board, with the ship listing badly to starboard, taking the microphone from the director Michael Anderson and shouting: 'Doesn't matter what your job is—get off the ship on to the tugs and take the cameras with you—ask no questions—and be bloody quick about it.'

In minutes the decks were cleared and Kerans gave instructions for some tanks to be flooded. *Amethyst* slowly righted herself and settled down on an even keel.

In my desire to secure absolute authenticity, I had requested an explosives contingent from H.M.S. *Vernon* to lay live charges that could be electrically detonated. The result was magnificent, but one charge had drifted towards *Amethyst*, settled under a raft and when detonated could not explode upwards, but was forced into the plates of *Amethyst*, which were almost paper-thin. The water poured in, causing her to list. And that is where Kerans took command and adjusted matters by flooding the opposite tanks.

Had she gone down, the damage would have been £500,000. As it was, it cost the underwriters only £3,500. Kerans was given a pink gin! I must admit it was a double.

For some time after the *première*, which I shall deal with later, Mountbatten—when referring to or introducing me at a gathering—would invariably say in his breezy, attractive manner: 'This is Herbert Wilcox, the man who nearly did what the Communists failed to do—sink *Amethyst*.'

Production was going according to schedule with scenes on *Amethyst*, anchored in the Orwell river, when a motor boat approached and through a megaphone the skipper called:

'Will Mr Herbert Wilcox report to his solicitors in London—at once.'

I was having a pink gin with Michael Anderson and Richard Todd at the time. Finishing the drink, I rushed off and up to London to learn that the bank would not accept the guarantee of £150,000 of R.K.O. London, unless it was supported by its parent company in New York. This support was not forthcoming. I had already spent £70,000 of the £150,000, so could count on no more from the bank.

I decided on a bold course. I saw Arthur Jarratt of British Lion and, in conjunction with the National Film Finance Corporation, switched distribution. All this in twenty-four hours, so that production was not held up. But what a scare I had, with visions of an unfinished film and *Amethyst* in mid-stream.

Excitement ran high on the River Orwell ('exactly like the Yangtse,' declared Kerans) when word came through from the Admiralty that H.M.S. *Essex*, also engaged on the production, had to leave without delay for Egypt where Nasser was making a nuisance of himself. *Essex* was needed by us to 'double' for *Amethyst* and simulate the run down the river, without which the film could not be completed.

I appealed to Whitehall in vain, and then called a meeting of all concerned, as we would have to attempt to shoot the run as *Essex* steamed out at full speed for Egypt. It would have to be done in one take, the captain of H.M.S. *Essex* informed us, and on his way out at that.

Never was a naval battle better planned. Michael Anderson, a brilliant director, assembled all concerned including the pukka naval officers. Everything was set, explosives were timed to go off at intervals of seconds, the speed of *Essex* fixed, and four cameras with synchronised watches and radio contact set up with Anderson in charge of all signal buttons.

Essex had to get full steam up by 10 a.m. to be at her Mediterranean rendezvous on time. Early to bed the night before was an order and on the job at 6 a.m.

To my horror a black fog descended over the Orwell and we could not even see *Essex* from the shore less than forty yards away. I consulted our head cameraman, Gordon Dines. No cameraman would, of course, think of photographing an invisible destroyer at speed in a black fog.

'Not to worry,' said Gordon, himself a commander in the navy during World War II. 'Signal *Essex* to fire one round when she starts down-stream, and ask the captain to keep her at twenty knots.'

Dines gave orders for all cameras to fix certain filters and, dead on time, *Essex* fired the warning round and soon was steaming down at speed, constant fire coming from her guns and lighting up the black fog with bursts of flame. For fifteen minutes, we followed the flashes and then *Essex* was on her way to pay her respects to Nasser.

Live charges had been laid by the explosive experts of H.M.S. *Vernon* covering the entire distance from the Orwell at Harwich to the open sea—a matter of five miles or so. H.M.S. *Essex* had to run this gauntlet in black fog! Drifting had brought some charges when detonated within a few feet of her.

The captain of *Essex* sent a signal to me that was not quite so friendly as our exchange of greetings at the cocktail and dinner-party I had given to him and his officers the previous night. Most certainly it would not have been accepted for transmission by Western Union!

The suspense in waiting for the laboratory report was intense. At all events I thought it was that or nothing.

'That' turned out to be one of the most exciting shots I have ever seen on the screen. The *Essex* just visible, her guns belching white and yellow fire and always in the centre of the screen. It was a great tribute to Anderson and Dines. Most directors and cameramen would have thrown in their hands.

When Lord Mountbatten saw the finished film of *Yangtse Incident* to approve its exhibition, he was so enthusiastic that he asked in what way the Admiralty could show their appreciation.

'A naval *première* with the Lords of the Admiralty in mess kit,' I requested.

'It shall be done,' he answered.

'With Prince Philip?' I asked.

He shook his head. 'He's on his way back from his tour with the Queen and only has one evening off.'

'We'll make it that evening,' I told him.

Mountbatten said he would see if he could arrange it. He did! As a result, we had the most extraordinary *première* with the Lords of the Admiralty led by Prince Philip.

Afterwards—Mountbatten gave instructions that a print of the film was to be sent to every naval establishment and, before each new course, was to be shown to all attending. He described it as: 'A film that shows without frills how an ordinary seaman behaves under stress and adversity.'

A great achievement, of which I am very proud, *Yangtse Incident*. It was selected for showing at the Cannes Festival, and Anna and I went over with a contingent to attend the showing. Once again through Lord Mountbatten, the Navy sent the cruiser H.M.S. *Birmingham* to show the flag in honour of the film.

The night of the showing was memorable. A dinner of top naval brass at the Carlton Hotel, then on to the cinema. At the end, the audience came out—having seen H.M.S. *Amethyst* on the screen—to see H.M.S. *Birmingham* fully illuminated and floodlit, with the sound of the film guns still in their ears. It was an effect Cecil B. de Mille would have given his birthright to get.

Why then does this film come into the lean years? In this way:

Our distribution company, British Lion, headed by Captain Sir Arthur Jarratt, was as enthusiastic about the film as the First Sea Lord. He gave instructions that it must be booked to record figures, however long it took.

The London *première* was on 1st April, 1957, and to give all his salesmen maximum time to achieve record results throughout the country, he set the release date for October and confidently assured me I could assume a profit of £400,000. It seemed the turning-point of all my problems.

Rigidly the distributors refused to accept early playing time. Meanwhile another naval film, *The Battle of the River Plate*, was completed, shown, and rushed out without delay. In my opinion, it was an inferior film to *Yangtse Incident* but it was still good at that and—following the *Amethyst* publicity—scooped the market.

By October, the edge and excitement had been stripped from our film and audience attendance fell far short of expectations. Instead of £400,000 profit, I have, at the time of writing, still not recovered the cost of the film. So one year's work went for nothing—except glory.

And then, Arthur Jarratt and British Lion parted company. This was indeed a blow.

Arthur Jarratt had complete confidence in me as a producer and director, and I in him as a distributor. We had the same views on entertainment and, if we didn't see eye to eye on an idea, it was out by mutual consent. Since I worked largely on hunches, it needed someone of Jarratt's immediate reaction to harness my imagination.

In one case, I was taking Anna to Ireland for a short holiday before starting my next film—a Joseph Conrad story. I read the first outline of the script whilst *en route* from Holyhead to Dublin. It was magnificent but grim. We were in the middle of a gay glamorous period with Anna and Michael top of the box office polls.

I told Anna my misgivings. 'Why do it?' she asked.

'We've spent quite a lot on it already.'

'Well, you won't get it back if you make a flop and you've no confidence.'

No answer to that one. I wandered off for a walk, stopped short and turned back to the hotel. A call to Jarratt.

'I should certainly switch if that's the way you feel.'

I told him my idea.

'Much better at this time,' he said. 'It's a deal. Get something down on paper and let me have it to show them.'

'Them' were Sir John Reith and the Board of the National Film Finance Corporation. What I wrote in forty-eight hours amazed Sir John. That he could read it at all amazed me. For when I write at speed, my brain is away to a flying start. And, as I always write in longhand, the problem is for anyone—sometimes myself—to know what it is all about.

I invariably think in cinematic picture images rather than words, and the pictures sometimes get little or no benefit from the words. In this case I had written the entire outline in forty-eight hours, so the handwriting must have reflected the stampede.

'Have you read this stuff Wilcox has written?' Sir John asked Jarratt.

'No,' answered Jarratt.

'And you've agreed to finance this without reading it?' asked the astonished Reith.

'Sir John, I viewed finished films for thirty years and still had difficulty in deciding whether to book them or not. Don't ask me to judge a treatment or even a screenplay before the film is made. I rely on the producer and his record, and I wouldn't attempt to pass judgment on anything submitted by experts like Carol Reed, Korda or Wilcox.'

'Extraordinary,' replied Sir John, 'But this is sheer rubbish—this *Spring in Park Lane*, as he calls it.'

It took £1,600,000 at the box office in this market alone, and still holds the attendance record for any British film—a record which can never be beaten now that 2,000 cinemas have been closed. If I had made the same film today, with entertainments tax removed and Eady money (the British film bonus) added, the United Kingdom result alone would have shown a profit of nearly a million pounds. Poor Sir John. I bear no grudge. I merely apologise that my handwriting did not reflect the potential!

The reverse of the medal was Jarratt's turning down of a subject I had submitted.

'I don't like it, Herbert,' he said, 'and I hope you don't make it. But if you do, don't ask me to put it out.'

I told him at once I would not make it.

'Got anything else in mind?' he asked.

I told him I had a vague idea of an epic embracing an English family and house, and proceeded to outline the story. Half-way through, he stopped me. 'It's mine,' he said, and we shook hands. It was *The Courtneys of Curzon Street*, starring Anna and Michael.

One story of my association with Arthur Jarratt is worth recording. It was because of *The Courtneys of Curzon Street* that Jarratt approached the late Harley Drayton, the eminent City financier, to advance £250,000 against the security of the film. Since it soon paid off, and revealed to Drayton that the entertainment world was a new medium of activity for him, he moved into British Lion and eventually became chairman. And a wonderful chairman he was.

An extraordinary man, Harley Drayton. A very hard business-man, but a man of compassion and inflexible principles, who understood the imponderables in our industry and the elements that could bring big results.

Of all the financiers I have met, Harley Drayton, Sir John Keeling and Lionel Fraser stand out most vividly in my mind. They seemed to reflect the legendary attributes of the City of London financier: integrity—conscience—principle—and imagination. I've also met some others!

None of the trio I have selected showed any external signs of the wear and tear of their pursuit of profit. Harley Drayton would, in film parlance, be perfectly cast as a country squire and a lover of farming, which he was. Less likely, though, would he be cast as a lover of old books, but he was, and possessed one of the finest collections in the country. Sir John Keeling would be the casting director's dream as a benign Chancellor of King's College, Cambridge; whilst Lionel Fraser looked about the handsomest and best-dressed actor-manager since George Alexander.

Being a devout Christian Scientist, Fraser was compassionate to a degree. I will not readily forget the one occasion on which he provided me with very substantial production finance. There was a technical hitch—he 'phoned and asked me if I was concerned at the delay. I had to admit I was. 'Well,' said Lionel, 'go ahead, Herbert, we will sign the contract later when I have straightened things out. You've got the money, good luck to you!'

Arthur Jarratt also supported my making of *Odette*, against the opinion of James Lawrie, who succeeded Sir John Reith at the National Film Finance Corporation.

It is as well to go back and recall that I made *Nell Gwyn* because of a glance at a music-hall bill; and *Dawn* because a shaft of sunshine lit up the word 'Dawn' as I passed Nurse Cavell's statue. These inspirational hunches and the flexibility of mind which promoted *Spring in Park Lane* and *The Courtneys of Curzon Street* are born of instinct. If analysed—or submitted to banks, accountants or distributors—the inspiration dies in the process. Because of this, what I did with Jarratt on *Spring in Park Lane* and *The Courtneys of Curzon Street* is no longer possible.

Of course, I'm not always right. I have made mistakes—many of them. But the hits outweigh them by a distance.

So, with Jarratt out, I had to seek new distribution and borrow privately, both in England and abroad, at high rates of interest. By this time, the decline of my fortunes was worsening daily. Robert Clark, the one man who could have changed the picture for me considerably, had unhappily become involved in conflict within his own company, Associated British Picture Corporation, with whom I had produced two outstanding successes, *I Live in Grosvenor Square* and *Piccadilly Incident*, whilst Robert was head of production.

Clark, like Korda, believed absolutely in British films. He was responsible for *The Dam Busters*, which is the only recent outstanding success that comes readily to mind in connection with the activities of Associated British Pictures Corporation, and Robert was sad indeed when circumstances separated him from his production interests in the industry.

As with Arthur Jarratt, Clark's dropping out of the scene was one more nail, and a big one at that, in my financial coffin.

Then, from out of the blue, came the turn of the tide when a top City finance-house offered me £200,000—primarily to produce the film of *Ross*, Terence Rattigan's play about Lawrence of Arabia which was running at the Haymarket Theatre, starring Alec Guinness. I was thrilled at the prospect for I have always admired Rattigan as a writer.

Moreover, when I was new in the British film industry, a literary agent, Raymond Savage, had brought a young author to see me with the view of producing a silent film of a book he had just completed. The young author was slight and short, about 5 ft. 3 ins. at the most and not very prepossessing. However, Raymond Savage, being a top agent, would not have brought him had he not been important.

The title of the book meant nothing to me, but Savage suggested the author roughly outline his story and relate one or two of the more spectacular incidents.

In a hesitant voice, which became stronger and deeper as he went along, the author gave me an outline of his book which I found extremely interesting but not good cinema and in spots rather sordid. In particular he told me of the homosexual advances of a Turkish chief and how in desperation one night he fought him off with what he called 'a knee kick', which resulted in the chief being disinterested in homo or any other form of sexual activity for a week or so, and the author being scourged and tortured for his attack. Since he was a British subject, masquerading as an Arab, which language he spoke like a native, his great fear was that during the torture he would cry out in English and not Arabic.

The book was *The Seven Pillars of Wisdom*—the author T. E. Lawrence.

I ventured the opinion that I could not see cinema audiences seeking entertainment being attracted to such a subject. Lawrence did not agree—neither did Savage. Lawrence told me that one day it would make an outstanding film. He failed to sway me—but how right he was.

Admittedly audience taste has changed and I have grown up. But, ironically, for some years now I had unsuccessfully endeavoured to secure the film rights, which were held by Korda. Not only the film rights of *Ross* as a stage play, but the *screenplay* of *Lawrence of Arabia*, written by Rattigan, were now available—and I had £200,000 in my banking account.

Knowing that an American production company was in the market I invited Terry Rattigan out to lunch and the conversation went something like this.

Wilcox: Are the film rights of *Ross* still available?
Rattigan: Well, they're on offer at 250,000 dollars.
(A little quick reckoning produced a figure in sterling of £85,000.)
Wilcox: If I offered you £100,000 cash, would you accept my offer?
Rattigan: You mean cash?
I assured him I did.
Rattigan: When?

I pulled out my cheque-book and made out the cheque for £100,000 (photograph shown in this book). I offered the cheque and held out my hand for a hand-shake. He shook hands but suggested the deal be completed between solicitors and accountants. It was—and announced world-wide.

I pulled out to New York to make a deal for world distribution and for casting of the name part, since Guinness considered himself too old to play it. On arrival in New York, Sam Spiegel announced *Lawrence of Arabia* and threatened to injunct me if I attempted my film.

I would have gone ahead and made *Ross*, defying Spiegel—and could have shown my film a year ahead of his since David Lean, although a great director, is very slow. However, the City wanted no part of litigation, and so I had to let the whole subject drop since no distributor would finance me with an injunction hanging over my head. Not a penny of the £100,000 did I recover.

So another year's work went for no return—and not even glory this time.

These setbacks meant that for two years my company was only kept active on borrowed money instead of income. Worse still, I was borrowing money to repay loans—a disastrous policy with an inevitable outcome.

I tried everything I knew to stop the rot. We sold Anna's beloved paintings much too soon. Although more than the capital I had borrowed had been repaid, plus handsome interest, there was still some interest outstanding and a bankruptcy petition was served upon me.

An action by an American distribution company in respect of a personal guarantee followed, which I lost. It was the last nail in my financial coffin.

A nightmare period. How I hated the early morning post. I used to wait for the postman's knock, get out of bed and collect all letters. This was primarily to protect Anna from reading any of them. I knew from the envelopes who they were from, and all would demand immediate payment. I tore them up unopened and threw the pieces into the waste-paper-basket.

Then I would go to the kitchen to make myself an early morning cup of tea. Waiting for the kettle to boil, I invariably looked out of the window—east—over the rooftops of London to St Paul's, the sun rising behind it—which normally inspired a moment of peaceful reflection. But at this time, blinded by constant worry, I looked with unseeing eyes. A period which I shall never forget.

Anna then sold our home in Park Lane, including the entire contents, and with the proceeds held off some of the creditors—but not all. I endeavoured to stave off the inevitable, but the pack closed in and eventually I had to throw in the towel.

On 1st July, 1964, I was declared bankrupt.

Hundreds of letters of sympathy poured in, many of them containing money. One of them so moved Anna and me that I always carry it with me. It is reproduced in this book. Some hundreds of pounds arrived in all, which was greatly appreciated by our own trade charity.

Another gesture I shall not forget came from Vivien Leigh. As a souvenir and thanks for his part as co-producer and star of *The Beggar's Opera*, I had given Larry Olivier a small painting by Corot. When he and Vivien parted, one of the joint possessions given to her was this painting. When my bankruptcy was announced, Vivien sought me out and asked if she might give it back to me. I thanked her, but refused it. It was a sweet and generous thought on the part of dear Vivien.

This year, when I found myself in hospital, very ill indeed, one of the first things I saw when I recovered consciousness was a glorious white azalea plant from Vivien. I must record that in all her brilliant career she owes nothing to me since, unfortunately for me, we have never worked together.

As I walked down Kingsway after leaving the court, I wondered what it would feel like to be a man without possessions—without a banking account. (At one time I had five). I also wondered about my friends.

I then made a firm resolution—never to embarrass any of them by referring to my situation, and to behave as if the whole affair had never happened. I would also resign from all my clubs.

Although my resolution was sound, I need not have worried. For the very few friends whom it seemed to embarrass were swamped by those who almost embarrassed me with their kind inquiries and offers.

Perhaps the most touching experience of that dismal period was when I took my four British 'Oscars' by taxi to the sale-room. The taxi-driver, helping me out with them, read the inscription on the *Odette* trophy.

'Are you Herbert Wilcox?' he asked.

I told him I was.

'I read about these in the papers. I think it's a bleeding shame, and so does my wife.'

'Thanks,' I said. 'But those are the regulations.'

'Why, we've seen all of your films with Miss Neagle and we'd go and see 'em again if we knew where.'

He looked at each inscription... *The Courtneys of Curzon Street*, *Piccadilly Incident*, *Odette* and *Spring in Park Lane* ...

'A bleeding shame,' he repeated.

By now I was feeling a little conspicuous and, carrying two 'Oscars', went into the sale-room followed by the driver with the other two.

'Thank you,' I said to him. 'How much do I owe you?'

'On me,' he replied.

I protested.

'If my old woman knew about these and thought I'd charged you, she'd give me a proper rollocking.'

I took the number of his taxi. When I get the 'Oscars' back, as I hope to do, I am going to invite my taxi friend and his wife round for a drink.

And now, in the year 1964, to start all over again when in my seventies! I faced the challenge strongly enough. My health was good; my brain never clearer.

I prepared several important dramatic subjects with top entertainment value, but could not get them airborne. The so-called realistic vogue was upon us, and not only I, but many others of those who had put British films proudly on the world's map far beyond the sound of kitchen taps and flushing lavatories, found themselves wondering when a return to glamour and good family entertainment would come.

I somehow believed it was just round the corner. Until then I could not compete. Had I tried, I should have been a dismal failure. Suddenly the tide was stemmed. Anna, in her first stage thriller, *Person Unknown*, toured the country and broke records everywhere. She also starred most successfully in two television plays. And, as a moving climax to this sudden spurt of recovery, she was asked by the Dean of Norwich to address the congregation at Norwich Cathedral on the occasion to mark the fiftieth anniversary of Nurse Cavell's death.

Anna borrowed Sybil Thorndike's Thomas à Kempis, *The Imitation of Christ*, since in quoting certain passages marked by Miss Cavell she felt she could more forcibly convey a picture of her thoughts awaiting execution. Buried at Life's Green in the cathedral precincts, within a stone's throw of the pulpit where Anna was speaking, Nurse Cavell seemed to come to life when Anna spoke of her heroism and referred to the annotations. Anna was superb. I have never been so moved.

Then Anna signed to do a West End musical with the pop-singer, Joe Brown. Inspirational casting of exciting chemistry—I had another hunch that this would be the end of the famine period and would sublimate a dream Anna and I have had for years of a West End theatre smash hit.

But then something happened. Something unexpected and frightening that almost caused this book to remain unfinished and also rob Anna of her heart's desire.

19

To appreciate how it all started, I must take you back to 1952. In the morning Anna had attended Buckingham Palace to be invested with the Order of the British Empire, of which she became a Commander. Since I had been similarly honoured the previous year, we became unique as husband and wife holders of the C.B.E. It was the culmination of a period of hard work and success. Smash hit film followed smash hit. 'Oscar' had followed 'Oscar', and now we were both officially recognised.

Anna and I were sitting in front of a coal fire in our lovely Park Lane home where, from our balcony running the length of the flat, we could see Richmond Hill ahead, the Surrey hills to our left, and Harrow-on-the-Hill to our right. Behind us was a glorious view of the City of London, dominated by the dome of St Paul's Cathedral.

On the walls of the living-room hung paintings by Van Gogh, Rembrandt, Renoir, Fantin-Latour, Gauguin, Brueghel, Corot, Utrillo, Boudin. On our sideboard were thirteen awards, including the Gold Cup of the Nations awarded at Venice, Anna's five Gold Medal Awards (a record for any actress or actor) and my four British 'Oscars'.

We reflected on our good fortune. There was not a cloud on our horizon.

'We've been very lucky,' I said. 'We've got everything haven't we?'
'There's one thing more I'd like to do,' said Anna.
'What's that?' I asked.
'Whilst my looks hang out,' replied Anna, 'I *must* do a musical play on the West End stage. I want to experience again the reaction of live audiences.'
'I know just how you feel,' I told her. 'Playing to a dead camera doesn't give you much back—except results. So let's have a go. But with your present status you must be prepared to carry the show.'
'Do you think I can?'
'No,' I answered, 'I don't think—I know. I must book Row D, Seat 13 right away for the first night (thirteen has always been our lucky number), and from there I'll start the booing!'

Tom Arnold, whom I first approached, jumped at the idea of a musical play for Anna—and within a month Robert Nesbitt was signed as producer and the book was being written.

The following year was Coronation year and would of course, they said, be a bonanza for show business generally. And the play, *The Glorious Days*, based on a patriotic theme, was perfect for the occasion. It opened at the Palace Theatre, Manchester, on 30th July, 1952, for a six weeks' run.

Anna and I invited eighty guests, whose opinions we valued, to come up from London. I had a special train laid on, with a five-course meal on board. Reservations were made at the Midland Hotel, with a celebration supper to follow the performance.

The first night was a success beyond our wildest dreams. Then followed a six-week record run with audiences from all over Yorkshire and Lancashire, despite a heat-wave which hit Manchester and caused scores to faint in the theatre. For eight months the provincial tour continued, with the same story in every theatre: Five weeks' record in Edinburgh, four weeks in Birmingham, endless curtains and a speech from Anna after every performance.

Now for the West End—the Palace Theatre. At our own expense we installed a new neon sign covering the entire front of the theatre (it is still there) and a supper party for 200 guests was laid on at the Dorchester. It promised to be an electric evening and we knew, from the success in the provinces, that it could not fail.

I was sitting in row D, seat 13, as I had throughout the tour. At the second interval, the theatre manager whispered to me: 'They've cancelled Anna's curtain speech (which was pre-arranged) and there is to be only one curtain.'

'Why?' I asked.

'Trouble in the gallery,' I was told, 'and we must expect some booing.'

(The big investiture scene called for supers who could wear military dress. Drama students had applied but were passed over in favour of regular stage supers. The students had apparently decided to gang up on the show.)

My joke about my seat was coming home to roost!

Anna and the cast gave a superb performance and the audience could not have been warmer or friendlier. A leg-pull by the manager, I decided. But no. The curtain came down without a speech from Anna, and the orchestra struck up the national anthem. The applause was deafening and many curtain-calls would have been justified.

I was furious and sought out both Tom Arnold and Robert Nesbitt.

It was they who had been tipped off about the disappointed drama students. Whether the students booed or not, I cannot say. But I swear I never heard one. So the reception Anna and the cast deserved was denied them.

At the Dorchester party which followed, Anna was bombarded with congratulations. At our table we had the senior director, or 'elder statesman', of a leading Sunday newspaper, who was ecstatic in his appreciation of Anna and the show.

It was a Saturday, and at about two o'clock, with the dancing at its height, I stole out and bought a copy of our guest's paper. On the front page, in bold headlines, I read: 'Anna's play booed. "I don't care," said Anna.' An alleged story by Anna that she didn't care was printed in the first person.

I showed the paper to our guest. He said nothing—but looked plenty. It was the first really dishonest piece of reporting I have ever experienced in the whole of my career, and it shook Anna, for neither she nor I heard the semblance of a boo. It appeared that the reporter heard in advance of the students' plot and took a chance.

Anna has never fully recovered her faith in the press for, apart from the non-existent booing, she was quoted as not caring, whereas she had never been interviewed at all. The other papers took it up and the story grew until it became distorted beyond reason. That, and the fact that Coronation year as a bonanza for the theatre turned out to be a fallacy, was too much opposition for any play to stand up to.

So *The Glorious Days*, a wonderful production and a tour-de-force for Anna—twenty-one changes of dress and fifteen songs and dances—put up its shutters after eight months and Anna returned to the film studios. It was a grave disappointment.

However, we never eased up in our search for another musical play. It was some years before we found the ideal subject. The book was by Hugh and Margaret Williams; the music by David Heneker and John Taylor; and it was to be presented by Harold Fielding, who had put on the smash hit musical *Half a Sixpence* with Tommy Steele in London and New York. Its name was *Charlie Girl*.

It was a tailor-made part for Anna, with singing and dancing, as an ex-Cochran Young Lady who has married into the aristocracy and lives in a stately home which has to be thrown open to the public to meet death duties. It was full of fun and entertainment, and had a popular young singer in Joe Brown.

Yes, this was it. If it was a hit, it would be the end of all our current problems.

Once again Anna swung into action. It was twelve years since she had appeared in a musical play. Meanwhile standards all round were considerably higher, and the critics had become even more unpredictable.

Singing lessons, dancing, dress-fitting, intensified publicity, plus studying a long and strenuous part. How Anna worked! She never stopped. But we both felt this was her great West End chance at last.

Sleepless nights followed exhausting days, but this I expected; Anna is a perfectionist if ever there was one, and even a minor defect or problem robs her of sleep until she has sorted it out and resolved it. There was no private life for her at this point. Work was the boss and called all the tunes. However, this really looked like third time lucky. After a short rehearsal period calling for extended hours and intensive work, all was ready for the ten-day try-out at Golders Green.

Following our usual custom, Anna and I invited a number of guests whose opinion we valued, not sycophants but professionals, who would not hesitate to say what they thought either way. Many of them were from the provinces. About fifty in all were invited.

Then the first shock! The scenery was so massive, having been built for the much larger stage at the Adelphi, that it took twenty stage-hands to handle it instead of the customary half-dozen, and sufficient stage-hands—even on a temporary basis—could not be found. Some of the scenery crashed down on to the stage, and the set designer was rushed to hospital for stitches in an ugly head wound. The next day a more serious accident was narrowly averted.

The show was due to open that day, a Thursday. Harold Fielding took a courageous step. 'I'm not opening until the Saturday,' he said. Money would be returned for the Thursday and Friday, both houses having been sold out. As an alternative to money returned, transfers would be made. But for Saturday evening, both houses were sold out and it was impossible to deal with the disappointed ones—amongst them our guests, some of whom were coming from long distances. We managed to head off as many as possible, but the strain was considerable.

However, we succeeded in getting some in for the opening, which was a tremendous success. I cannot recall such enthusiasm from a sophisticated and discriminating audience.

From seat 13 in row D, I glowed with pleasure. We were home and dry. The long dream of Anna and myself for a triumphant return to the West End was to be realised at last. It was already booked for the opening night at the Adelphi. Yes! This was it!

'Now at least we've seen what we've got,' said Fielding. 'The next ten days are going to be really tough to get it right. Hope Anna's not too tired!'

'Not tired—just dead,' I felt like saying, but I didn't.

There was much to be done. So, apart from giving the actual performance, rehearsals went on all day and the changes were to be tried out on the last night at Golders Green Hippodrome. I did not attend any rehearsals of the changes since I had my own affairs to deal with during the day. And in any event I wanted to see the effect on a full house on the Saturday night.

Throughout the week the weather was foul, but I had to face it to lighten Anna's load and see that she had some food to snatch between rehearsals and performance. It was a gruelling time for her, but there was not a whisper of complaint.

On the Friday some last-minute changes were made after the performance, so Anna and I did not arrive home until the early hours. Having done nothing, I felt all in. What she must have felt like I cannot imagine. However, I could hardly wait to see the changes, all of which Anna thought greatly improved the show.

In the morning, I got up to make tea for us both. But something was wrong. I couldn't move, neither could I breathe. I don't mean breathe deeply—I mean breathe at all.

'Snap out of it,' I told myself. '*She's* done the work—not you.'

And I forced myself out of bed, only to fall flat on my face on the floor. Fortunately Anna, exhausted as she must have been, was asleep and heard nothing. I felt a sharp pain in my chest. Having enjoyed excellent health since World War I, I knew I could lick this, whatever it was.

I started to dress. Three times during the process I tumbled back on the bed, fighting for breath as the pain in my chest became worse. I must have eaten something which didn't agree with me. Omelette and a brandy? Couldn't be that. Somehow I made some tea and took it to Anna. She looked at me.

'Are you all right? You look ill.'

The pain in my chest at that moment was so bad that I screamed. Anna had never heard me scream. She jumped out of bed and helped me to my room.

'Rest on the bed. I'll call the doctor.'

I thought I could take as much pain as the next one, but not this.

My chest was being crushed as if it were in a vice. I could draw no breath. Anna was dialling. 'Don't worry, I'll be all right.' She took no notice. 'Don't call him,' I pleaded. 'He won't let me go to the theatre tonight and I want to see the changes.' 'How soon can you get here?' asked Anna. 'Herbert's ill.'

The doctor was round in minutes.

'Deep congestion—both lungs,' he told me. 'Get to bed.'

'Not tonight—I must be at the theatre.'

'You must get to bed and stay there,' he told me.

'Impossible for him to be with you tonight,' he told Anna.

'But I must,' I protested.

'I'll be all right,' said Anna. 'I'll miss you, but . . .'

They put me to bed. During that day, Anna's devoted secretary, Joyce—herself only recently recovered from a serious heart operation—kept me fully informed and did everything to cushion the strain for Anna and me.

About half past seven that night there was a call from Anna. The first house was over. The reaction of the audience could not have been better. The changes all came off. She would 'phone me after the second house.

Later I heard the 'phone ringing, but I couldn't reach it. That pain again—would it never ease up? I struggled and eventually picked up the 'phone. Too late—she'd already hung up. It seemed hours later—it was a matter of minutes—that the 'phone went again. It was near to me this time.

'It's all over, darling—wonderful. I'm on my way.'

Through a mental haze I later found myself asking Anna about the various changes. 'They all came off,' she assured me. 'But there's still more to be done before the opening.'

'Now you must get to bed,' I told her. 'You've got your L.P. recording tomorrow at C.B.S.'

'Yes, I must get some sleep.' She kissed me and left.

It was not night that followed. It was nightmare. I don't suppose I slept more than five consecutive minutes that night. I was ashamed of my groans and sometimes my shouts which invariably brought Anna in to me. She gave me sips of brandy. I couldn't sit down, couldn't sit up.

'What a cissy,' I managed to say.

'I think I should 'phone the doctor,' said Anna.

'What's the time?' I asked.

'Quarter past five.'

'Let's wait till seven. The pain seems a little better. It comes and goes. You must get some sleep—your recording . . .'

Anna went to bed until seven. At six I found myself pounding on her wall. She could not have been asleep for in a flash she was with me. I felt it was the end. I could stand no more. She stayed with me and on the stroke of seven 'phoned the doctor. He, too, was ill. He had a temperature of 103° but he 'phoned a deputy who was with me in a few minutes. He tested my lungs, confirmed bad congestion, and went to the phone.

'I want an ambulance—emergency—Brunswick Mews.'

The pain was now unbearable.

'Help me get him to the divan,' the doctor asked Anna.

'I'm giving you morphine,' he told me. 'If you've never had it, you'll be conscious of a strange feeling, but it will ease the pain.'

I made no protest. I became drowsy, I looked up at Anna. I swear she was smiling. And this after no sleep, with an important gramophone recording in an hour or so and two performances last night. And here was I screaming like a scalded cat because of a pain in my chest.

They got me into the ambulance and I saw Anna's face still smiling and blowing me a kiss as they closed the doors. The doctor followed in his own car. Yes, he knew what he was talking about. I do feel strange—as if floating in the air.

The engine in the ambulance was beating out the tunes of Anna's show. I saw Anna dancing the oriental dance with David Tagouri, then singing 'I Was Young'. The whole show whirled through my mind. 'I must pick up my ticket,' I thought. 'Row D, seat 13.' Twice before I've sat in that seat. But this time—this is it.

Yes, everything was strange—and all because of a small needle in the artery of someone who should have been able to throw off the effects and setbacks of the last week with that old *cliché*: 'That's show business.'

There it is again—that pain—only worse than ever. I'm going to be sick. Must think of something. Odette. Yes, that's who I'll think about. Pain? You don't know what it is. What about Odette? Toenails torn out—red-hot poker on her spine. Her face came vividly to me as I struggled for breath. She was answering the question I once asked her: 'You never know, Herbert, what you can bear until you're put to the test. You'd be all right.'

All right! Just a pain in my chest, in friendly hands, speeding to a hospital. The doctor in his car is following us and I am moaning and groaning. What do the Americans call it? Yellow—no, not that—oh yes, chicken! But I had to admit the pain was really bad.

I remember reading something J. A. Spender wrote: 'The maximum of pain is unconsciousness.' That's it. When it gets too much, I'll faint. So shut up moaning! Dear God, would they never get me there? Or was this the end? It had all the signs. Yes, there they were: headlines started dancing across my mind. 'Herbert Wilcox dead.' 'Death of Wilcox.' 'Film Producer Dies.' (Didn't like that much.) 'Famous Film Man Dead.' (That's better.) Then more headlines: 'Anna's triumph.' Anna now singing—taking the final curtain. My chest was now burning like a furnace. Yes, this must be it.

Then the ambulance pulled up at the hospital.

I don't remember much about entering the hospital except the tolling of a toneless bell, and a calm compassionate face in a sister's white habit moving noiselessly and giving instructions to the ambulance men.

Then the morphine took over completely. When I opened my eyes, I was lying on a bed with wires stuck on my legs, on my arms and on my chest. The doctor (a different one?) was watching a meter intently. The pain in my chest had gone. I moved slightly and the doctor looked at me as he continued his work.

'I feel better. I can breathe—the congestion?'

'Still there,' he told me.

'But the pain?'

'Yes, that's gone.'

Then, as he started removing the wires which were electric leads: 'Apart from the congestion, you've had a coronary thrombosis,' he said quietly.

I said nothing.

'You heard what I said?' he asked. I nodded. 'Don't worry, you've *had* the thrombosis. You've plenty of time ahead of you, but you must take it easy for some time.'

'How long?' I asked.

'Four to six weeks,' he told me. 'Absolute rest.'

'But Anna's first night! I must be there.'

'When is it?'

'December 15th.'

'Next week? Not the slightest chance. You'll be here in bed for a month. Nothing solid to eat. Drink plenty and sleep.'

I hadn't missed a 'first' of Anna's for over thirty years. And now it was the very thing we had set our hearts on, and I was not to be there. My mind flew to her at this moment, recording at C.B.S. Four solid days of rehearsals ahead. Three dress rehearsals, a royal charity performance before Princess Alexandra, and then the first night.

She must not know.

I told the doctor (he was a heart specialist) and the sister that if Anna heard about the thrombosis she might crack under the extra strain. Nor must the press hear about it.

The specialist and Sister could see my obvious distress. They agreed that nothing should be said to Anna until after the first night; and to all inquiries, just news of my progress but no details should be given.

The 'phone rang and, before they could stop me, I grabbed it. As I thought, it was Anna. 'Oh, much better,' I told her, 'the pain's gone. How did you make out? Oh, I'm so glad. Get round when you've finished.'

I turned to the specialist and to the sister. 'Thank you very much,' was all I could think to say. The effort had exhausted me, and I was given a few whiffs of oxygen by Sister.

Two people had to know the facts—my solicitor and my accountant. There were so many loose ends and unfinished jobs. So they both came to see me. And my secretary shared the secret as she recorded the many things that had to be done. I felt better for having tidied things up, since it was quite evident that, but for the grace of God, the thrombosis would have finished me.

Every day, despite constant rehearsals, Anna came to see me. It was thought best that she was not announced but just poked her head in, in case I was asleep. Although her visits were at varying times, I was invariably aware of her coming and had a smile ready for her when she slowly opened my door.

On 15th December, she came in early, as rehearsals and dress fittings were set almost up to curtain time.

'It'll seem strange without you,' she said.

'First time I've missed since *Good Night, Vienna*.'

'I'll let you know how it goes.'

' 'Phone at the interval,' I asked her as she kissed me 'good-bye'.

'Good luck, you'll knock 'em, I'm sure.'

How I prayed for her success.

After *The Glorious Days*, two disastrous years which resulted in my bankruptcy, her disappointing venture with the Fred Astaire Dancing Schools, which not only cost her her savings but prevented her from being seen by the public for over a year—and left her with substantial personal guarantees to the bank ... and now my illness. How she has stood up to it all baffles me. But a great success tonight and the problems and disappointments would be largely forgotten, if not melted right away. That evening of 15th December, telephone by my side, I lay in bed and watched the clock as it so slowly crept to 7.30 p.m.

Curtain time!

I had arranged with Anna's dresser that I would 'phone the stage door at 7.40 when Anna was due to make her entrance.

'She's just gone on and they've gone mad,' she told me. 'They're still applauding—must be over three minutes.'

'Thanks, Betty. Don't let her know I 'phoned. And 'phone me after her number with Hy Hazell.'

I almost dropped the 'phone—the exertion was so much. I rang for the nurse.

'Can I have a "cocktail"?' I asked. She gave me one. An oxygen bag over my face for about three minutes. I lay back. I could not have been happier. Anna's made it, I thought—despite me, despite everything.

I watched the clock and mentally followed the play. Any minute now—it was 8.10.

There it goes. 'Yes Betty, I'm here.'

I listened as she told me the duet had stopped the show.

'Good! Don't tell her you 'phoned me. She's ringing at the interval and will want to tell me herself.' The 'phone dropped out of my hand. Great reception—stopped the show. This is undoubtedly it!

The nurse popped her head in. 'You rang?'

'Oh, did I? Oh yes. Another cocktail, please—a double this time.' She put the oxygen mask over my mouth and I took some deep draughts.

Twenty minutes to go to the interval. I was mentally following every scene, humming every tune, living every minute of the play as I watched the clock. Yes, now it's Anna's big number in that Hartnell dress. Any minute she would ring. I closed my eyes and tried to relax.

There it goes. Anna was almost unable to get it out. 'Audience—everything wonderful.'

'Only one thing wrong, darling.'

'Yes, I know. I'd better go now—'phone you at the end.'

' 'Bye now.'

I lay quite still. It looked as if she was in for the hit of her life.
The nurse looked in. 'I think I'd better take that 'phone.'
'Over my dead body.'
'Well—you said it!' she replied. 'You look as if a few whiffs wouldn't hurt.'

I was exhausted and there was over an hour to go. I must have dropped off as I woke with a start with the 'phone bell ringing.

Anna was almost in tears. 'Fourteen curtain-calls,' she told me, 'and I had to make an impromptu speech.'

'Now, go out, have supper and enjoy yourself. Have fun,' I told her.

'No! I'll be with you as soon as I can get away.'

'Anna's great night,' I murmured. 'And the first time I haven't been with her. What rotten luck! But how lucky I am to be alive.'

Again the nurse: 'What news?'

'Wonderful,' I said.

'Another cocktail?' she asked.

'No thanks, nurse. It's her greatest success. Ask Sister if I can have that half-bottle of champagne and two glasses. She'll be here soon.'

Over our drink I was able to live through the whole evening. The 'phone never stopped from our good friends who had attended the opening.

The first caller was John Woolf, son of my old friend and film partner, the late C. M. Woolf. He was wildly enthusiastic and, knowing of his sincerity and judgment of entertainment, Anna and I felt the show was home and dry. So—another glass of champagne!

The calls never stopped, but Sister soon put an end to that and, about 2 a.m., told Anna she thought I had had enough.

Enough! I could have gone on all night. However, Anna agreed with Sister and went. A night to remember. 15th December, 1965.

Next morning, Anna was late in ringing, so I 'phoned her.

'What's the time?' she asked.

'10.30,' I told her.

'Good heavens, I must have slept for eight hours.'

'You needed it. Come over as soon as you can.'

I didn't tell her I hadn't slept a wink all night. With the tension lifted, I should have slept peacefully, but the thought that kept me awake was: 'When and how shall I tell her?'

I had made up my mind I would tell her myself. But how? She was due to play eleven performances in Christmas week. When these were behind her, I would tell her, I decided.

The following day, the specialist was due to take another electrocardiogram. I had suggested 4 p.m. as I knew Anna was having a singing lesson at that time, then going straight on to the theatre.

The specialist adjusted the electric contact on legs, arms and chest, and completed his examination of me. I saw from his face that the news was good, but over his shoulder I also saw my door slowly open. To my horror, there was Anna, and as usual with a smile on her face. The smile faded as she took in the scene with a strange doctor.

The specialist had removed the contacts and, as though he had seen or heard nothing, smiled and said—a little louder than necessary:

'Excellent! You've twenty years ahead of you if you don't climb too many mountains.'

He had finished his job now and was packing his case.

'Darling, come in and sit down.'

Anna mechanically did so. I introduced her to the specialist. 'Do you mind if I tell her now while you are both here?'

And so I told her the whole story. Anna said nothing.

'I trust we did the right thing,' said Sister.

'Thank you, Sister—you did.' Anna thanked the specialist as he left, followed by Sister.

Throughout the ordeal she had been through on my account, coupled with the strenuous work and endless rehearsals, Anna had stuck her chin out like the trouper she is. But now she looked at me for a moment, and then threw herself on her knees beside the bed. Her arms went round me as she murmured, 'Thank God!' And then she cried as I have never known her cry.

That night at about ten o'clock, the company manager 'phoned from the theatre. 'Miss Neagle asked me to call and say that she'd like to look in on her way home and say "good night"—if you'll still be awake.'

'I'll be awake,' I told him. 'How's it going?'

'Marvellous,' he said. 'A packed house and the record for the theatre is sure to go this week. (It did.) 'Miss Neagle is on the top of her form tonight. She must have had some good news at the hospital today.'

I put the 'phone down. Good news at the hospital! Coronary thrombosis!

She had already seen her beloved father and her brother, Stuart, both taken by heart trouble.

'On the top of her form—'

What a trouper! What a woman!

POSTLUDE

'Twenty years ahead of you, provided you don't climb too many mountains.' That's what the specialist told me.

In this book I have, so far as human memory is able, faithfully covered the proverbial threescore years and ten. I have reached up and touched the stars, and I have plumbed the depths.

Since God has granted me a respite before my accounting, I am moving into a new, exciting period of activity. Whatever the future holds for me may merit recording, or it may not.

So I'll settle for what has already happened—whilst my flirtation with death and Anna's indomitable spirit are uppermost in my mind.

STOP PRESS—Tuesday, 17th May, 1966

'... a gentleman who has attained a considerable degree of eminence as a producer and director of films.

'It is very much to the credit and is a refreshing feature of the case to see the manner in which his wife has discharged liabilities and assisted him.'

The words about myself and Anna were used by the registrar today granting my discharge from bankruptcy.

I hurried from the court to Claridges to keep that promised lunch date with Anna. Under the ever-watchful eye of Luigi we enjoyed curried chicken and a glass of Montrachet. Delicious!

The picture and story in the *Daily Express* of 18th May, which I have reproduced, tell the full story.

Peace of mind! Blessed peace of mind!!

The constant worry over the past few years had destroyed almost everything—except Anna's faith in me and my determination to live and rise again to the heights.

Worry not entirely on my own account—but about Anna. I had exposed her to the same danger I had so recently survived, for which she was less well equipped to cope, or to face the resultant indignities and demoralisation.

But—

> *'It's not going to happen again, old girl,*
> *It's not going to happen again.'*
>
> Rupert Brooke.

After our lunch, I once again retraced my steps and walked from Claridges to Farm Street Church for a brief moment of reflection and thanks—where twenty-three years ago I passed on my way to meet Anna at Caxton Hall.

As I walked, Korda's words about *Henry VIII* came sharply to mind.

'Herbert—one film can make a company.'

Maybe that's my next. 'After forty-seven years, haven't you had enough of the rat race?' I can hear some say. Not if you feel as I do—in spirit and enthusiasm, much the same as when I entered the film industry in 1918. But that much wiser—and I trust, no less adventurous.

THE BEGINNING

INDEX

INDEX

Index

Note: Illustration references are to plate numbers, not pages; see list on pages x-xii.

Agar, Herbert, 77
Aitken, Max, 182
Albert Hall, the, 58
Aldwych farces, the, 88, 89, 138
Ambler, Eric, 196–7
American Institute of Cinematography, 116, *illus. 38*
Amethyst, H.M.S., 196–8, 200, *illus. 57*
Anderson, Michael, 197, 198–9
Anglia TV, 106, 172
Aquitania, the, 72
Arlen, Michael, 154, 171
Arnold, Tom, 10, 209–10
Associated British Picture Corporation, 68, 69, 203
Associated Rediffusion, 194
Astor Hotel, New York, 100
Astra Films Ltd, 48
Australia, 38, 91, 140, 162, 180
  Australian Army, 38–9, 42
  Sydney, 38, 139

B.B.C., 90, 161, 175–6
Baird, John Logie, 92–3, 135
Baker, George Washington, 126–7
Balfour, Harold (Lord Balfour of Inchrye), 37, 38, 45
Bank of England, the, 106–7, 166, 167
Bankhead, Tallulah, 154
Barrie, J. M., 93–5
Barrymore, Lionel, 58, 59, *illus. 17*

Battle of the River Plate, The, 173, 200
Batory, Polish ship, 129, 176–7
Baughan, E. A., 62, 79
Beaverbrook, Lord, 71, 74, 75, 79, 118, 119, 180–2, *illus. 52*
Beck, Reggie, 165
Beggar's Opera, The, 163–7, 206, *illus. 51*
Bergman, Ingrid, 184–5, 187
Bergner, Elizabeth, 93–5, 158
Berkeley, Reginald, 73
Bernstein, Sidney, 194
Bevin, Ernest, 175
Bickell, Jack, 178
Bingham, Barry, 77
Birmingham, H.M.S., 200
Bishop, W. A., Air Marshal, 37–8, 173–4, 175, 177–8, *illus. 15*
Bitter Sweet, 97
Black, Alfred, 173
Black, George, senior, 51, 55–6
Black, George, junior, 173
Black Waters, 84
Blackmail, 85
Bliss, Sir Arthur, 163
Bloom, Claire, 168
Bloomer, Steve, 15
Blue Angel, The, 148
Blythe, Betty, 54, *illus. 18*
Blue Danube, The, 138–9
Bogart, Humphrey, 156
Bond, J. P., 141

Boot, Henry, 109
Bow, Clara, 170
Brabourne, Lord, 31, 173
Brighton Hippodrome, 10–11
British & Dominions Film Corporation, 71, 72, 86, 104
British Board of Film Censors, 79–80, 81
British Film Academy, 183
    see also 'Oscars'
British Film Industry Benevolent Home, 70
British International Pictures, 85
British Lion Film Corporation, 146, 196, 198, 200–1, 202
British National Pictures, 69, 71
British Red Cross, the, 126, 127
Bromhead, Col., 74
Brook, Peter, 163–5
Brooke, Rupert, 26–7, 222
Brown, Joe, 208, 211
Brown, Group Capt. Roy, 42, 178
Brown, Capt. Sam, 179
Buchanan, Jack, 85, 90, 91–3, 104, 118, 135, 158, *illus. 26*
Buckmaster, Col. Maurice, 152, 188
Buffs, the, (East Kent Regiment), 28–31
Bullock, F. William, 105
Bullock, John, 105–6, 107
Burgin, Dr Leslie, 109
Burnup, Peter, 70

Camberwell Green, London, 16, 17, 18–19, 20
Camberwell Palace Theatre, 17, 18
Campbell, Lady Jean, 181–2
Canada, 38, 45, 116, 129, 174–5, 177–80
Canadian Broadcasting Corporation, 129
Caneron, Kate, 116–17
Canadian Red Cross, 129–30
Canadian Royal Air Force, 174, 175, 177

Cannes Festival, 200
Capitol Theatre, Haymarket, 91
Cardiff, Jack, 173
Carminatti, Tullio, 109
Carroll, Sydney W., 116–17
Cavell, Eddie, 73
Cavell, Edith, 73, 78–9, 82, 124, 185, 208
Cavina, banana boat, 178–9
Cazalet-Keir, Thelma, 81
'Celebrity Parade', 177
Chaliapin, 86–8
Chamberlain, Sir Austen, 74
Chaplin, Charles, 17–18, 69, 132, 137, 190–1
Charlie Girl, 211–14, 217, 218–19, 220
Chicago Tribune, the, 124
Christiansen, Arthur, 75–6
Christie, Al, 84
Chu Chin Chow, 54, 55, 57, *illus. 18*
'Churchie', wardrobe mistress, 150
Churchill, Odette, 181, 183, 184, 185–8, 215, *illus. 46*
Churchill, Peter, 184, 186–8
Churchill, Sir Winston, 37, 127, *illus. 15*
Ciro's restaurant, London, 67
Citizen Kane, 133–4
Claridges Hotel, London, 107, 119, 128–9, 141, 151, 152–4, 156, 160, 221
Clark, Robert, 203–4
Clemenceau, Georges, 82
Clore, Charles, 140
Cloutier, Suzanne, 136
Cochran, C. B., 53, 55, 56, 82, 85, 93
Collier, Constance, 132, 190–1
Collins, Michael, 30
Comoedia, 82
Conan Doyle, Sir Arthur, 95
Connery, Sean, 156, 173
Conrad, Joseph, 163, 201
Constant Nymph, The, 93

Convent of the Sacred Heart, Brighton, 7
Corda, Maria, 158
Corinthians, the, football team, 14–15
Cork, County, 2, 4, 29–31
Courtneys of Curzon Street, The, 27, 51, 202, 203
Courville, Albert de, 55, 85
Cowan, Maurice, 144
Coward, Noel, 72, 95, 97, 130, 137, 177
Cowdin, Cheever, 105, 107
Cox, George, senior, 14
Cox's Bank, 43–4
Cromer, Lord, 188
Cudlipp, Hugh, 77–8
Cutts, Graham, 51
Czinner, Paul, 93, 94

Daghakowski, Capt., 177
Daily Express, the, 118, 221, *illus. 37*
Daily Mail, the, 75, *illus. 39*
Daily News, the, 79
Daily Telegraph, the, 79
Dam Busters, The, 203
Daniels, Bebe, 175–6
Dannenberg, Joe, 60–1
Davis, Bette, 183
Dawn, 27, 73–4, 79–82, 203
Day in the Life of the Prince of Wales, A, 111
de Mille, Cecil B., 61–2
Decameron Nights, 58–9, *illus. 17*
Dempster, Hugh, 165, 184
Denham studios, 72, 113, 130, 144, 158–9
Deutsch, Oscar, 108
Dietrich, Marlene, 148
Dines, Gordon, 199
Donovan, Bill, 127
Dorchester Hotel, London, 210–11
Dowling, David, 28
Drayton, Harley, 72, 194, 202–3
Dunn, Sir James, 71
Duke, Ivy, 58

Eady money, 202
Eaton, Margaret, 38
Edward VII, King, 9, 13, 26, 27, 111, *illus. 3*
Edward VIII, King, 22, 76, 111, 115, 154–5
Egypt, 21, 198
Elizabeth II, Queen, 31–2, 121, 159–60, 191–2, *illus. 54*
Elizabeth the Queen Mother, Queen, 188
Elphinstone, Lord and Lady, 115–16
Elstree studios, 68–9, 71, 85, 86, 108–9
Elsworthy, Dolly, 65
Embassy Club, the, London, 154–5
Emerson, R. W., 140
Ephraim, Lee, 56
Escape Me Never, 73–4, 172
Essex, H.M.S., 198–9
Evans, Sir Francis, 62, 190
Evans, Lady Mary, 62, 190
Evening Argus, 9, 32

FANYs (First Aid Nursing Yeomanry), 185–6
Fairbanks, Douglas, senior, 17
Farm Street Church, London, 142, 222
Farrow, Leslie, 104, 107, 109
Faulkner, W. G., 51
Fenwick, Keld, 43–4
Fermoy, County Cork, 4, 29–31
Fielding, Harold, 211, 212–13
Film Finances, 165
Fitelson, William, 68
Fitzherbert, Mrs, 5
Flames of Passion, 52–3, *illus. 16*
Ford, Florrie, 17
Foreign Office, the, 74, 120, 162, 175
Forever and a Day, 126, 127, 128, 178
Fowler, Gene, 97
Fox, William, 96–7

Foxwell, Ivan, 173
Fraser, Lionel, 202-3
Fred Astaire Dancing Schools, the, 217
Frederick, Pauline, 72-3, 137
Fredman, E. W., 51
Fresnes Prison, France, 187
Fry, Christopher, 163

Gabor, Zsa Zsa, 6
Galsworthy, John, 95-7
Garbo, Greta, 183
Garson, Greer, 183
Gaumont British, 104, 108, 158
General Cinema Finance, 108
General Film Distributors Ltd, 111
George VI, King, 120-1, 127, 185, 188-9, 191, 192, *illus. 48*
Giannini, A. P., 59, 128-9, 196
Giannini, Dr, 59-61, 126, 190, 196
Gielgud, John, 135
Gillespie, Colonel, 56
Gish, Dorothy, 17, 65-6, 69, 70, 83, 85, 91, 96, 137, 154, 169-71, *illus. 23, 24*
Gish, Lillian, 17, 65-6, 183
Glorious Days, The, 10, 156, 210-11
Glyn, Elinor, 170
Gold Cup of the Nations, 189, 209
Goodhead, Eric, 144, 147, 148
Good Night, Vienna, 88, 90-2, 97, *illus. 26*
Grade, Lew, 194
Granada TV, 194
Grant, Cary, 122-3, 124-5
Green, Abel, 78-9
Grenadier Guards, the, 22, 28
Grierson, John, 178
Griffith, D. W., 47-8, 50, 51, 65, 101, 102-3, 133
Guinness, Alec, 74, 137, 204, 205
Guisberg, Freddie, 87-8, 132-3
Guy's Hospital, London, 35, 36
Gwyn, Nell, 101-2

Haigh, Kenneth, 78
Hall, Radclyffe, *The Well of Loneliness*, 170-1
Hambros, the, 157
Hammerstein, Oscar, 126
Hanbury, Ralph, 128
Hardwicke, Cedric, 100, 103, 126, 136, *illus. 31*
Harlem, New York, 116
Harris's cook shop, Brighton, 5-6, *illus. 4*
Harrison, Rex, 63-4, 144
Hart, Capt. Liddell, *illus. 58*
Harvey, Sir John Martin, 62, 63, *illus. 19, 20, 21*
Hassell, Christopher, 161
Hastings, Aubrey, 12
Hawkins, Douglas, 13-14, 28
Hawkins, Jack, 104, *illus. 31*
Haymarket Theatre, the, 98
Healy, Mary (mother of author), 2-4, 5, 11-12
Hearst, William Randolph, 77, 133
Helm, Brigitte, 54, 138, *illus. 27*
Hepburn, Audrey, 167-8
Hepburn, Katharine, 183
Herbert, Sir Alan, 141
Herbert Wilcox Productions Ltd. 111
'Hi Gang', 175-6
Himmler, Heinrich, 161
Hirst, Sir Hugo, 71
His Master's Voice, 86-7, 132
Hislop, Joseph, 86
Hitchcock, Alfred, 71, 85, 191
Hobbs, Jack, 20
Hoffe, Monckton, 97, 98, 177
Holliday, Mr, 149-50
Hollywood Reporter, the, 125
Holmes, Joe, 47-8
Holt, Paul, 118, *illus. 37*
'Hortense', 169
Housman, Laurence, *Victoria Regina*, 111, 152
Howard, Sydney, 85, 88, 158

Howard, Trevor, 63, 184, *illus. 46*
Hughes, Howard, 84
Hurley, Alec, 122
Hutton, Barbara, 123, 125

I, Claudius, 114–15
I Live in Grosvenor Square, 63, 144
In Which We Serve, 130, 137
Innes, Tom, 75, 180
Intolerance, 50
Ireland, 2, 4, 29–31, 33, 201
Irene, 125

Jagger, Dean, 63
Jannings, Emil, 54, 59, *illus. 17*
Jarratt, Sir Arthur, 146–7, 198, 200–3
Joel, J. B., 7, 8, 26
Johnson, Amy, 131, 174, 175
Jowitt, Lord, 75
Joynson-Hicks, Sir William, 63

Karno, Fred, 17
Kearney, Neville, 189, 190
Keeling, Sir John, 202–3
Kempis, Thomas à, *The Imitation of Christ*, 73, 208
Kemsley, Lord, 193, 194
Kennedy, Joseph, 127
Kennedy, Margaret, 93–4
Kerans, Commander J. S., 197–8, *illus. 57*
Keys, Nelson, 7–8, 71, 98, 154, *illus. 23*
King, Cecil, 75, 76
King, Ruth, 76
King of Paris, The, 136
Kit Kat Club, Haymarket, 138
Knight, Castleton, 82
Knoblock, Edward, 72
Korda, Alexander, 111–12, 113, 114, 121, 135, 156–60, 165–6, 167, 202, 205, 222, *illus. 49, 50*
Kraus, Werner, 54, 59, *illus. 17*
Kurfürstendamm, Berlin, 54–5

Lady with a Lamp, The, 31, 191–2, *illus. 53, 54*
Lanchester, Elsa, 85
Langley, Herbert, 51, 52
Laughing Ann, 163
Laughton, Charles, 85, 114–15, 137
Lawrence, T. E., 172, 204, *illus. 58*
Lawrence of Arabia, 205
Lawrie, James, 203
Lawson, Cissie, 17
Laye, Evelyn, 90
Lean, David, 172, 205
Lebreton, R., 82
Leicester Square: the Alhambra, 51
 the Empire, 144
 the Odeon, 132
 the Warner, 93, 100, 104, 116, 118–19, 127, 144, 191–2
Leigh, Vivien, 125, 206
Lejeune, Caroline, 90
Lewis, Rosa, 44
Leyton, George, 10
Lichtman, Al, 100–1
Lilacs in the Spring, 72
Lisbon Story, 56
Little Damozel, The, 98, *illus. 28*
Little Tich, 17
Littler, Emile, 51, 172–3
Lloyd, Frank, 126
Lloyd, Marie, 17, 122–3
Lockwood, Margaret, 134, 163, 168
Logan, Ella, 78
London County Council, 53, 81–2
London Film Productions, 157, 158, 160
London Hippodrome, 63, 90
London Palladium, 55, 82
London Pavilion, 93
London Plaza, 68, 98, 188, *illus. 47*
London, H.M.S., 189–90
London Melody, 109
Longest Day, The, 173
Lonsdale, Frederick, 95, 157
Lothian, Lord, 124, 125, 127
Louie, Anna Neagle's dresser, 130

Louisville Courier, the, 77
Low, David, *illus. 30*
Loyalties, 95–7
Luigi, of Claridges, 154, 221
Luigi, of the Embassy Club, 154–5
Luke, Lord, 104, 109
Lynn, Ralph, 85, 88–9, 158
Lyon, Ben, 175–6

McCary, Leo, 85
McClory, Kevin, 173
McCormick, Col., 124
McGowan, Sir Harry, 71
Madame Pompadour, 68
Major Barbara, 131
Male and Female, 94
'March of Dimes', the, 126, 127
Margaret, Princess, 31, 121
Margesson, Capt. Arthur, 143
Mario, of the Caprice, 154
Marney, Derek de, 114
Marsh, Mae, 52, 53, *illus. 16*
Marshall, Herbert, 72
Mary Poppins, 145, 161
Maschwitz, Eric, 90
Masefield, John, 26
Massey, Vincent, 175
Maugham, W. Somerset, 95
Maxwell, John, 71, 85
Melchett, Lord, 71
Menuhin, Yehudi, 86, 132–3
Metcalfe, 'Fruity', 154
Metro Goldwyn Mayer, 149
Metropolis, 138
Milland, Ray, 125, 128
Miller, Gilbert, 168
Mills, John, 144
Mollison, Jim, 131, 152
Montego Bay, Jamaica, 181–2
Morden, Col. Grant, 108
Morgan, Michèle, 184
Morley, Robert, 63
Mountbatten, Earl, 152, 192–3, 196–7, 198, 199–200

Mountbatten, Lady Edwina, 31–2, 191–2, *illus. 54*
Mumsie, 72
Murray, Gladstone, 129
My Teenage Daughter, 78

Nathan, George Jean, 66
National Film Finance Corporation, 198, 201, 203
Neagle, Capt. (grandfather of Anna), 142
Neagle, Anna; meets author, 90–1, 97–9; wedding, 141–2; family, 142–3; invested, 209; 1, 31, 62, 63, 72, 76–7, 77–8, 100–4, 109, 111, 112–18, 121–3, 124–32, 138, 140, 144–50, 152, 154–6, 159–61, 167–9, 174–82, 183–93, 196, 200–2, 204, 205–6, 208, 209–20, 221–2; *illus. 1, 26, 28, 29, 31, 32, 33, 34, 35, 39, 41, 42, 43, 44, 46, 47, 48, 54, 57, 61, 62*
Neagle, Capt. Arthur (uncle of Anna), 142–3
Neagle, 'Auntie', 1, 141, 142–3, *illus. 42*
Neilan, Marshall, 84
Nell Gwyn: silent version, 10, 65–8, 169, *illus. 24*
talkie, 10, 100–2, 112, *illus. 29, 30*
Nesbitt, Robert, 210
Neubabelsburg studios, Berlin, 54, 58–9, *illus. 17*
New York Daily News, the, 116–17
Newman, Tom, 18
Newton, Robert, 131–2
Nightingale, Florence, 31, 191, 192
Norman, Montagu, 106–7, 167
Northcliffe, Lord, 75
Norton, Richard, (Lord Grantley), 109–10
Norwich Cathedral, 208
Nurse Edith Cavell, 124, *illus. 39, 40*

Ocean Times, the, 146

O'Connor, T. P., 74
Odette, 118, 136, 138, 183–6, 187–8, 193, 203, *illus. 46, 47*
première, 188–9, *illus. 48*
Oliver, Vic, 175
Olivier, Laurence, 63, 124–5, 163–5, 167, 206, *illus. 51*
Only Way, The, 62–3, 65, *illus. 19, 20, 21*
Osborne, John, 78
'Oscars', 144, 145, 183, 207, 209
Othello, 134

Palace Theatre, London, 210–11
Paramount Pictures, 70, 90, 94
Paris Exhibition, 75–6, 116
Parker, Dorothy, xiii, 169
Parnell, Val, 55
Parsons, Louella, 190
Passmore, Stanley, 146–7
Pathe Pictures, 71
Patton, General, 153
Payne, Jack, 88
Pearce, Guy, 114
Pearce, Pat, 114–15
Peep Behind the Scenes, A, 50
Peg of Old Drury, 103–4, 121, *illus. 31*
Perinal, George, 93
Person Unknown, 208
Peter Pan, 94
Philip, Prince, Duke of Edinburgh, 31, 159–60, 191–2, 199–200
Piccadilly Incident, 144
Pickford, Mary, 17–18, 69, 147
Pinewood studios, 68, 72, 108–10
Place in the Sun, A, 155
Plunder, 140
Pommer, Erich, 54, 58, 59
Pope, Group Capt., 178
Portal of Laverstoke, Lord, ('Wyndham'), 104, 106–7, 108, 109, 113, 118, 119–20, 152
Posford, George, 90
Powell, Morgan, 117
Private Angelo, 136

Private Life of Henry VIII, The, 113, 158–9
Provincial Cinematograph Theatres, 71
Prudential Assurance Co., 157, 158

Quaglino, 154
Queen Elizabeth, the, 146–7, 180–1, *illus. 45*
Queen Mary, the, 77
Quigley, Martin, 70, 101, 102

R.K.O., 113, 124, 125, 126, 128, 196, 198
Rains, Claude, 128
Ranjitsinhji, K. S., 14, *illus. 10*
Rank, J. Arthur, 104, 107, 108–9
Rattigan, Terence, 95, 204, 205
Ross, 137, 204, 205, *illus. 58, 59*
Raymond, Jack, 136
Reed, Carol, 202
Reith, Sir John, 201–2, 203
Rhys-Davis, A. P. F., 37
Richardson, Ralph, 136
Robert Burns, 86
Robertson, Alan, 98
Robertson, Capt, H. W. (father of Anna Neagle), 113, 143, 220
Robertson, Stuart, 220
Robey, George, 17
Rogers, Will, 154, *illus. 23*
Romulus Films, 106, 172
Rookery Nook, 88
Roosevelt, Franklin D., 126–7
Rose Marie, 99
Rothermere, Lord, 75, 194
Royal College of Nursing, 31, 191, *illus. 56*
Royal Flying Corps, xiii, 34–45
Royal Fusiliers, 17th Battalion, 22–3, 24–6, 27–8

St John, Earl, 68
St John and St Elizabeth, Hospital of, London, 1, 216–20

St John the Baptist, church of, Kemp Town, 5
Salmond, Sir John, 45
Sarnoff, Gen. David, 153
Savage, Raymond, 204
Saville, Victor, 47–8, 126
Savoy Hotel, London, 87, 98
Say It With Music, 88
Schaefer, George, 126, 128
Schenck, Joe, 60–1
Schiff, Otto and Ernest, 71
Schildkraut, Joseph, 138
Schlesinger, I. W., 71
Seattle, U.S.A., 178
Seidl, Lea, 90
Selwyn, Archie, 79, 82
Shaw, George Bernard, 79–81, 95
Shepperton studios, 163
Sidewalks of New York, The, 83
Sigrist, Bobo, 173
Simpson, Mrs (later Duchess of Windsor), 111
Sinclair, Hugh, 94
Sixty Glorious Years, 120–1, 122, *illus. 32, 33*
Skouras, Spyros, 63
Smart, Jack, 48
Smith, C. Aubrey, 52, 126, 128, *illus. 16*
Smith, F. E. (Lord Birkenhead), 79
Smith, G. O., 14–15
Smith, Homer, 177
Solomon, Jack, 71–2
Southern Love, 57–8, 59, 166
Sovrani, 6, 154
Spender, J. A., 26, 216
Sphere, the, *illus. 21*
Spiegel, Sam, 205
Spring in Park Lane, 89, 145, 147, 156–7, 159–61, 168, 183, 202, 203
Square Story, 161
Stand Up and Sing, 90, 92
Standard Films, 71
Sternberg, Josef von, 115
Stoll studios, 99
Strode, Warren Chetham, 186
Stroheim, Eric von, 103
Sunday Express, the, 80, 116, 117
Sunday Times, the, 80–1, 116, 117
Sutton, Sir George, 75
Sweetings restaurant, Brighton, 7, 8
Swift, Frank, 15
Switzerland, 105
Syms, Sylvia, 78

Tagouri, David, 215
Taylor, Elizabeth, 51, 148–51, 152, 155–6, *illus. 55*
Ten Commandments, The, 61–2
Thalberg, Irving, 108
They Flew Alone, 131–2, 174, 175, 178
Thomson, Roy, 75, 182
Thorndike, Dame Sybil, 73–4, 79–81, 82, 137
Three Weeks, 170
Thunderball, 173
Times, The, 51
Tiptoes, 154, *illus. 23*
Titanic, S.S., 153
Todd, Richard, 198, *illus. 57*
Tonight's the Night, 29
Toronto Star, the, 174
Trent's Last Case, 134–5
Tweedsmuir, Lord, 45, 116
Twentieth Century Fox, 63, 96, 173

United Artists, 61, 100, 105, 158
Universal Pictures, 105–8
Universum Film Company, 54, 58
Up for the Cup, 88
Ustinov, Peter, 135–6, *illus. 46*

Vanderbilt, A. G., 7, 26, *illus. 5*
Vansittart, Sir Robert, 120, 121
Variety, 78
Venice Film Festival, 116, 189–90
Vernon, H.M.S., 197, 199
Victoria, Vesta, 17

Victoria the Great, 9, 75–6, 93, 111–19, 120, 159, 183, *illus. 34, 35, 36, 37, 38*
premières, 44–5, 116–18, 189–91, *illus. 35*
Vienna, 57, 58
von Richthofen, Baron, 41–2, 43, *illus. 13, 14*

Walbrook, Anton, *illus. 32*
Walls, Tom, 85, 88–9, 140, 158, *illus. 25*
Walton, Sir William, 93
Warner, Jack, 165–7
Warner Bros., 125, 166–7, 173
Wasserman, Lew, 108
Watts, Stephen, 117
Webb, Teddy, 16, 17, 20
Welles, Orson, 133–5
Wells, H. G., 95, 121–2
Wembley Stadium, 15
Westminster, Duke of, 141
White, Pearl, 46
Who's Afraid of Virginia Woolf?, 102, 156
Wilcox, Charles (brother of author), 4, 12, 46, 47–8
Wilcox, Mrs Herbert, I, 29, 33–5, 39, 40–1
Wilcox, Mrs Herbert, II, 40–1, 46, 62, 67–8, 71, 90, 99, 140–1, 161
Wilcox, Mrs Herbert, III, *see* Neagle, Anna
Wilcox, John (son of author), 62, 67, 70–1, 90, 161, 163
Wilcox, Joseph John (father of author), 3, 4, 5, 9, 11, 12, 13, 15–16
Wilcox, Joseph Michael (brother of author), 4, 12, 38–9
Wilcox, Lil (sister of author), 4, 12, 13, 15, 21–2, 25, 28
Wilcox, Mary (mother of author), 2–4, 5, 11–12

Wilcox, P. W. (brother of author), 4, 12, 23, 24–5, 28, 38
Wilcox, Pamela (daughter of author), 62, 67, 70–1, 90, 140, 161
Wilcox, Patricia (daughter of author), 70–1, 90, 140, 162
Wilcox, Sheila (daughter of author), 162
Wilding, Michael, 27, 77, 144–51, 152, 155, 159–61, 167–8, 191, 201, 202, *illus. 44, 54, 55*
Wilkinson, Brooke, 81
Williams, Elmo, 173
Williams, Hopie, 69–70
Williams, J. D., 67, 68–70, 71, *illus. 22*
Wilson, Harold, 130, 146–7
Winans, Walter, 7, 26
Wolfson, Sir Isaac, 72, 193–5
Wolfson, Lady, 50
mother of, 49–50
Wolheim, Louis, 84
Wolves, 85
Wonderful Story, The, 27, 51, 52, 53
Woods, Al, 58
Woolf, C. M., 74, 82, 104, 106, 107, 108–9, 110, 111, 112–13, 119, 158, 195
Woolf, 'Jimmy', 172
Woolf, John, 106, 172, 219
Woolf, Maurice, 111, 112–13
Wootton, Stanley, 25
Wynter, Dana, 168

Yangtse Incident, 51, 196–200, *illus. 57*
Young, F. A., 172, *illus. 32*
Young, Terence, 156
Yugoslavia, Queen of, 153

Zannuck, Darryl, 173
Zinkeisen, Doris, 98
Zukor, Adolf, 70